Transformed by Desire

A Journey of Awakening to Life and Love

Bible Study

by

Patty Mason

Transformed by Desire: A Journey of Awakening to Life and Love / Bible study
Formerly known as: *For the Love of the Bride*

Copyright © 2010 by Patty Mason
Revised February 2011
ISBN 978-0-9829718-1-9

This book is available on-line through distributors worldwide.
To order: www.LibertyinChrist.net

To request permission, please send your request to:
Patty@LibertyinChrist.net

Dedication

This Bible study is dedicated to my
Eternal Husband, Jesus,
and to my loving, earthly husband.
Thank you for opening your heart to share
your love with me, and for allowing the room
in our marriage for this glorious endeavor.

*"Make the price for the bride and the gift
I am to bring as great as you like, and I'll pay
whatever you ask me"* (Genesis 34:12).

About the Author

Patty Mason is an award-winning author, speaker, Bible teacher, and the founder of Liberty in Christ Ministries. For many years she has been inspiring women of all ages through her writings and her talks. Patty has reached women all over the world through Sisters on Assignment, Christian.tv, CWebTV, Sermon.net, Light Source, and WLGT Blog Radio Live.

Patty lives in Nashville, Tennessee, with her husband and children. She is also the author of the Bible study, Know that I AM God, and the devotional, God's Heart; Drawing Close to the Heart of God.

"I am a wife and mother who is madly and passionately in love with Jesus. Everything I have the privilege to write, share, or teach is a direct result of my love affair with Jesus. As a writer, speaker, Bible teacher, and women's ministry leader, I love sharing Jesus. It is my mission to teach others how to know Him in a richer, more intimate way."

If you would like to learn more about the author, or her ministry, visit www.libertyinchrist.net.

Foreword

"What does someone's life look like when they are passionately in love with the Master? We read about it in the Scriptures in the lives of people like David, 'a man after God's own heart' (1 Samuel 13:14), or that of Paul who lived his entire life wanting to know more and more of Christ. You will come to realize, in this Bible study, that Patty's life simply radiates these same passions for Christ. Transformed by Desire is her journey of desire with Christ. It is first hand, it is authentic, and it is transparent. From its inception to its present day ongoing passion, you'll experience both the joys and sorrows that come as God's desires for His bride are born and nurtured.

It has been my privilege to be Patty's pastor for over ten years. I have observed and greatly benefitted from her relationship with Christ, and that ongoing relationship is reflected in the pages of this book. If you are looking for more of Him, you have found an invaluable resource. Be ready to be challenged, stretched and courted by your Bridegroom.

Rev. David L. Noel, Senior Pastor
First Alliance Church, Columbus, Ohio

Table of Contents

A Prayer for Our Journey

*"Has anything so great as this ever happened,
or has anything like it ever been heard of?"*
(Deuteronomy: 4:32).

My prayer is for all of you who are reading this Bible study. With each of you in mind and heart, I pray that you will experience a spiritual awakening. I ask for each of you to be given eyes to see and ears to hear all of what Christ desires to communicate to you. May you not close this book untouched or unchanged. Earnestly, I pray that the Holy Spirit will use the words in this book to woo your heart in new ways, paving the way for a turning point in your relationship with Jesus. May you be granted glorious revelation and abundant wisdom to grasp how wide, and high, and long, and deep His love is for you. May your heart be opened wide to journey in the sacred romance with your First Love as He teaches you to indulge in the richness of that extravagant love. I ask the God of Truth to enlighten your understanding of the covenant relationship to which He calls you. I pray that you will taste the unequaled pleasure of entering into this relationship unhindered. May you see your beauty from His perspective; and may you embrace each day clothed in His righteousness and salvation, lifting high the shield of faith and exerting the sword of the Spirit.

I pray that you will know how great His desire is for you and that your desire for Him would grow daily. I pray that you will fall deeper in love with Jesus each day as you journey with Him, embracing every moment with the maturity of unshakable love, yet holding on to that sense of new love. May you experience the joy of sharing cherished times of intimacy with Christ. May you know the inexpressible joy of tasting His unfathomable affections. I pray that you will know, firsthand, the warmth of His embrace and the sensation of His personal touch on your life. I pray that you will know the sound of His voice and will share with Him times of laughter. I pray for Jesus to take you in His tender embrace and bestow on you His passionate kiss of compassion, mercy, forgiveness, joy and love. And I pray for your freedom and your release from the bondage of past hurts and pain. And I pray that daily you will reach out for Him with overwhelming hunger, allowing Him to heal your mind, heart, soul and spirit, so that you may fully embrace all that He has in mind for you.

Embracing Desire:

The Journey that Changes Everything

"May he give you the desires of your heart…"
(Psalm 20:4).

What are the desires of your heart?

What do you yearn for? What are the longings that you ache to fill? What have you kept buried within your soul that needs to be uncovered? Everyone has desires. No matter who you are, or where you come from, you carry desire deep within your heart. But have you allowed those desires to surface? Have you shared the desires of your heart with Jesus? Have you ever answered the question: What are the desires of my heart?

I recall the day when this question was first presented to me. In a pre-Bible study assignment, I was asked to write a letter to Jesus and share with Him the desires of my heart. At first I thought it was an unusual request, one that I hadn't thought about before and certainly didn't expect from God. Nonetheless, I saw this question as a unique opportunity, and I took on the challenge, eager to see what God had in mind.

What are the desires of my heart? I pondered the question; and the more I thought about the possibilities, the more excited I became. Suddenly my mind began to fill with thoughts and dreams. Like a powerful wave crashing on the shoreline, the desires of my heart began to flood my soul. Some were childhood desires I had long since forgotten; others were fresh, still they were longings I had never shared with anyone. It was like a secret part of me just waiting to be revealed. Until that day, I had no idea how I had repressed the desires of my heart; but now, God was touching a place within me that begged to get out, to be set free, to spread it wings and fly.

That day, as I sat at my computer, a sense of determination arose. I wanted much. I wanted more out of life than I was getting. I wanted to love and be loved. I desired deep, significant friendships, rather than superficial relationships. I wanted to dive into the deep end of the pool…to laugh…to grow…to dance. I wanted to be free and embrace more fun in life. I wanted to know God, not just things about God. I hungered to know every line of His face and the number of hairs on His head. I yearned for meaning and a sense of purpose in my life. I wanted to have more passion, to live the life I was born again to live.

I didn't worry about how my desires surfaced. I didn't fret over whether or not they were perfect, or correct. I didn't concern myself with whether or not God would answer my letter, and give me everything I longed for. I just wrote—with great passion, I might add—about everything I wanted out of life and my relationship with Him. It was liberating.

When I finished, I folded the letter, placed it in an envelope, and tucked it in the back of my Bible study book. I didn't look at the letter again until the end of the study. On the last day, I broke open the seal and began to read those desires, the ones that easily poured from my heart several weeks earlier. To my amazement, Jesus took my requests and gave me more than I could have imagined. Tears streaked my face as I read aloud each desire that had received His touch. I couldn't believe it. Jesus took every aspiration and began to fill them. He wasn't filling my longings in exactly the way I thought He would, but He was certainly taking them beyond my wildest expectations. It was then that I received a far greater image of the God I serve. Laying my desires at Jesus' feet, and seeing Him respond to those desires, completely changed my walk with Him, and subsequently, changed my life.

Others noticed the change in me, and soon I began to share this life-altering message with other women. It was wonderful to watch the Lord move in the hearts of others, to witness the miracles of transformation as He moved each of them into deeper levels of intimacy with Jesus.

Many of them had been walking with the Lord for many years, yet they had no joy and felt spiritually dry. Once they shared with Jesus the desires of their hearts, He completely transformed them with His love, bringing floods of joy and purpose into their lives. Another woman God brought into my life was extremely depressed; she wouldn't leave her home, and she had lost the will to live. But once she opened her heart to Jesus, He revealed to her His desire to embrace her in a loving romance. The effects of that romance transformed her life into one filled with purpose. She is now out of the house and ministering to other women who are hurting as she once was, bringing them encouragement and hope.

Another precious woman I knew was drowning in self-hatred. She felt ugly, and she thought others found her undesirable. She longed for acceptance. Once she opened her heart to Jesus, He transformed her life by revealing His heart toward her, showing her how much He loved and valued her. Now she walks with confidence, knowing she is precious and dearly loved.

Beloved, a journey of desire means discovering the transforming power of God's love for you, as He reveals the passion of His heart to transform you into His likeness. It's the awakening of your soul and the renewing of your mind, as God unfolds the true desires He implanted deep within your heart. Therefore, open your heart and mind; share with Jesus those deep desires of longing. Dare to dream; dare to embrace the truest desires of your heart; dare to be all of whom you were created to be in Christ Jesus. Dare to answer the question: *"What are the desires of my heart?"*

Introduction

The Invitation to Desire

Song of Songs 1:1

"This is Solomon's song of songs, more wonderful than any other"
(Song of Songs 1:1, NLT).

1. God asked Solomon: "What are the _____ of your heart?"

2. God took Solomon's desires _____ his request.

   a. Ask for the desires of your heart, but _____ (James 4:2b-3).

3. The Song of Songs is a _____ book of the Bible.

4. All Scripture is _____ (2 Timothy 3:16).

There once was a servant girl who worked in the king's vineyard. Every day she would rise early and make the journey to the valley to serve the king. Day after day she worked hard, tirelessly serving her king and tending to his harvest. She wanted to do well, hoping that the king would be pleased with her. Oh, how she desired to win his approval. She noticed his warm smile each time he would walk past her, and she would work harder anytime she thought he might be watching her. Diligently she served him, hoping to gain his acceptance, not realizing that he was already pleased with her. What the servant girl didn't understand was the king desired a relationship with her. She was completely unaware of the longings in his heart to show her his love and tender affection.

Week One

The Journey of a Lifetime Begins with Desire

- Day One: *God Desires to Fulfill Your Desires*

- Day Two: *God Desires Relationship*

- Day Three: *God Desires Worship*

- Day Four: *God Desires to Come First*

- Day Five: *God Desires Communication*

- Reflection and Response: *God Desires You*

In this first week we are going to:

Begin to identify our God implanted desires
"What do you want me to do for you?"
(Matthew 20:32).

Begin to recognize God's desire for relationship
*"God, who has called you into fellowship with his Son
Jesus Christ our Lord, is faithful"* (1 Corinthians 1:9).

Understand what true worship is
"God is Spirit and his worshipers must worship in spirit and in truth"
(John 4:24).

Learn to put Jesus first in our lives
"Mary chose what is better" (Luke 10:42).

Grasp the importance of communication with God
*"Very early in the morning, while it was still dark, Jesus got up, left the house
and went off to a solitary place, where he prayed"* (Mark 1:35).

Day One

God Desires to Fulfill Your Desires

"Ask and it will be given to you; seek and you will find; knock and the door will be opened to you. For everyone who asks receives; he who seeks finds; and to him who knocks, the door will be opened" (Matthew 7:7-8).

Ask—seek—knock. I love these intriguing words, because they awaken desire. They invite you to come and open your heart and experience the promise of something more. When God created you, He implanted specific desires in your heart that only He could fill. He longs for you to open your heart and ask, so that He can help you discover those desires, bringing them out into the light of His love.

For an example, in the story found in Matthew 20:29-34, what desire did these men communicate to Jesus?

_____

When God created you He implanted specific desires in your heart that only He could fill.

Jesus already knew what these men needed, but He wanted them to express their desire to receive their sight. He wanted them to ask. When they cried out to Him, Jesus stopped and said to them, "What do you want me to do for you?" (v.32). Just like these blind men, you, too, need to express to Jesus the desires of your heart, even the ones you may have kept buried since childhood. Jesus longs for you to open your heart and offer Him your deepest desires. Like a little child, He beckons you to come and freely give Him that part of yourself.

As children, we are full of dreams and desires, and, as children, we feel a freedom to express ourselves—a liberty that bursts with delight and a playfulness that is unhindered. Unfortunately, as we travel along this road called "life" we lose that freedom. We become burdened with heartache, worries and problems that drown our desires. We become filled with the things that keep us bound and chained to a life of emptiness. We were created for more, much more, but in order to experience all God has in mind, we must seek Him with the heart of a child.

Fill in the blanks according to Matthew 18:3, NIV:

I tell you the truth, unless you _____ and become

_____ _____ _____ you will

_____ _____ the kingdom of heaven.

When I was a child, there were two things that simply delighted me: one was to write, the other, to dance. I felt a freedom in both, being able to express my heart and emotions openly without fear of rejection. I discovered at an early age that I had a talent for writing, and my love for dance was evident even in the way I walked. Unfortunately, as the years went by, I put my writing on the shelf and I lost the dance in my step. I still dreamed of writing a book one day, but as I got older, and marriage and children began to consume my life, I felt more and more detached from my dream. And dancing, well, I married a man with two left feet, so dancing, too, became a mere memory. But then one day Jesus awakened those lost desires within my heart, renewing them and bringing them back to life; and now I'm using them for His glory.

What were the desires of your youth? What were your favorite things to do as a child?

_____

_____

_____

Hear His heart, the Lord is asking you, *"What are the desires of your heart?"* I have been given the privilege of some of the most unimaginable riches of intimacy with Christ because I asked, sought after Him and knocked. In our prayer lives, we ask the Lord for many things, good things; but we don't ask Him for what He truly longs to shower upon us—the best of all things, the richness of Himself. Strive for something of greater worth than gold (see Psalm 73:25). God is not Santa Claus, available to grant your every request, but He does long to fill the voids in your heart. He wants to give you what only He can give you. It is an incredible thought, but Jesus is waiting and greatly yearning to fill your deepest desires; but, many times, you don't receive.

What did James tell the church in James 4:2-3 about receiving from God? Why were they not receiving? Check all that apply.

____ Because they didn't ask God

____ Because they asked for too much

____ Because they asked for their personal gain

Beloved, if you want to receive the truest desires of your heart you must be joined to God in a loving relationship and bold enough to ask for what you crave. You need to be willing to let go of fear and unbelief, and trust Him completely; then, you shall receive what you asked for in prayer.

Fill in the blanks according to John 15:7, NIV:

If you _____ _____ _____ and my words _____

_____ _____, _____ whatever you wish, and it will be given you.

What did Jesus tell His followers in Matthew 7:11?

_____

_____

_____

The Father gives good gifts to those who ask Him. Therefore, ask—seek—knock.

◦❦

What does Psalm 37:4 say about receiving the desires of your heart?

_____

_____

_____

If you open your heart, He will share His passions with you.

As you walk with Jesus through this journey of desire, make it your pursuit to delight the heart of God, and give Him the room to share with you the desires of His heart. Jesus has desires too; therefore, be willing to ask Him the same question, "Lord, what are the desires of Your heart?" If you open your heart, He will share His passions with you. He will make Himself known to you in a very real and special way, revealing His glory, His life and His love in your life.

The journey of a lifetime begins with desire—yours and God's. Therefore turn toward Jesus; give Him the opportunity to share with you the desires of His heart, as He continues to invite you to share the desires of yours. As He responses to you in each lesson, revealing the longings of His heart, take the time to respond back to Him. Make good use of those journals; take every occasion to connect with Jesus through pure desire—yours and His.

Don't worry about want others may think or say. Your journey of desire with Jesus is a personal one, customized to your specific needs and longings. Do not compare yourself, or your journey, with anyone else. Do not become upset if your journey is not a carbon copy of the one I share in this book.

Each journey is a unique relationship—a personal dance. Jesus responds to each of us individually. He knows what will move our hearts in-line with His own. There can be common experiences for those who are in tune with Christ; but based on individual backgrounds, personal hurts and rejections, levels of hunger, and commitment to Christ, experiences will vary.

For some, once they made the decision to ask, seek, and knock with their whole heart, the transformation came rapidly. For others, the changes and revelations came slowly—more gradually. That's okay. Don't get frustrated. Christ knows your heart, and He understands the longings of your soul. Give Him the room to move freely; unhindered and without any precon-ceived notions of what this journey is supposed to look like, or how it will turn out. Let go and let God reveal to you the desires of His heart, as He births the desires in yours.

So, let's get started. Seek Him, knock, ask and believe. Tell Jesus your deepest desires, even the ones you may have kept buried. Come with the heart and expectancy of a child. Be bold. Be specific, and lay those desires before Him.

Dear Jesus,
The desires of my heart are…

_____

_____

_____

_____

_____

_____

_____

_____

_____

_____

_____

_____

_____

Day Two

God Desires Relationship

*"We proclaim to you what we have seen and heard, so that
you also may have fellowship with us. And our fellowship is with
the Father and with his Son, Jesus Christ"* (1 John 1:3).

In order for us to begin to understand the desires of God's heart, and learn to embrace our own desires, we will need to start at the beginning of the story. "In the beginning God created…" (Genesis 1:1).

In the beginning, according to Genesis 1:26-27, who did God create in His own image?

_____

_____

According to Genesis 2:8-10, where did the relationship between God and man begin?

_____

_____

Now turn to the end of the story. According to Revelation 22:1-6, where will the relationship climax?

_____

_____

In the beginning God created man in His own image—both man and woman He created them. And in the beginning, a relationship between God and man developed in a garden. And one day this relationship will climax in a garden where the "dwelling of God is with men, and he will live with them" (Revelation 21:3).

God desired relationship then, He desires it now, and He will continue to desire it for all eternity. The Holy Trinity (Father, Son and Holy Spirit) is saying, "Relationship, relationship, relationship, relationship." From the beginning, relationship with man has always been the first desire of God's heart; an unfathomable, personal, intimate union, one that is stronger and deeper than any earthly relationship.

Understand the magnitude of this concept. The Holy Trinity does not need us. God is complete in and of Himself, but He desires the exceeding joy that comes from giving and receiving love in an intimate relationship. God longs for fellowship, and He yearns for each of us to desire that same fellowship with Him. Yet, how many times do we forsake fellowship because of sin and unforgiveness? How many times do we forfeit intimacy because of religious mindsets and rules? How many times do we remain distant because of fear or lack of commitment?

We see an example of this in Exodus 20:18-21. According to these verses, how would you describe the relationship between God and the Israelites?

_____

_____

_____

How would you describe the relationship between God and Moses?

_____

_____

_____

Thousands of years ago, at Mount Sinai, God revealed His desire for relationship with the people of Israel, but when He appeared in great power, they remained distant. More than anything God desired fellowship. He longed for them to consecrate themselves and be His people. Still the Israelites stood in the distance, afraid to come near to God.

This is not want God wants at all. Yes, it is good to fear the Lord. Proverbs 1:7 says, "The fear of the Lord is the beginning of knowledge." But we must not fear Him the way the Israelites did; this kind of fear will keep us from drawing close to God.

Normally when we think of the word "fear," we think of dread, terror, or alarm. But God doesn't want us to be terrified of Him. We are to fear the Lord with awe and wonder. We are to fear grieving Him (see Ephesians 4:30), to have a fear of not doing His will and not walking in His ways. But we are not to fear who He is or what He desires to do in our lives; rather, we are to possess the fear of not knowing Him. Proper fear of the Lord will allow the relationship to flourish, because "the fear of the LORD leads to life" (Proverbs 19:23).

From the beginning, relationship with man has always been the first desire of God's heart: an unfathomable, personal, intimate union, one that is stronger and deeper than any earthly relationship.

Think of your relationship with the Lord. What is your fear factor? Are you afraid to approach Him like the Israelites? Are you standing in the distance, and watching others enter into the place where God is? Or are you like Moses, in awe, yet, unhindered in your approach? Or perhaps you are somewhere in between. Briefly explain where you think you are, and then express where you would like to be.

_____

_____

_____

Nothing has changed. Just as God desired relationship in the Garden of Eden, and at the foot of Mt. Sinai, God still desires fellowship with those He loves. God the Father desires a close and cherished relationship with His beloved children and God the Son desires to draw near to His beloved bride. This is the truth of God, yet, so many just don't get it. I know I didn't. In all the years I was growing up in church, I learned the rules, I learned what was expected, but I didn't learn to love God. I was taught to respect and honor God; to worship Him with song, and serve Him by performing services and tasks, but there was no relationship.

In some respects I was like the Pharisees, the religious leaders of Jesus' day. They knew the law, and they performed their rituals by the way they were taught; but they never entered into a personal relationship with God. Please do not do what I did and get caught up in the religious mindset, ritualistically following the rules, but not following the Savior in love.

The desire of God's heart proclaims, "Love me. I don't want your rules and religious rituals. I want a close relationship with you." God doesn't want songs of praise from our lips if our hearts are far from Him (see Isaiah 29:13). He doesn't want our rituals and sacrifices; He wants our love (see Hosea 6:6).

I was well into adulthood before I understood that God wanted an intimate relationship with me. Since that time, the Holy Spirit has been reconditioning my way of thinking and reprogramming what I was taught. First John 4:16 says, "God is love." In fact, He wrote the Book on it. Unlike before, I now see the Bible as the greatest romance ever to be placed on parchment. All throughout Scripture, I see Christ as the beloved Bridegroom. I see His heart toward His bride and His constant pursuit of her. I see everything in Scripture as being either about Him, about her, or about their relationship.

All through its pages, story after story, I see living mentors who serve as a parallel, each one reminding me of the relationship that God longs to share with man.

Glance through Scripture and name a few of these living mentors: I'll get you started. *David and Jonathan, Ruth and Boaz….*

_____

_____

My perspective may be difficult for you to grasp right now. It is far easier for us to acknowledge God as Father, than to think of Him as a Bridegroom, who is in love with us. But allow the Holy Spirit to open your heart and mind as He did mine. God the Son desires a loving and committed relationship with you as His beloved. And from this devoted relationship He will share with you mysteries, unlock hidden treasures, and reveal Himself to you in both His person and personal love.

Beloved, if you are to receive the utmost that God desires to shower upon you, if you are to be awakened by the desires that God has implanted in you, so that you can begin to live the life you are meant to live, you must first recognize the desire of God's heart to be in an intimate relationship with you as His beloved. And in order to partake of close fellowship with God, you need to put three essential elements of relationship into practice: worship, giving Jesus first priority, and communication. If you are not putting these fundamental applications into practice on a continual basis, your journey of desire will be limited.

Therefore, for the remainder of this week, we will look at these three elements, giving the Holy Spirit the opportunity to develop our relationship with Jesus. We want to receive all of what God offers. We want exceedingly and abundantly more than we could ask or imagine. Let's keep praying for God to show us the true fullness to which we have been called—an unimaginable relationship of love with Him.

Which aspect of relationship do you most easily relate to?

____ Father/child	____ Shepherd/sheep
____ Master/slave	____ Friend/friend
____ Teacher/student	____ Bridegroom/bride

Explain why you feel this aspect of relationship with God best relates to your level of familiarity with Him.

_____

_____

_____

_____

_____

_____

_____

_____

_____

_____

Do you believe that your relationship with Jesus can be better? Do you yearn for something more in your relationship with Christ? Share with Jesus the desires of your heart:

_____

_____

_____

_____

_____

_____

_____

_____

_____

_____

_____

_____

_____

_____

_____

Day Three

God Desires Worship

"God is Spirit and his worshipers must worship in spirit and in truth"
(John 4:24).

Yesterday we began to understand the cry of God's heart is relationship, relationship, relationship, and not just any relationship, but a love relationship with Him as His beloved. We also recognized that in order to partake of this close fellowship with God, we need to put three essential elements of relationship into practice. We'll look at worship first.

What is worship? When you think of worship what comes to mind?

_____

_____

What do you think God is longing to receive through our worship?

_____

_____

Why is worship important?

_____

_____

Worship is far more than any of us realize. Worship is not singing a song or attending church. Although singing to God is a tool for worship, singing is not worship. Worship is a condition of the heart. It is a lifestyle; a moment-by-moment ardent love expressed to God. Everything you do should be done as though you are doing it only for Jesus. And when I say everything, I mean everything (even the laundry). Worship is loving Him with everything you have, with everything you are. Worship is the cornerstone of your relationship with God.

In Mark 12:28-31, how did Jesus describe worship?

_____

_____

How does Romans 12:1 communicate this kind of worship?

_____

_____

"Love the Lord your God with all your heart, soul, mind and strength; and love your neighbor as yourself" (Mark 12:29-31). We must embrace the first of these commandments, before we can hope to celebrate the second. This is important, and, to emphasize this, these two commandments are mentioned in the Bible at least eleven times. The word *love* is used more than 800 times, and there are ten different forms for the word *love* including *love, lover, beloved,* and *loving*. With so much talk about love, do you think God is trying to tell us something? Worship is all about love—receiving love and giving love.

God wants us to worship with passion and devoted attachment, and by being completely and utterly enthralled with Him. He longs for us to offer our entire being, mind, soul, spirit, heart, everything we have as a living sacrifice, holy and pleasing to Him (see Romans 12:1).

So how do we do this? How do we love God with our entire being? How do we embrace a lifestyle of ardent adoration, devoted attachment, and sacrificial love that is pleasing to God? First of all, in order to embrace true love, we must be willing to *surrender* our mind, body, soul and heart to God. True love, even in a human relationship, requires complete trust of another and total *abandonment* of oneself. It actually requires us to become completely *vulnerable* to another. Love is not something we can control. It is about *submitting*, a yielding willingness to be in the hands of another.

Put this way, love sounds scary. Yet, we, as women, fall in love all the time. We want to be in love; in fact, we long for it, and dream about the day we will find our soul mate. When we are in love it is wonderful, and our minds and hearts become consumed with the other.

I remember the first time I fell in love. This young man was like heaven on earth to me. Every time I saw him, my heart would race, my palms would sweat and my soul would melt. I felt giddy and light, moved by the sheer delight of being with him. When I wasn't around him, I thought about him—all the time. He became my world.

There is something special, even sacred about first love. Maybe that is why Christ Jesus calls Himself the First Love of the church (see Revelation 2:4). God wants us to fall in love with Him like our first love. He wants us to *surrender* to Him. He longs for us to *trust* Him to love and care for us. He requires us to *abandon* our lives completely for a better life. God wants us to be *vulnerable*, weak in our own strength so that we can be made strong

God wants us to worship with passion and devoted attachment, and by being completely and utterly enthralled with Him.

in His (see 2 Corinthians 12:10). He yearns for us to *submit*, to totally let go of everything and allow Him to mold us in His loving hands. When we do this, when we come to the end of ourselves, when we learn to *surrender, trust, abandon, submit* and become *vulnerable*, we find the greatest treasure of all—pure love.

Look through the Psalms and select a couple of your favorite verses that you feel communicate *surrendered, abandoned, submitted, vulnerable* and *trusting* worship to God.

_____

_____

King David was an awesome example of this kind of worship, and, according to God, David was a man after his own heart (see 1Samuel 13:14). David was not perfect in his quest for righteousness, but he dove into the unfailing love of God. David knew beyond a shadow of doubt that he was dearly and wonderfully loved by God, and he abandoned himself entirely to that love. David loved God with everything he had, and he opened his heart to receive the love of God in return. We must learn to do the same.

This brings us to the second way we can embrace a lifestyle of ardent adoration and worship: receiving a revelation of Christ's love for us (Ephesians 3:18-19). I am not talking about knowing that God loves you; most Christians believe that. I am talking about experiencing the love of God. Has the truth of God's personal love for you penetrated your heart? Have you been awakened to the truth that God desires you, longs for you, dreams of you, and waits with great anticipation for the day you will be together forever?

It is vital that you first receive His love for you. In order to worship Him the way He longs to be loved, or to love others, you must first get a revelation of God's love for you personally.

Have you ever heard God tell you that He loves you? Have His words, "I love you" penetrated your heart? If so, share your experience. If not, pen your prayer below. Express to Jesus your desire to receive a revelation of His love for you.

_____

_____

I remember the first time I heard the Lord tell me He loved me. It was so precious I wept over it for days. These words came to me after a time of discipline from the Lord. The verse: "Those whom I love I rebuke and

In order to worship Him the way He longs to be loved, or to love others, you must first get a revelation of God's love for you personally.

discipline" (Revelation 3:19) is a verse that one normally doesn't get too excited about; but, for me, Revelation 3:19 was like receiving a hug after being turned across Daddy's knee. You see, for years I knew and understood that God loved me, but it wasn't until I heard those sweet words come from His heart that I began to grasp the magnitude of His love, and the impact of that revelation was life altering for me.

According to John 4:13-14, what did Jesus desire for the woman to ask Him for? Why was it important for the woman to receive from Him?

_____

_____

Value what God longs to give you: His personal and intimate love. You cannot embrace a lifestyle of ardent adoration in your own strength. Jesus said in John 4:23-24, "Yet a time is coming and has now come when the true worshipers will worship the Father in spirit and truth, for they are the kind of worshipers the Father seeks. God is Spirit and his worshipers must worship in spirit and in truth."

In this Scripture, Jesus is saying that you need God to love God. If you are to embrace a lifestyle of ardent adoration, devoted attachment, and sacrificial love that is pleasing to God, then you must learn to worship Him in the power of the Holy Spirit, who is Spirit and Truth. Jesus desires for you to give Him your undivided heart—not half or a part of your heart, but all of your heart, soul, and mind. The only way you can do this is by first receiving from Him (see 1 John 4:19). The only way you can love God and others in the way He truly desires, with an agape love—a love which is selfless, a love which loves in the other's best interest—is to first *abandon* yourself to His love. *Surrender* to it completely. Become *vulnerable* and *submissive* in His embrace; and *trust* His Holy Spirit to fill you with His power and love.

What do you find is the hardest part of ardent worship? To *surrender, abandon, submit, trust* or become *vulnerable*.

_____

Why do you think that this part of worship is difficult for you?

_____

_____

Day Four

God Desires To Come First

"Mary chose what is better, and it will not be taken away from her"
(Luke 10:42).

As you work your way through this study, you will quickly realize that I am a woman, who like Martha, likes to get down to business. Therefore, let's consider our second foundational element in developing a relationship with Christ—putting Him first by making Him the priority of our everyday lives. To learn this all-important concept let's enter the home of Mary and Martha.

Read Luke 10:38-42.

I love Martha and Mary, primarily because I can relate to both of these ladies. You see, at some point during my journey with Jesus, I have actually walked in each of their shoes.

Which sister do you relate to more? Why?

_____

_____

As a new believer, I was just like Martha—all about the work, while unknowingly forsaking Jesus, by not being Mary. For years I worked hard, earnestly believing I was doing what God, and the church, wanted me to do. At first, I was extremely excited, as I diligently served the Lord. As the years went by, however, I began to realize that a level of frustration was rising. I felt like I was on a hamster wheel, running around and around in circles and getting nowhere. It was like I was trying to push a boulder uphill. I had no joy, no peace, and no fruit. In time, I burned out.

Please do not misunderstand. God does desire our willing service, and He takes great delight in watching us serve, but in no way is our servanthood to come before, or take the place of, a personal intimate relationship with Christ. Since I took no time for an intimate relationship with Jesus, I became frustrated. Yes, it is important to take care of others, to serve and to share your heart and home; but the most important thing is Christ. Do not let ministry be a distraction in your pursuit of intimate fellowship. Please, do not tirelessly serve the church, day-after-day, year-after-year, yet, never enjoy a close relationship with Jesus.

According to Luke 10:40 what had Martha's attention?

_____

Too many times in life it is far too easy to allow all of the preparations to be a distraction. We have a lot to do; there are places to go, people to take care of; unfortunately, these distractions can, and do, get in the way of our relationship with God. Some days there are too many things to get done, and our hectic schedules often take priority over what is best.

Jesus tried to get Martha to understand this. Write His words to her in Luke 10:41-42:

_____

_____

One of the most important lessons to be learned is the discovery Mary made— the joy of simply being with Jesus.

Now, after hearing this comment, do you think that Martha pulled up a chair and joined the group? Most likely, she returned to the kitchen, huffing and puffing, as steam from her anger vented through her ears. How do I know? I used to be Martha. I understand the woman. I appreciate her need to get things done and not receive help in accomplishing all the tasks. I recognize Martha's desire to please everyone, especially Jesus. I know Martha's heart in wanting everything to be perfect—the house, the food, herself…ha, ha. When I served, I wanted everything to be ideal, but all too often, because my focus was on the preparations, I didn't reach the point where I could relax and enjoy the moment. Mary chose what was better. It was a hard lesson for me to learn, but I did learn. Throughout the years, I have learned to drop the frying pan and just be Mary. I have learned to take the time to build an individual and cherished connection with Jesus first. As a result, when I now serve, I have joy.

There are many lessons we can learn from Mary and Martha, and we will focus on them again a little later. One of the most important lessons to be learned is the discovery Mary made—the joy of simply being with Jesus.

Mary took the time to get to know Jesus. She sat at His feet and built an individual and cherished connection. She intently looked up at Him, enthralled, captivated, hanging on His every word. Glory! Mary did not lift a finger to help. She sat there, to her sister's dismay, and entered into fellowship with Jesus. God wanted the intimate relationship with both sisters to be top priority. From there He would guide them to serve Him (see John 15:5.)

Understand the scope of this scenario, Jesus loved both of these women dearly (see John 11:5). And both of these women had a relationship with Jesus, but only one took the time to truly enter into and develop an intimate relationship. Each sister loved Jesus, yet each chose a different way of expressing her love to Jesus; remember, Jesus said, "Mary chose what is better" (Luke 10:42).

We must first learn to be Mary, before we can even consider entering into servanthood, as Martha did. Our service needs to be a result of the relationship. Like a set of dominos falling, we need to come before the Lord every day to sit at His feet, to listen, to love. He then, in turn, fills us with what we need in order to serve Him, and others, effectively. Intimacy and service go together. You cannot have one without the other. Just like Mary and Martha are sisters, intimate relationship and service are sisters. You cannot effectively have one without the other.

Martha dove into the work, without even talking with Jesus, except to tell Him what she expected—not only from her sister, but from Him. Martha asked Jesus to bless the work of her hands. When we don't take time to know the Lord and His desires, we get consumed in our own agenda, and we begin to ask Jesus to bless our work. Jesus is telling us that He wants to bless us with the plans that He has for us (Jeremiah 29:11). In order to know those plans—to know what God desires—we must first know His heart. And the only way to know God's heart is to experience it, first, in a loving relationship.

Different people within the body of the church have different functions and passions, but in order to know and understand your function, you must be plugged into Jesus.

Turn to John 15:5. What did Jesus say would happen if a man remained in Him?

_____

_____

What fruit can you produce if you are apart from Him?

_____

_____

God wants the intimate relationship first. He wants us to be connected to Him. We are His beloved, and corporately we are His bride, and He desires a bride who will trust Him and abandon herself completely into His love. From there He will guide her to serve Him.

Day Five

God Desires Communication

"My heart has heard you say, 'Come and talk with me.' And my heart responds, 'Lord, I am coming'" (Psalm 27:8, NLT).

Our next fundamental element in developing a relationship with Christ is communication. Any good relationship is built on solid and steady communication. Without it, the relationship falls apart. Although there are many ways the Lord can speak with us, we will focus on two key elements that are essential in communicating with God: intimate prayer and His Word.

Let's begin today by praying to receive wisdom on the value of communication. Then please read Luke 11:1-4.

I find it interesting that immediately following our previous story with Mary and Martha, and the lessons we learn there, Scripture turns our attention to prayer. Jesus placed great value on prayer. While He was here, gracing the earth with His human presence, He continually indulged in private moments of intimacy with His Father.

What does Luke 11:1, Mark 1:35, and Matthew 6:6 tell us about prayer and the way Jesus prayed?

_____

_____

Why do you think it is important to pray with God behind closed doors?

_____

_____

According to Luke 11:1, what did the disciples ask Jesus to do?

_____

_____

The disciples walked with Jesus, in person, up-close and personal. They observed Him, on many occasions, praying. And one day, when he was finished, they asked to be taught how to do it the way He did. They were awestruck by the way Jesus prayed. I think what they were saying to Him was, "Lord, teach us to pray like that!"

Week One: The Journey of a Lifetime Begins with Desire

Prayer is meant to be union and fellowship with God through His Holy Spirit. It is intended to be a two-way conversation where we share with Him in intimacy. He desires our heartfelt, personal prayers that first take time to love Him, showering Him with adoration and affection, offering up thanksgiving and praise. Prayer and worship go hand-in-hand. Just like fellowship and service, you cannot have one without the other. Otherwise, prayer becomes a list of wants and needs.

Prayer wasn't always a priority for me. I recall the days when I sensed the Lord beckoning me to come and spend time with Him. In my mind I would respond: *Just a minute, Lord. Let me finish what I'm doing and I'll be right there.* Trouble was, most of the time, something else would begin pressing me, drawing my attention to accomplish another task, and again the Lord would wait. So, as the day went on, I would try to squeeze Him in where I could, if I could.

Then, there were the occasions when I found prayer boring. Can you relate? I even remember one prayer meeting in particular where I actually fell asleep. There were also the times when I couldn't seem to connect with God—at all. It was like I was offering up prayers, but they seemed to be bouncing off the ceiling. When this happened, I would leave my prayer time feeling drained and dirty. Let's face it, at that time, I didn't like prayer; in fact, I avoided it.

Yet, despite all of these obstacles, Jesus showed me the beauty found in prayer, when He brought a wonderful friend into my life—one who taught me how to pray intimacy. Up until that time, I didn't know how to draw near to God in prayer. I didn't know how to worship Him through prayer. We'll talk more about this later in the workbook, but worship ushers in the presence of God. Until you experience the presence of God in prayer, until you know what it is to come face-to-face with Him in intimacy, prayer is monotonous, and at times, empty; it is nothing more than rattling off requests and demands.

Now, unlike before, I long to meet with God every morning in prayer. I don't come out of duty or obligation, but out of the love in my heart, simply desiring to be with Him. Morning prayer is "our time." It is a wonderful time of intense passion and tenderness. I express my love for Him, and He washes over me like a wave with His grace, peace, love, and joy. During this time, if something is weighing on my heart, I confide in Him, but for the most part, it is a time of worship and simply being together. It is also a time when I surrender everything to Christ and ask for His protection from the enemy. I ask for the placement of the armor on myself and others, and I commit my heart and life to Him for that day.

Any good relationship is built on solid and steady communication. Without it, the relationship falls apart.

Then, as I go throughout the day, when something comes up, or I am feeling anxious, I pray. When I settle in for the night, again I reach out for Him, ending my day with loving devotion and thanksgiving. Basically, I have learned how to pray without ceasing; continually engaging God in continuous communication (see 1 Thessalonians 5:17-18).

Read Psalm 63:1-9. From these verses what pattern of prayer can you see in David's life? Match the verse by drawing a line to the corresponding answer.

v. 1	he ended the day in prayer
v. 2, 3, 5, 8	he engaged God in continual prayer
v. 4	he cried out for intimate time with God
v. 6	he shared intimacy with God
v. 7, 9	he prayed for protection and help

Once I understood what God desired to receive, and how He longed to share times of closeness with me, my attitude about prayer changed dramatically. As a result my prayer life increased in volume and passion; this new approach deepened the bonds of relationship between us to unparalleled levels of intimacy.

Prayer is extremely central to Jesus (see Matthew 21:12-13 and John 2:13-17), and He longs to talk with you. He desires to be an active and vital part of your everyday life. Once this revelation pierces your heart you too will learn to pray without ceasing; you will begin to continually engage God in continuous communication.

Prayer does not always have to be formal. Talk to Him as you would a close friend. Talk to Him while driving in your car, doing dishes, and standing in the checkout line at the grocery store. Prayer is key in helping you develop your relationship with Christ. Sing to Him, love Him, play with Him, and share your heart. Ask for advice, permission, and help; and if you need a shoulder to cry on, turn to Him. He is there.

Learn to see prayer for what it really is—a pleasure. Once you begin to experience the joy and freedom found only in prayer, prayer will never be the same. You will never be the same.

Now, let's shift our focus to the second key element that keeps the bonds of communication flowing and the relationship growing—God's Word.

Turn with me to Psalm 119. What does the psalmist tell us about God's Word in each of these verses? I'll get you started:

vs. 14   *it is worth rejoicing over* _____

v. 28   _____

vs. 42-43   _____

v. 72   _____

v. 81   _____

v. 89   _____

v. 105   _____

I love God's Word. It is like air to me, but I must admit that it wasn't always this way. I recall the years when I would read the Bible *only if* I was in a Bible study. I wasn't disciplined enough to stay in the Word on my own. I could not seem to feed myself. Even when I was in a study, there were days when I would do my homework just to get it done. I would read through the lessons quickly, treating it like it was something I had to do, rather than something I enjoyed.

Over time Jesus brought me into a place where I learned to see the value of His Word; to receive it as a gift rather than a burden. Unlike before, the Bible has become a virtual banquet for my soul; an unending table filled with wonderful foods and rich desserts (see Psalm 119:103). It became His heart poured out in a love letter filled with faith and hope; the promise of something better. Unlike anything I had ever experienced, God's Word communicated love in such a way that it transformed my heart and renewed my mind; it touched me, changed me, and drew me closer to the heart of God.

Allow me to challenge you to dive into and devour the living breathing Word of God. Read it. Meditate on it. Dissect it and ask the Holy Spirit for better clarity and understanding. Allow it to become a part of you. Stand in awe and watch it come to life and unfold before you. Allow God to communicate to you personally. Let the Holy Spirit catch you getting excited about what He has to say; then rejoice in what He shows you.

Take a minute to take inventory. In no way do I mean for this next exercise to be condemning, but allow it to challenge you. Give the Holy Spirit the opportunity to grow you and strengthen you in this area of your relationship with Christ.

Circle the response which most accurately relates to you.

1. On an average day how much time would you say you faithfully spend reading and mediating on the Word of God?

    All day

    Most of the day

    About an hour

    Less than 30 minutes

    Not at all

2. How much time do you spend daily in intimate prayer? Not offering requests and petitions, but in genuine intimate prayer filled with praise and love?

    I pray without ceasing

    Off and on throughout the day

    When I think about Jesus

    Rarely

    Never

3. At what point of the day do you first speak to God?

    Before I get out of bed in the morning

    After breakfast or while I am on my way to work

    Lunchtime

    Sometime in the afternoon

    Before I go to sleep at night

God's Word communicated love in such a way that it transformed my heart and renewed my mind; it touched me, changed me, and drew me closer to the heart of God.

How beautiful is the Word of God coupled with the passion of intimate prayer. Take some time right now, before you close the book on today's lesson, to engage the Lord in intimate prayer. Pray His Word back to Him. Remember prayer does not have to be formal. The words don't have to be flowery or perfect; just talk to Him. Tell Him how you feel about Him. If you don't know what to pray, open to the book of Psalms and read it aloud as a prayer to Jesus.

If you don't feel any special connection with Him right now, don't panic. Don't start thinking that something is wrong with you. It took time for me to grow in these areas of communication, and it will take time for you, too. Begin by telling Jesus how you are feeling. Then, ask Him to help you develop a love language that the two of you can share.

Use the space below to share the desires of your heart with Jesus for deeper, richer times of intimate communication.

_____

_____

_____

God Desires You

Through the power of His Holy Spirit, Christ will bring you into an intimate relationship. He will teach you the steps to the dance that will become your own. And you, as His beloved, will learn to take His hand, to follow His lead, and dance with Him—moving with Him as one in beauty and grace.

Listen to the heart of the Bridegroom: "Come dance with Me, My Bride." He extends His hand. "I long for you. My desire is for you to be close to My heart. I love you with an everlasting love. My commitment to you, My everlasting covenant, is offered to you. Dance with Me. Allow Me to love you. My desire is great. My passion is vast. Come to the waters and drink. Come to Me and eat. Eat until your heart is full and overflowing with My love for you. My love for you is strong, My Bride. My heart is full, spilling over with love for you. Come, My Bride, it is time to dance. Dance with Me. I long for you. Dance with Me. See the spring has come and My love for you pours like the rain. This is the season of the Bride and the Bridegroom. The time is near. The coming of the Lord is close at hand. My Bride, make yourself ready. Prepare the way. Remove the obstacles out of the way of my people for I am coming (see Isaiah 57:14). Open your heart to Me. Let Me come in and allow Me to move you with My passion. Follow Me and I will lead you in the dance of true romance. I will lead you into the chambers of My heart. Take My hand. I will draw you close and hold you in My arms, and together we will dance."

Reflection and Response

When was the first time you became aware of God's personal and intimate love for you?

Share your story. If you have not yet received this revelation, share your heart with Jesus to experience His love, which surpasses knowledge.

_____

_____

_____

_____

_____

_____

_____

What areas of relationship with Jesus do you find the most challenging? Why?

_____

_____

_____

_____

_____

_____

In what areas of relationship would you like to go deeper with Jesus?

_____

_____

_____

_____

_____

_____

Week One

Lesson One

The Journey Begins with Desire

Song of Songs 1:2-8

1. The maiden desires to _____ what she has _____ about the king.

2. The maiden desires to _____ his love for _____

3. The hindrances that can keep us from receiving what we desire:

    a.) Feelings of _____

    b.) Feelings of _____

    c.) Do not _____ yourself and your _____

4. The maiden wants _____

In a large ballroom, the king stands before his precious bride, ready to take her hand, yearning to draw her to himself. With great longing in his heart to dance with her, he reaches out; his heart is full of love. Suddenly, the bride begins falling apart. Large pieces of her body begin to fall to the ground. Like a china doll the pieces shatter from the impact into thousands of tiny fragments. His heart broken, the king kneels beside her; his hands cover his face as he weeps over her.

His hands reach out and pick up her shoes, setting them upright in position. Slowly, carefully, one tiny fragment at a time, the king begins rebuilding his bride from the foundation up. Piece by piece he continually and meticulously puts each piece back in its proper place, until she is completely restored. As the final touch, he places on her head a crown; a crown of beauty and life (see Isaiah 61:3). Once again she is whole, perfect, and prepared as a bride beautifully dressed for her husband (see Revelation 21:2). The glorious bride will once again rise to be a queen (see Ezekiel 16:13). Brought back together, one piece at a time, she is unified as a whole, together in one body, and one with God (see Ephesians 4:4-6).

Week Two

The Freedom to Reject Him

- Day One: *God Desires to be Chosen*

- Day Two: *God Desires to Show Mercy*

- Day Three: *God Desires to Forgive*

- Day Four: *God Desires to Redeem*

- Day Five: *God Desires Reconciliation*

- Reflection and Response: *God Desires You*

In this second week we are going to:

See the heartbreak of God
"Yet my people have forgotten me, days without number" (Jeremiah 2:32).

Recognize that we have all gone astray
"All of us have strayed away like sheep. We have left God's path to follow our own"
(Isaiah 53:6).

Be wooed by Christ's pursuit
*"I will heal their waywardness and love them freely,
for my anger has turned away from them"* (Hosea 14:4).

See the power of redeeming love
*"This is real love. It is not that we love God, but that he loved us and
sent his Son as a sacrifice to take away our sins"* (1 John 4:10, NLT).

Receive a glimpse of Christ's Passion
*"For God so loved the world that he gave his one and only Son,
that whoever believes in him shall not perish but have eternal life"* (John 3:16).

Day One

God Desires to be Chosen

"Now…choose for yourselves this day whom you will serve, whether the gods your forefathers served beyond the River, or the gods of the Amorites, in whose land you are living. But as for me and my household, we will serve the LORD" (Joshua 24:14-15).

In Week One we opened the door for the invitation to desire. We gave Christ the opportunity to share with us the desire of His heart to enter into an intimate relationship with each of us as His beloved. This week we are going to take a hard look at the heartbreak of God due to Israel's unfaithfulness, as we examine our own hearts. This will not be easy, but let me encourage you to press in. The goal is a close and loving relationship with Christ. Let's give the Holy Spirit the room He needs, so that He can move us from our disobedience and into a right relationship with God.

Christ's desire for His bride is immeasurable, His heart is overflowing with love for His church, and He longs to enter into a loving and committed covenant relationship with the bride He loves. Unfortunately, all too often, many of us do not share this same desire for fellowship. This lack of commitment pierces Christ's heart. Yet, in order to grasp the heartbreak of God, we must, first and foremost, understand the depth of Christ's love and His great longing to be loved in return. Without this revelation, our view of God's heart will be incomplete; as a result, we will not fully enter into all God has in mind to share with us.

In order to examine the heartbreak of God, once again, let's start at the beginning of the story. In the beginning God created Eden. It was an ideal place full of beauty; it was a perfect garden where God desired to partake of intimate fellowship with man. Everything, including man, was faultless and pure. Until, one day, man chose his own path; he turned away from God's perfect order and turned toward his own way of doing things. Through his act of disobedience, sin entered the garden and the heart of man. God gave man the opportunity to repent of his sin, to take responsibility for his wrong actions and turn back to Him. Man, however, chose to make excuses; so, God expelled him from the garden, fellowship was broken, and so was the heart of God (see Genesis 3).

Since that day, God has been in pursuit of mankind, wanting nothing more than for man to return to Him with all of his heart. But true love cannot be forced—it must be given willingly. So, God bestows on mankind the greatest privilege of all: freewill, the freedom to reject Him.

Christ's desire for His bride is immeasurable, His heart is overflowing with love for His church, and He longs to enter into a loving and committed covenant relationship with the bride He loves.

We see this over and over in the Old Testament. Repeatedly God shared His tender care and mercy, reaching out to the people He loved. Again and again we see how His people continually strayed from Him, choosing a sinful lifestyle instead.

Begin today's lesson by opening your heart to God in prayer, then turn to the book of Jeremiah. In the following verses, how does God express His heart-break over the unfaithfulness of His people?

Jeremiah 2:5:

_____

Jeremiah 2:20-25:

_____

Jeremiah 3:14:

_____

Jeremiah 3:20:

_____

Jeremiah 7:13:

_____

The people desired their errant lifestyle. His people removed their wedding ring and garments and gave their love to another. Yet, even with all of His efforts to woo them back, they remained self-indulgent in their search for love in all the wrong places. Daily they continued to offer affections to false lovers and idols; anyone and anything that they believed would give them what they hungered for.

Even today, many people are just like the Israelites of the Old Testament. People are lovers of themselves, money; they're boastful, proud, abusive, disobedient, ungrateful, and unholy. They are without love, unforgiving, slanderous, without self-control, and brutal, lovers of pleasure for their own gain rather than lovers of God (see 2 Timothy 3:2-4). Nonetheless, no matter what people do or don't do, God never seems to give up. Even in their rebellion He implores them to come back to Him.

Consider the allegory found in Ezekiel 16:8-19 and answer the following:

In this metaphor, we see an association between the Lord and the Israelites, His chosen people. What relationship did the Lord desire to share with them? (v. 8)

_____

_____

In what ways did the Lord reveal His care and provision? What happened as a result of His provision, care and love? (vv. 13-14)

_____

_____

Over time what happened to their hearts? Check the correct answer:

_____ They fell more in love with the Lord

_____ They turned away from the Lord and began to worship false idols

_____ They loved themselves more than anything else

What happened with the provision from the Lord? Check all that apply:

_____ They took the beautiful garments and decorated places of idol worship

_____ They took the jewelry and turned the pieces into male idols

_____ They adorned their idols

_____ They burned the food and spices as fragrant incense before their idols

Ezekiel 16 gives us a foretaste of the type of relationship that God desired to share with His people. We can see how, at first, His people freely accepted His offer of provision and willingly returned His love with tender devotion. In Jeremiah 2:2 the Lord calls to mind the sweetness of that time: "I remember the devotion of your youth, how as a bride you loved me and followed me through the desert, through a land not sown." But as the story goes on, pride and arrogance filled the heart and head of the bride, and she decided to take her beauty on the road, sharing her affections with others and breaking His heart. Overzealous in her actions, she offers herself willingly and freely to false lovers; lovers whom she feels will fill and complete her, but who only give her a counterfeit sense of love.

Even today, we, all too often, act just like this. We move away from the relationship Christ desires and forsake our First Love for the things of this world. Because we don't understand what God truly longs for we miss out on the utmost of all relationships. We become consumed with chasing after the things in life that we think will fill our needs. We are starved for love and affection, and so desperate to fill the void and ache in our souls, that we find ourselves doing just about anything and everything in an attempt to feel even remotely whole; but, only Christ can fill the ache and longing of our souls.

God is the Creator of all things, the Author of all eternity, and He has written our life story to include Him. The trouble is that we can't seem to include God. Rather than turn to Him, trust Him, and allow Him to become our fulfillment, we stubbornly turn to other things, trying to find our way in life without Him. In our fallen state, we desperately pursue a substitute for God, and we open our souls to anything that we think will stop the emptiness. However, anything we chase after, other than God, is what the Bible calls an idol.

An *idol* according to *Webster's Dictionary* is defined as "an object of worship; a false god (false lover); an object of expressive devotion."[1] An idol is anything or anyone who creates a wedge between you and Christ, taking up the room in your heart that rightfully belongs to Him. Money, the pursuit of success, your career, things, television, a hobby, sports, even ministry—*anything* that you love and desire more than God is an idol.

Did you realize that even fear and worry are idols? You may not love and desire fear and worry, but if you are focusing more on your situation by worrying and being fearful, that is an idol. Remember, an idol is anything or anyone who creates a wedge between you and Christ.

Even your personal relationships can hinder your relationship with God, if you allow people to take up the room in your heart that rightfully belongs to Christ. Please do not take this the wrong way, but even your children can be idols. I know sweet women completely devoted to their families, tirelessly rearing their precious children. But they are so consumed with their children they spend no time with Jesus.

Having three children of my own, I know and understand the energy and time it requires to take care of children; but, you must not forsake the One who loves you with the "I-don't-have-time-for-God-because-my-children-need-me" attitude. Yes, your children, especially young children, need the love and care that comes from their mother, but who is caring for you? Beloved, you cannot give out what you do not have.

We become consumed with chasing after the things in life that we think will fill our needs... but, only Christ can fill the ache and longing of our souls.

If you are not taking the time to nurture a loving relationship between yourself and the Lord, you are robbing both Him and yourself. Ask the Lord to help you to be creative with your time. Set up regularly scheduled appointments when the two of you can meet privately. Allow Him the access to your heart that He deserves and craves. Permit Jesus to fill your heart with His love (see Romans 5:5), and then you will be able to love beyond yourself. You will be able to love even when it is difficult to show love (see 1 John 4:19). When you come to Christ and allow Him to fill you and care for you, you then will begin to receive the wholeness that you so desperately crave.

What are you hungering for that is not being filled?

_____

_____

_____

_____

_____

What area(s) of your life are you trying to fill with things other than God?

_____

_____

_____

_____

_____

Share with Jesus the desire of your heart.

_____

_____

_____

_____

_____

_____

_____

_____

Day Two

God Desires to Show Mercy

"They exchanged the truth of God for a lie, and worshipped and served created things rather than the Creator" (Roman 1:25).

Yesterday we took a sobering look at the heartbreak of God because of Israel's unfaithfulness, worshiping everything but Him and trying to fill her soul with things that would never satisfy her. Today we are going to continue to look at this topic, while at the same time see the pain that Israel undoubtedly caused herself by looking for love in all the wrong places. Our God is faithful, even when we are not. For God to be unfaithful He would have to forsake Himself.

Pray that your heart would be tender toward all He desires to show you; then dive into today's lesson by reading Nehemiah 9:16-31. Despite all God had done for them, how do you see the people being unfaithful to God?

_____

_____

Despite the unfaithfulness of His people, to rebel and not listen, to turn away and call upon idols, how do you see God remaining faithful?

_____

_____

How do you see God trying to regain the people's attention, trying to get them to turn back to Him? (vv. 27-28, 30-31)

_____

_____

Can you relate personally in any way? (In day three of this week I will share with you my personal testimony and how I can relate personally to this scenario.)

_____

_____

Proud and stubborn the Israelites refused to obey, they refused to listen. They did not remember the miracles God had done for them. They rebelled and chose a leader to take them back into captivity (v. 17). They abandoned everything good and made for themselves an idol and said, "This is our god…" (v. 18).

As hard as it may be to face, we, like the Israelites, have also been disobedient, willful, rebellious toward God and sinful. At some point in our lives, most, if not all of us, have totally rejected the love of Jesus. This happens when we do not receive God's salvation by grace through faith. Other times, even after we accept God's gift of salvation, we take for granted Christ's tender care and mercy, treating Him like a genie in a bottle, continually asking for the life that we think will bring us happiness with no obligation on our part toward Him.

Let's consider another primary example of unfaithfulness found in Jeremiah 3:6-11.

In this scenario God called both Israel and Judah unfaithful; yet, in verse 11 He said that faithless Israel is more righteous than unfaithful Judea. Why? (The answer is found in verse 10.)

_____

_____

Do you realize that it is worse to be half-hearted with the Lord than not to acknowledge Him at all? Don't return to Him in pretense, going through the motions of loving God, but not surrendering your whole heart to Him.

Fill in the blanks according to Revelation 3:15-16, NIV:

I know your deeds, that you are neither _____ nor _____ — I wish you were either one of the other! So, because you are _____ —neither hot nor cold—I am about to _____ you out of my mouth.

If you have strayed from the Lord, whether you have never given your life to Jesus or you have somehow strayed from your pure devotion to Him, allow me to encourage you to return to the Lord with all your heart and be on fire for Him! It's not too late. He loves you with all His heart, and He is anxiously waiting for the day you will turn your whole heart toward His.

Beloved, God the Father implanted longings and desires in your heart that only Christ can fill. He has placed these desires in your heart so that you can connect with His Son, and He can take His rightful place in your life.

When these longings and desires go unfilled, however, you will begin desperately looking for love and happiness anywhere you think you might find it, even harmful places, only to come up empty and void of your longings and desires. You will search for the purpose and the meaning of life, never realizing that true unconditional love, acceptance, intimacy, approval, friendship, and fulfillment are all right in front of you.

Christ will not force any of us to return His love. When God created us He could have made us to involuntarily desire Him, forcing us to choose Him, but He didn't. God has chosen us, and He desires that none should perish (see 2 Peter 3:9). What He longs for is for each of us to make the decision to offer ourselves to Him freely, devotionally, and without reservation.

Also understand that although God will not force us to accept His love, He will bring loneliness, pain and hardship in an attempt to get us to turn back to Him just as He did with the Israelites. God uses this method because, most of the time, people will seek the Lord only when they are in great need. At the time that their hearts are overwhelmed and broken is often the time they will turn to God and cry out for His deliverance. When we are at the end of ourselves, in complete desperation, deeply desiring to end the sorrow and suffering, is when we turn to God.

Please understand that this is not His first choice of action. He does not like to take this approach (see Joel 2:13). He would rather we come to Him and acknowledge our sin, to ask for forgiveness, so that He can pour His mercy and grace on us. It breaks His heart to see us suffer (see Jeremiah 42:10); but, please recognize that He will do it because His deepest desire is to have us with Him forever. He would rather we suffer for a short time here on earth and come to repentance, than end up in eternity without Him.

The bottom line: Christ's desire to be with you is so strong, He will do whatever He needs to do to get you to stop and notice Him. The good news is that God is merciful; He doesn't want to leave us without hope or a way out. He is not surprised by the sinful nature of man. He knew that man would turn away from Him; so, before God created man He devised a plan for his rescue.

End today's lesson by sharing the desire of your heart to turn to Jesus with pure devotion.

_____

_____

_____

_____

He loves you with all His heart, and He is anxiously waiting for the day you will turn your whole heart toward His.

Day Three

God Desires to Forgive

When you are in distress and all these things have happened to you,
then in later days you will return to the LORD your God and obey Him.
For the LORD your God is a merciful God; he will not abandon
or destroy you or forget the covenant with your forefathers,
which he confirmed to them by oath" (Deuteronomy 4:30-31).

In our previous lesson I promised that I would share my personal testimony with you. I can relate all too well to the scenario in Nehemiah 9:16-31. Dear One, never for one moment think that I am preaching at you with no personal conviction of my own. For most of my life I was like the Israelites of the Old Testament. I rejected Jesus, caught up in what I like to call that "catered religion." Basically, I made it up as I went along. I went to church when I felt like it and on holidays. I almost never read the Bible. I prayed only when I really needed something; otherwise, I never gave God the time of day. Oh, let me assure you, I believed in Jesus. I believed that He existed and that He even died for my sins; but I had not yet accepted Him as my personal Lord and Savior. I had no relationship with Him. And all the while as I was going about my life, He waited, trying gently to get me to see that He was right in front of me, showing me over and over that He wanted that close and personal relationship with me (see Isaiah 65:1-3), but I ignored Him; so, again, He waited. Until one day….

My Story …

I am miserable in the course of my life. I am always searching for some meaning and purpose. I am bored and feel like my life isn't worth much. This is a time in my life when everyone around me thinks that I have it all: a wonderful husband who loves me, three beautiful and healthy children, a nice home, no major money worries, and a successful career; but I don't think I have it all. Nothing in my life gives me the happiness I am looking for; not things, family, money, career—nothing. I am angry and frustrated at myself because I know that I have a good life and I am throwing it away with both hands. It's been almost a year now and I continue on this downward spiral, sinking deeper into depression. Feelings of rage overwhelm me and I am out of control. I spend my days sleeping, screaming, and crying. I am frustrated and I feel totally hopeless—so lost and completely alone…. As the days drag on into months, I sink deeper and deeper into the pit of depression. I just want to die.

God allowed the depression to swallow my life for almost a year. Oh, how I cried out to Him for His help during that time, begging Him to remove the anguish and heartache. I asked over and over, "Why has this happened to me?" At that time I didn't understand that I had totally rejected God, that I had turned to false idols to fill my needs.

How does Jeremiah 13:22 and 25 answer the question: "Why has this happened to me?" Check all that apply.

___ Because of sin

___ Because of trusting in false gods (idols)

___ Because of forsaking God

Make no mistake, this was a very difficult time in my life; but please understand, love is the hand that turns the wheel, the driving force behind Christ's passion. God's love permitted the devastating depression to come into my life because He knew that it would bring me to Him.

You see, God doesn't give up on those He loves, even though we sin against Him, turn to idols and reject His love and favor. God will continually, until the return of Christ, reveal Himself to those who do not know Him in order to show the world His mercy and forgiveness (see Isaiah 65:1-3).

Oh, how grateful I am that true love never dies; it always prevails. How thankful I am that He will not always accuse, nor will He treat us as our sins deserve or repay us according to our iniquities (see Psalm 103:9-10). Christ will fight for the love of the bride. He will never leave any of us without hope, even in the pit of sin and despair. God, in His infinite mercy and goodness, did not give up on me when I was deep in the well of depression, and He will not give up on you. God reaches out His hand to all and offers His forgiveness, but we must be willing to accept it.

Christ desires to win our hearts. He wants to reveal to us His true intensions and draw us into His loving embrace, where we will be His, just as He had planned from the beginning.

Day after day, I blindly go through each hour. The needs and care of my toddler son is the only thing that keeps me clinging to life. Deep in my heart I want to die. I want to be free from this desolation and pain. I want out of this well of darkness that has engulfed my life. This morning I got into the shower and began thinking about reaching out to God one more time. Maybe if He knew how desperate I was—I had to try. Suddenly tears began to pour from my eyes as if it was the water flowing from the showerhead. Naked, drenched, and ashamed, I went before the throne of God feeling like I had been ground into the ashes from which I came. "Help me!" I begged, "Only you can help me!"

Suddenly, my heart told me to go to "MOPS" (Mothers of Pre-schoolers, a Christian Women's organization). An older woman was the speaker that day. She shared about the sorrow of a life filled with a lack of purpose and joy, and that the only way to experience pure joy was through Jesus. God was speaking to me. I could hear Him through this woman. After the meeting, I approached her to receive one of her booklets. She greeted me with such love and tenderness. I did not know this woman, but a strong sense of compassion rushed over me, and I suddenly began crying, and before I knew it, I was telling her everything. My sentences were confusing. I was making no sense, not even to myself; but somehow I sensed she understood. Attentively, she listened as I continued to dump my life at her feet. Then, suddenly, without warning, she touched my arm and it stopped. The tears and run-on sentences just stopped—like someone had come and shut off the faucet. The pain in my chest and heart was gone. The nausea in my stomach has vanished, and my soul feels light. The dark cloud which has been covering my life for the past several months in darkness and gloom is gone. I don't know what happened. All I know is that the power that I felt rush through my body was like nothing I had ever felt before. It was beyond mortal; it was beyond human. It could have only come from God.

Since the healing I can't stop thinking about Jesus. So, today, when I saw an advertisement for a Christmas play I had an overwhelming desire to go. Tonight was the final night and it was last minute, but I went and took my two young daughters. Even with no tickets in hand, we were welcomed and shown to three available seats. The play was beautiful with its mix of Christmas hymns, children's delights and the birth of Christ. Throughout my life I had seen the reenactment of the birth performed in a variety of ways, but this time it was different. Something so tender touched my heart, I was overcome with joy and tears. At the end of the play, the pastor of that church asked if there was anyone who wanted to receive Christ as his or her personal Savior. Truthfully, I did not understand what he was talking about, but one thing I was certain of: I needed Jesus. This was the one truth I understood. As the pastor prayed, with tears running down my face, I echoed his every word. It was a heartfelt moment filled with a great longing to make Jesus a part of my life. I am so grateful for His healing hand upon my life; I can no longer live without Him.

At the lowest point of my life, when the depression had all but destroyed me, when I was in a state of mind where I just wanted to die, God reached into my well and pulled me out, instantly healing me and setting my feet on the solid ground of His love.

What does Hosea 6:1-3 promise if we return to the Lord? Check all that apply:

    ____ He will bind up our wounds

    ____ He will restore us

    ____ He will reestablish us to live in His presence

    ____ He will come to us and revive us

Christ desires to win our hearts. He wants to reveal to us His true intensions and draw us into His loving embrace, where we will be His, just as He had planned from the beginning. We don't realize that our sins, like cumbersome chains, hold us bound to a life of slavery (see John 8:34). "Our offenses and sins weigh us down, and we are wasting away because of them" (Ezekiel 33:10). Yet, in our weakness, God is determined to save us, to set us free from ourselves; to give us the freedom to love and be loved.

When I was going through the depression I lost hope. I felt like everything had been taken from me, and I was completely alone. No one understood; and no one could help. And in that make-it-or-break-it moment, on the day I was planning on committing suicide, I cried out to the Lord in complete desperation. Then, without warning, like a knight in shining armor, Jesus heard and answered my cries for His healing hand. In the blink of an eye, He graciously and mercifully healed me from the darkness that had consumed my life. And when I came out of that pit of depression, I came out a different person—zealous and so utterly grateful for what God had done for me that I gave Him my heart and began to return His love (see Psalm 116).

End today by filling in the blanks to Deuteronomy 4:30-31, NIV:

"When you are in distress and all these things have happened to you, then in later days you will _____ to the LORD your God and _____ Him. For the LORD your God is a _____ God; _____ _____ _____ _____ or _____ you or _____ the covenant with your forefathers, which he confirmed to them by oath."

Loved One, God has not forgotten His covenant, and He has not forgotten you. Hallelujah! Get excited about that, return to Him and embrace His forgiveness with everything you've got!

Millions of people suffer from the effects of depression every day, and many different things can be the cause of depression, such as hormonal imbalance. I am not a doctor; I cannot answer most questions about depression, but hear my heart. If you are one of those people who are caught in the clutches of depression, reach out to the Lord—He can heal your mind, body, soul, and spirit. But understand that God is Sovereign and the way in which He chooses to heal you is completely in His hands. God is a miracle God, and, as in my case, He can reach out His hand and heal you in an instant. God's primary purpose, however, is to bring wholeness into your life. He may not heal you exactly the way He healed me; but you're not alone, Dear One. Look to Him—He is the answer to all things.

Day Four

God Desires to Redeem

"…Christ loved the church and gave himself up for her to make her holy, cleansing her by the washing with water through the word, and to present her to himself as a radiant church, without stain or wrinkle or any other blemish, but holy and blameless" (Ephesians 5:25-27).

Can you imagine being presented spotless, pure and without blemish to our Lord Jesus Christ? I cannot wait, but mostly I look forward to the wrinkle-free part since age is now showing itself in noticeable ways. The concept of salvation by grace through faith is mind-blowing to me. I cannot even try to comprehend the plan of deliverance that was put into place before the very creation of the world. To dwell on the fact that God decided to share a covenant relationship with us is inconceivable to me. Yet, before the Word spoke, "Let there be light" (see Genesis 1:3), He devised a rescue plan to save the life of His chosen bride from the mess she would undoubtedly find herself in.

This is what *real* love is. Not that we loved God, but that He loved us and sent His One and Only Son as a sacrifice for our sins (see 1 John 4:9-10, NLT). I can hardly fathom it—the complexity, yet the simplicity, of it all. Jesus was chosen before the creation of the world to be the sacrifice for our numerous sins and waywardness (see 1 Peter 1:19-20).

Think about it, even with our errant lifestyles, He left His heavenly realm and came dressed as a beggar, longing to show His worth, great compassion, forgiveness and kindness. Then, in the most gracious act of mercy, He pays the ultimate price to redeem us, not with perishable items such as gold or silver, but with His own blood (see 1 Peter 1:18-19). The story of Hosea is a wonderful example of this kind of redeeming love.

Please pray for your heart to be awakened to the sacrifice of Christ, and then read Hosea 2:2 through 3:3.

In what ways was Gomer unfaithful to her husband Hosea? List a few of them.

_____

_____

How do we again see the heartbreak of God in this story? (esp. v. 2:13)

_____

_____

Despite the bride's rebellion, what was God's intended purpose? What did He plan to do?

_____

_____

Despite Gomer's rebellious nature, there is a plan to bring her back. In Hosea 3:1, what does the Lord tell Hosea to do?

_____

_____

What parallel is drawn for us in this verse?

_____

_____

According to Hosea 3:2, what was the price Hosea paid to redeem his unfaithful wife?

_____

_____

According to 1 Peter 1:18-19, what was the price Jesus paid to redeem His bride?

_____

_____

Even though Gomer, Hosea's wife, was unfaithful to him, God tells Hosea to go and redeem his wife; to take her back, and love her as God loves His people. Through Hosea, God tells those He loves, "I will not give up on you. Even though you have strayed far from me, I will bring you back. I will make a covenant with you, and you will be mine.

According to Hosea 2:18-23, what does the Lord tell His people He will do? Check all that apply.

____ Make a covenant with them

____ Enter into a betrothal with them

____ Restore the relationship between them

____ Respond to them and make them fruitful

How precious is the true heart of Christ? Can we even begin to understand the extent of His love; how overwhelmed with love and desire He must have been for His bride, and still is?

"In that day," at the appointed time, the time set on the Kingdom calendar, the Bridegroom comes and says, "I will betroth you to me forever; I will betroth you in righteousness, justice, love and compassion (vs. 19-20). I will be faithful to you and you will respond to me." Then, He redeems her. He pays the price, making a way for her to be renewed in right relationship with Him. He blesses her and makes her fruitful; He calls her His own, and He becomes her God (v. 23).

Through His sacrifice of real love, the Bridegroom made a promise, took a vow—an oath that He will not forsake, abandon, desert, leave, disown, renounce, relinquish, give up on, or turn His back on—for He is faithful to all His promises (see Psalm 145:13). This oath, this promise of real love, is what God calls His covenant.

The Covenant is a relationship of love and loyalty between the Lord and His chosen people, His bride. *Vine's Concise Dictionary of Bible Words* relates God's covenant purpose in this "that man be joined to Him in loving service and know eternal fellowship with Him through the redemption that is in Jesus Christ."[2] The word *join* means "to glue or cement together; to unite; to join to oneself—as a wife is to her husband; to yoke together with union in wedlock."[3]

In order to draw on more of the significance of the covenant offered to us through Christ's redeeming sacrifice, we also need to look at the events of the Last Supper. On the night before His death, Jesus gathered His twelve disciples together and offered them the bread and the cup and said to them, "This is my body, which is for you; do this in remembrance of me. This cup is the new covenant in my blood; do this, whenever you drink it, in remembrance of me" (1 Corinthians 11:24-25).

Part of the symbolism of partaking of the cup of the covenant is a Jewish custom. When a bride accepted the groom's proposal and drank from the cup of the covenant, she then became His betrothed. The word *betroth* is defined as "giving one's truth, or pledging one's faith to marry."[4] "In ancient Jewish customs, a betrothal was as formal and legally binding as a marriage. When a betrothal was arranged, a meeting would take place between the two families where a contract was drawn up by the parents or a close friend of the groom. In the presence of witnesses, the groom would present the bride with a piece of jewelry (such as a ring) or something of value. The groom would then give a statement of his intentions to firmly observe the contract. Then the couple would mutually pledge themselves to each other

Through His sacrifice of real love the Bridegroom made a promise, took a vow—an oath that He will not forsake, abandon, desert, leave, disown, renounce, relinquish, give up on, or turn His back on...This oath, this promise of real love, is what God calls His covenant.

by drinking from a cup of consecrated wine. First, the groom would sip from the cup and then hand it to his bride. By doing this, the groom was saying, 'I offer you my life.' If she drank from the same cup, she was agreeing to receive his live, and offer her life to him in return. By accepting the cup, the bride was agreeing to the betrothal and entering into a covenant with him."[5]

That night, Jesus offered up His life (bread) and blood (cup of the New Covenant) to His first disciples. Today, He offers it to us. As we partake of the communion elements, Jesus, in essence, is saying, "I offer you my life. Will you be joined to me?" If you accept, and drink from the cup, you are agreeing to the terms of the covenant contract.

Also during the betrothal ceremony (the Last Supper), Jesus made His followers another promise: According to John 14:2-3, what is the promise?

_____

_____

_____

_____

_____

Again, this is another Jewish Custom. Traditionally, when a betrothal was arranged, it was customary for the groom to leave his bride behind and go to prepare a place for her. Usually, a room was added to the existing home of the groom's parents where the marriage would one day be consummated. When the addition was complete, the groom would return for his bride and take her to live with him.

After the betrothal ceremony was complete, Jesus explained to His followers that He was going to His Father's house to prepare a place for them. When He was finished, He would return so that they could be with Him forever. Let's take a moment and remember that our Jewish Bridegroom is also a carpenter. We can only imagine what kind of home He is building for us!

The next time you celebrate communion, ponder the symbolism and significance of the betrothal with a new heart. This is an act of love and loyalty; it is not to be gone into lightly (see 1 Corinthians 11:27-34). Through His sacrifice, His broken body and shed blood, Christ offers you His redeeming love, making a way for you to be joined to Him in a covenant relationship. The only question that remains is: Will you accept?

Day Five

God Desires Reconciliation

"And through him to reconcile to himself all things, whether things on earth or things in heaven, by making peace through his blood, shed on the cross. Once you were alienated from God and were enemies in your minds because of your evil behavior. But now he has reconciled you by Christ's physical body through death to present you holy in his sight, without blemish and free from accusation" (Colossians 1:20-22).

God's desire is to bring us into right relationship with Him, to reconcile us to Himself through Christ's bloodshed for us on the cross. Love is what drove Christ to the cross. Love wore the crown of thorns and repeatedly took beating after beating, marking His precious body with the scars and wounds of our sins. He willingly shed His blood, desiring to cleanse our past. A profound love for each and every one of us drove the nails deep into His hands and feet (see Matthew 27:11-50).

How does John 3:16-17 and 1 John 3:16a express this love of God?

_____

_____

When you receive Christ as your personal Lord and Savior, you become His; and He and His eternal inheritance becomes yours. Your life here on earth, in the flesh, is temporary; a fleeting moment compared to the length of eternity (see Psalm 39:4-5). Your flesh body will one day pass away, and your life here on earth will be over. But if you belong to Christ, though your body dies, your spirit will live.

Pray for the power of His love, mercy and forgiveness to be revealed to you, and then begin today's lesson by reading John 3:1-21.

What did Jesus tell Nicodemus in verse 3?

_____

_____

What was Nicodemus's response to what Jesus told him? (v. 4)

_____

_____

Fill in the blanks according to John 3:5, NIV:

Jesus answered, "I tell you the truth, _____ _____ can enter the kingdom of God unless he is _____ of water and the _____

Which Spirit is Jesus referring to? (v.5)

_____ The Holy Spirit   _____ a human spirit

Fill in the blanks according to John 3:6, NIV:

Flesh gives birth to _____, but the Spirit gives birth to

_____

Whose spirit is born by the power of the Spirit?

_____ The Holy Spirit   _____ a human spirit

In your own words explain John 3:16-17:

_____

_____

How does being "born again" (vs. 3:6-7) connect with John 3:16-17?

_____

_____

Nicodemus asked Jesus a very important question, one that you may have asked yourself: "How can a man be born again?" "How do I receive God's gift of salvation by grace through faith?" "How do I know that one day I will be in eternity with Christ?" Let's turn again to God's Word for the answer.

According to Romans 10:8-13 what are we to confess with our mouth?

_____

What are we to believe in our heart?

_____

Why is it important to confess with your mouth that "Jesus is Lord?" (v. 10)

_____

_____

There are three keys points that I want to stress from these verses. First, we must confess with our mouth. Second, we must believe in our heart; and third, we must proclaim: "Jesus as Lord." The belief that Paul is talking about here is a deep-seated faith, one that is grounded in the heart and bubbles up and spills over through the mouth proclaiming, "Jesus is Lord." These are not just words. It is the response of a life committed to Christ, and the desire to make Him Lord.

Read these verses carefully. It is not enough to believe "in" Jesus. Even Satan believes "in" Jesus (see James 2:19). Remember, I told you earlier that I believed in Jesus. I believed that He existed and that He even died for my sins; but I did not have a relationship with Him because I had not yet received Him as my personal Savior. I had not yet made Him Lord of my life.

Through Jesus' sacrifice on the cross, God made a way for us to be reconciled to Himself. By His gift of grace and mercy, He made a way for us to be born of His Spirit making us His own (see John 1:12, Ephesians 2:8). Jesus told His disciples, "I am the way and the truth and the life. No one comes to the Father except through me" (John 14:6). The sacrifice has been made through Jesus, but in order to make it our own, we must, like any gift, receive it. We must believe in our hearts that Jesus died for our sins, that He was raised to life, and then we must confess this belief with our mouths by proclaiming that Jesus is Lord.

If you have never accepted God's gift of salvation by grace through faith in His Son, Jesus Christ, allow me to extend an invitation. God's word tells us: "For the wages of sin is death, but the gift of God is eternal life in Christ Jesus our Lord" (Romans 6:23). Right now He is willing and able to forgive all your sins. There is no action of sin that He cannot forgive. There is nothing you have done that is beyond His mercy. He desires to embrace you forever. Allow Him to cleanse you from your sins and heal you. Christ was pierced for your transgressions, and crushed for your iniquities, so that you could be given the opportunity to be with Him forever (see Isaiah 53:5).

If you, however, did at one time receive His gift, but somehow turned away from Him, turning back toward the sinful nature and the ways of the world, recommit your life to Christ. Once again proclaim with your mouth from your heart, "Jesus is Lord."

Through Jesus' sacrifice on the cross, God made a way for us to be reconciled to Himself.

God wants to deliver you from whatever is keeping you from him, and restore the relationship that He longs to share with you. He desires to reconcile with you, and His word promises that if you confess your sins, He is faithful and just and will forgive you of your sins and purify you from all unrighteousness (see 1 John 1:9). But you must be willing to respond and receive His gift of love and life. Jesus offered His life for you on the cross. In His personal and precious act of surrender and sacrifice, with His arms spread wide, He is saying to you, "I love you this much." And now He waits for your response.

So, how will you respond? Will you receive His gift of love and life? Will you confess Him to be Lord? Will you share with Jesus the desire of your heart to be reconciled to Him? Will you make the decision to humble yourself and tell Him that you are a sinner in need of His grace and forgiveness? If you are ready to make that decision, go ahead and tell Him.

I am giving you the space below to date and pen your prayer as a record. (If you have already made the decision to call upon the name of the Lord for salvation, and you are following Him with pure devotion, please take this opportunity to pen your prayer for someone who needs to make the decision to make Jesus a part of his/her life.)

_____

_____

_____

_____

_____

_____

Beloved, if this is your first time responding to the Lord, receiving His gift of eternal life by grace through faith (Ephesians 2:8-9), please contact me or share with someone who can help you grow in your faith. It is important that you "continue to live in Him, rooted and built up in Him, and strengthened in the faith" (Colossians 2:6). You must now begin to receive sound doctrine, from both God's word and a local body of believers, so that you may "grow in the grace and knowledge of our Lord and Savior Jesus Christ" (2 Peter 3:18).

Since I received Christ as my personal Savior and Lord, He has changed my heart, attitude, and life, in ways I never dreamed possible. When you plug into Jesus and do not hold back, allowing Him to become Lord of your life, beautiful changes begin to take place within you; and you begin to travel with Him on an incredible journey. By taking His hand and trusting your heart to Him, you begin the adventure of a lifetime; an adventure of transformation and love so tender that you will wonder how you ever managed without Him.

We were created to be loved. We were created to know and experience the inexpressible joy of giving love and receiving love. All people need love, and women, especially, simply cannot resist romance. Jesus offers high levels of both. Therefore, dive into the relationship that He offers, because if you do, you will not be able to resist Him. For this reason, in Week Three, we will begin to look at a new way of understanding our relationship with Jesus. Once we are reconciled to Him, His desire is to woo our hearts and draw us into an even deeper intimate relationship with Himself.

God Desires You

Listen; hear the heart of the Bridegroom: "What good is being on a throne if I can't be with the one I love? I want to be with you, My bride. Don't you understand, I love you more than anything in heaven and on earth? I love you more than anything I have created, and My heart's deepest desire is for you to love Me more than anything else. I gave up everything to come and be with you—everything—and that included My Throne. I came to earth to win your heart, My bride, and lay down My life for you so that you could be with Me forever. Don't you realize, My love, you are the most important thing to Me, and I desire to sit upon the throne of your heart.

"My desire for you is strong; stronger than death, even death on a cross. Yet, the pain I endured was nothing compared to the empty void growing within My heart. My love burns within Me like a fire (see Song of Songs 8:6). I must be with you, and I will stop at nothing to possess you; all of you. My desire for you is mightier than the mountains, stronger than the raging sea, and higher than the heavens. Steadfast and sure are the arrows of love that yearn to fly from My heart to yours, and I long to draw you into a deeper, intimate, and committed relationship where love never dies."

Reflection and Response

Describe a time in your life when you knew you turned away from God.

_____

_____

_____

_____

What idols did you build during that time? How has the Lord helped you to tear them down?

_____

_____

_____

_____

_____

How does understanding the heartbreak of God help you to draw closer to Him?

_____

_____

_____

_____

How has your life changed since you made Jesus your personal Lord and Savior?

_____

_____

_____

_____

_____

Week Two

Lesson Two

The Greatest Song of Love

Song of Songs 2:4

"He has taken me to the banquet hall and His banner over me is love" (Song of Songs 2:4).

There are two key words hidden in this verse: _____ and _____

What is a banner?

The word for Standard is _____ (pronounced _____).

The word "Nec" is taken from the Hebrew word "Nacac" which means to be _____; displayed; to be conspicuous as a signal; to raise a beacon; to lift up as an ensign.

_____ was lifted up on _____ to stand as a banner for the peoples.

_____: The LORD is my _____ (Exodus 17:15).

What is love?

This is how we know what love is: _____ (1 John 3:16).

"For God so loved _____ that he gave his one and only Son, that whoever believes in him shall not perish but have eternal life" (John 3:16).

"He has taken me to the banquet hall and His _____"
(Song of Songs 2:4).

Gently she combs her hair as she looks into the mirror, watching her reflection gaze back at her. She is nervous, yet her heart yearns for him; longing to be with him, alone in his chambers. The room is still; the only sound that can be heard is the gentle ticking of the clock on the wall. Time seems to be moving slowly; 'Oh, when will they come?' she wonders. Carefully she gets up from her dressing table where she has made herself ready. Stepping back, she turns to face the mirror in order to see herself in full length. It seems like only yesterday she was a simple maiden working in the king's vineyards; darkened by the sun. But now she stands within the palace walls adorning herself for her king. How beautiful. She smiles as she gazes at her glorious gown interwoven with threads of gold. But then she hesitates. 'What will he think? Will he think I am beautiful?' Feelings of inadequacy begin to pierce her heart; "I am not worthy of him," she whispers into the night air.

Unexpectedly, she is startled by the knocking on her bedroom door. "He is waiting for you." The virgin companion speaks through the door. Her heart leaps into her throat, for the time has come; now she will be led to her king. Gracefully, she moves toward the door; taking hold of the knob she quietly opens to her waiting companions. "Good evening." They smile at her. "He is ready for you." Softly she smiles back at them, hoping that her elegant expression will hide her fears. No one speaks as they move swiftly along the corridor; her heart beating in time with their quickening steps; and the rustling of her embroidered dress flows with the rhythm of their pace.

The king's attendants firmly stand on both sides of the double doors that mark the entrance of his chambers. She has been here before; she is familiar with the room and knows the one who waits for her; yet, she is trembling as the attendants open the doors and announce her presence. Desiring to please her king, she gracefully enters the room. He looks up, smiling at her. At the sight of him her heart floods with delight, full of joy and gladness. He moves toward her, not taking his eyes from her exquisite form for a moment. Lovingly, he reaches out and takes her hand. The delight in his eyes quiets her fears; and she feels like she can breathe again. 'He is pleased with me,' she thinks to herself. Affectionately, he takes her in his arms, looking deeply into her eyes; he gently brushes her cheek with the back of his hand. 'It will be okay,' she murmurs to herself, 'He loves me so, I can see it in his eyes.' His touch is soothing to her skin and she allows her heart to be captured in his love. A sense of peace fills her heart as he leans down to kiss her delicate lips gently. Silently the virgin companions slip from the room; and the attendants softly close the doors.

Story inspired by Psalm 45:10-15.

Week Three

The Romance of New Love

- Day One: *God Desires for You to Fall in Love with Him*

- Day Two: *God Desires to Commune with You*

- Day Three: *God Desires to Draw Near*

- Day Four: *God Desires be Welcomed*

- Day Five: *God Desires Your Banquet of Love*

- Reflection and Response: *God Desires You*

In this third week we are going to:

Observe how Christ woos the heart of His Beloved
"Christ's love compels us" (2 Corinthians 5:14).

Begin to understand the purpose of being in intimacy with Christ
"I will build you up again, and you will be rebuilt, O Virgin Israel"
(Jeremiah 31:4a).

Understand what it takes to enter in
"But if from there you seek the LORD your God, you will find him if you look for him with all your heart and with all your soul" (Deuteronomy 4:29).

Prepare to Welcome the King
"…he came to a village where a woman named Martha opened her home to him" (Luke 10:38).

Offer up our banquet of love
"If it pleases the king," replied Esther, *"let the king …come today to a banquet I have prepared for him"* (Esther 5:4).

Day One

God Desires for You to Fall in Love with Him

"Let him kiss me with the kisses of his mouth—for your love is more delightful than wine. Pleasing is the fragrance of your perfumes; your name is like perfume poured out. No wonder the maidens love you! Take me away with you—let us hurry! Let the king bring me into his chambers" (Song of Songs 1:2-4).

Do we, as the church, dare to dream of the possibilities that are offered to us in this unfathomable relationship? Do we dare to embrace what Christ offers us in its purest form of holy intimate love? Do we understand that Christ desires to be our Bridegroom, and share with us what many have called the sacred romance? And in this sacred romance Christ has chosen a name for His church, His bride; she is to be called "Beloved," because she was created to be-loved.

The sanctified romance begins through the power of the Holy Spirit as the Bridegroom begins to woo and romance His bride. The word *woo*, according to *Webster's Dictionary* means "to make love to, to court, to endeavor to gain."[6] Christ is a wooer who desires to gain your heart, to court you and draw you into His everlasting love. He beckons you, through the transforming power of the Holy Spirit, and forms a precious union with you of one heart and one spirit (see 1 Corinthians 6:16b-17).

The word *union* is "an act of joining two or more things into one; ...a marriage."[7] And the word *unite* means "to join; to make into one; to form a whole; ...to be joined together; to grow together; to act as one."[8] And this profound union is confirmed for us in Ephesians 5:31-32, where our relationship with Christ is compared to that of a husband and wife being united in marriage.

Before we dive into today's lesson, I want to take a minute and encourage you if you are hesitating in embracing the concept of the relationship between the bride and Bridegroom. At first, this concept may seem foreign. It may be far easier for you to see God as your heavenly Father than it will be for you to behold Christ as your loving Bridegroom. I understand that what I am sharing may be surprising or even sound unrealistic, even shocking. Perhaps you were not aware that this kind of intimate fellowship is offered with Christ. That's okay. Others have been surprised as well; completely astounded when I shared with them that Christ desired an intimate

Do we understand that Christ desires to be our Bridegroom, and share with us what many have called the sacred romance?

Week Three: The Romance of New Love

union with them. I recall one woman in particular who asked me if I was having some kind of fantasy. I assure you, this is not a fantasy but an amazing reality of love so pure, so profound that it could only come from God. And once she let go of her doubts and concerns, and opened her heart to the sacred romance, she was radically transformed into a passionate follower of the Lord Jesus Christ.

Like this woman, as I lead you through the romance of new love, you must be willing to keep an open mind. Christ wants to be our All-in-all. Therefore, we must learn to accept the biblical concept that those, both Jew and Gentile, men and women, young and old, who belong to Christ, corporately make up the Bride of Christ. And, we, as the bride, are the very objects of His affection. Christ desires to broaden our perspective; that is why, all throughout Scripture, we are given examples of this wonderful union with Christ. And perhaps the most profound example is given to us in the Song of Songs.

Begin today's lesson by asking for the Spirit of wisdom and revelation as stated Ephesians 1:17, and then read Song of Songs chapter 1 through 2:6 and answer the following:

Who is this story about?

_____

How does the maiden describe herself?

_____

_____

Based on her description, how do you think the maiden feels about herself? What do you think she means when she tells us, "My own vineyard I have neglected? (vv. 5-6).

_____

_____

To what does the lover in this story compare the beloved (the maiden)? What does this tell you about the heart of the lover for the beloved? (vv. 9-11, 15)?

_____

_____

As the lover leads the maiden into his chambers, how does she respond to him in her heart? (vv. 12-14; 16)

_____

What changes do you see take place in the confidence level of the beloved?

_____

_____

Don't hold back. Fall in love with your Savior, because the one who embraces Jesus as the Lover of her soul has an inner-life that exceeds that of most believers.

King Solomon, under the influence and inspiration of the Holy Spirit, penned the Song of Songs (See 2 Timothy 3:16-17; 2 Peter 1:20-21). This is a journey of love shared between the lover (King Solomon) and his beloved (Shulammite maiden). In this portion of Scripture I see some wonderful parallels of Christ and His bride. Solomon, I can see as a type of Christ figure, who through his love and devotion to his beloved displays the heart of Christ for His bride. The Shulammite maiden can be seen as us, the church, the Bride of Christ who is on a journey with her lover. Each of us is on a different portion of this journey; remember that although the church as a whole is the Bride, the relationship that we partake of with Christ is individual. I realize that, for many, this portion of Scripture has been given as an example of a godly marriage, and I believe that that is one interpretation; however, there is another possible analogy that cannot and should not be overlooked—the sacred romance.

At the beginning of the story the king (lover) sets out to win the heart of the maiden (beloved), but at first she is astonished that he would even notice her. Clothed with hurt feelings and a sense of unworthiness because of the treatment of others, she implores him to not look at her, (v. 1:6); but in his great love, he assures her of his desire for her (vv. 1:9-11, 15). Then taking her heart in his hands, the king leads the maiden into his chambers. It is a place where they are alone, and soon the maiden finds herself captivated by the king's affections and faint with love (v. 2:3-5).

Christ does the same with us. At the beginning of the sacred romance, the Holy Spirit leads the beloved into a period of time with her Bridegroom that I like to call the "honeymoon season." The honeymoon season is a special time where Christ tenderly takes His beloved (and sometimes hurting beloved) into a quiet place where He begins to pour His holy love upon her. Overwhelmed, the beloved is melted by His tender affections because in many ways she is experiencing His intense love for the first time. During this incredible season of the sacred romance, it is Christ's desire for His beloved to feast on His abundant love.

Week Three: The Romance of New Love

Look again at Song of Songs 2:3-6. How do you see this invitation to feast on His love being offered to the beloved?

_____

_____

_____

How do you see the beloved responding to his out-pouring of love? (vv. 3-5) What does she exclaim? Be specific.

_____

_____

_____

In verses 3-6, how many times do you see the beloved using the words I, me, and my? _____ At this point in their relationship, how do you view the heart of the beloved?

_____

_____

_____

Falling quickly, the beloved melts into what seems like a dream, and she finds herself enjoying a love that she never dreamed possible. Her mind is racing and her heart spilling over with joy that he would value her. Completely love-sick, the beloved faints into his love; because at this point in their relationship her love is a bit self-focused. Yet, even in her immaturity, he greatly enjoys her.

During the honeymoon season the Bridegroom is getting you hooked for life. He is taking you to a place in your relationship where you become so awe-struck with Him that you cannot live without Him. Do not underestimate the honeymoon season. Though the words I am using to describe this incredible time are romantic and passionate, if you submit to the love Christ desires to shower upon you, it will change your life beyond anything you could ask or imagine.

Beloved, God longs for you to be deeply devoted to Him; loving Him with all your heart, soul, mind and strength; filled with wonder and awe for who He is; completely taken, captivated by the heart in a holy relationship; consumed by a burning passion, a hunger, and a thirst that can only be filled though a close personal relationship with Christ. Christ is the Lover of your soul; and, in turn, you are to be an ardent and devoted lover to Him—communing with Him in Spiritual intimacy.

Don't hold back. Fall in love with your Savior, because the one who embraces Jesus as the Lover of her soul has an inner-life that exceeds that of most believers. Take some time right now and express the desire of your heart to Jesus. If you have already fallen deeply in love with Jesus, spend some time in intimate worship. If you are struggling to embrace this concept take this opportunity to ask Jesus to help you see He attempts to woo your heart.

_____

_____

_____

_____

_____

_____

_____

_____

_____

_____

_____

_____

_____

_____

_____

_____

_____

_____

_____

Day Two

God Desires to Commune with You

*"There I will meet with thee, and I will commune with thee from
above the mercy seat, from between the two cherubim
which are upon the ark of the testimony, of all things
which I will give thee in commandment"* (Exodus 25:22, KJV).

Yesterday we began to look at how the Holy Spirit begins to woo the heart of the beloved into the arms of Christ where He begins to reveal His desire to share His intimate love with her. We began to witness the parallel of the sacred romance to the Song of Songs and how this portion of Scripture reveals the heart of Christ for His bride. We saw how He begins to take His sometimes hurting and immature beloved into a quiet place where he begins to pour His love into her. Today we are going to start to understand what begins to happen to the soul of the beloved during this honeymoon season and how vital it is to her spiritual growth and healing.

Once you let go and begin to receive Christ's love through intimate communion, transformation begins to take place. Your soul is nurtured, spiritual growth and healing begin, and you start to become whole in Christ. Understand that a great deal is happening here. In the transforming power of the Holy Spirit you are becoming one with Him in heart, mind, and spirit. Through intimate communion, you reflect the Lord's glory, being transformed into his likeness (see 1 Corinthians 6:16b-17; 2 Corinthians 3:18).

Begin today's lesson by asking Christ to reveal His heart to you. May you be blessed on your journey today.

Remind yourself of Ephesians 5:31-32. Write the verse below:

_____

_____

The word *intimate* means "innermost; deeply familiar; close; and cherished."[9] The word *commune* means "to converse together intimately; to have spiritual intercourse."[10] Christ desires to make His joy and yours complete by fellowshipping with you in intimate spiritual unity.

Before we move on, allow me to take a minute and caution you. Please do not look at this divine romance, or what I am sharing with you, and come to the conclusion that it is of a sexual nature. As we consider the depth of relationship that Christ desires to share with His bride, we must consider it from a heavenly perspective and not an earthly one. It is imperative that we keep in mind the things of God and not the things of man (see Matthew 16:23). The intimacy I am speaking of with Christ is purely of a holy spiritual nature.

Now, once you begin experiencing Christ in intimate communion, once you realize how incredibly loved you are by Your Bridegroom, and that you are the object of His affections, the effects become life altering. This time with your First Love is necessary and vital to your spiritual growth. We all need to be loved, and you need this time in your Lover's embrace if He is to redeem your past and strengthen your future. It is here, in this season, that He begins equipping you for every season you will ever face; because, the truth is, once you have been immersed in the love of Christ, you will follow Him anywhere He desires to lead you (see 2 Corinthians 5:14).

Stop trying to figure it all out. Stop striving; let go of the mindset that says you have to have it all together. Allow Jesus to take you aside and love you in the place where you are right now, even if it is in the midst of pain and immaturity.

Don't be afraid. Do not be one who cannot seem to draw near to Christ because of fear of rejection, past hurts, or bitterness. Remember, only Christ Jesus can fill the needs, true desires, and longings of your heart. Only He can fill the emptiness and bring satisfaction to your soul. When you are alone with Him, totally submitted to Him, restorative healing begins, and little by little you become whole.

Jesus is reaching out to you right now, speaking to your wounded heart. Hear Him calling you, "Come with me by yourself to a quiet place and get some rest" (Mark 6:31).

King David called this quiet place the secret place. This is the place of God's infinite beauty and love. It is the place of God's personal touch upon you; a place where His rivers of peace and tranquility flow. It is a place where you are lifted out of your earthly circumstances and given a higher perspective. It is a place of exclusive passion expressed between the Lover and the beloved. A place of true worship set aside for God alone (see John 4:23-24).

Yearn for the intimacy of the King's chambers (see v. 1:4b). Desire God's manifest presence; you are touched and changed every time you come into the tangible presence of God. When you look into the face of God, every-thing changes. You cannot transform yourself; you can only be changed in the presence of God. The more time you spend with God in the secret place, the more profoundly your life will change. Rest in this promise and claim the assurance of God's Word that says, "He heals the brokenhearted

Once you let go and begin to receive Christ's love through intimate communion, transformation begins to take place.

Week Three: The Romance of New Love

and binds up their wounds" (Psalm 147:3). In the presence of His exquisite love, your broken heart and old wounds are dressed with His healing balm.

According to Isaiah 61:1-4, what was Jesus sent to do? List as many as you can.

_____

_____

Which plan of restoration means the most to you? Why?

_____

_____

Jesus came to bring freedom and healing to those living in despair, loneliness, disgrace, and hurt. He wants to set you free from your past and renew your heart with His love. He longs to turn the ashes of brokenness into something beautiful. Let Him do that. Come into the intimacy of the secret place, so that the rebuilding and restorative work can be done. Allow Christ to pour the oil of His love and praise over you so that He can turn your sorrow and pain into joy and gladness (see Isaiah 61:1-3).

According to Jeremiah 31:3-4, how does the Lord draw us to Himself?

_____

Why does He do this, what does He desire to accomplish?

_____

What is the response of those who come to Him?

_____

_____

Jesus came to bring freedom and healing to those living in despair, loneliness, disgrace, and hurt. He wants to set you free from your past and renew your heart with His love.

No matter where you are right now in your journey with Jesus, turn your face toward His and share the desires of your heart. Hear the desire of His heart to be made one with you. Hear Him inviting you to come and find rest for your soul. Let Him draw you with His loving-kindness. Allow Him to lead you into the secret place and show you how to commune with Him so that He may restore you. Allow His divine love to wash over you, bringing restoration, healing and wholeness.

Day Three
God Desires to Draw Near

"Come near to God, and he will come near to you" (James 4:8).

So, how do we enter this intimate place where the Lord's restorative healing begins? As we search for the answer to this question, begin with a receptive heart and ask the Lord to continue to lead you into deeper places of intimacy with Him.

Read Isaiah 29:13 and compare it with Psalm 63:3-5. In both of these portions, what are the people doing?

_____

_____

Describe the condition of David's heart in Psalm 63:3-5. Is it the same as the people described in Isaiah 29:13? Explain your answer.

_____

_____

In Isaiah 29:13, what is their worship made of? Check all that apply.

___ Pure devotion

___ Pomp and pretense

___ Rules and rituals

If we desire to enter the secret place, our worship cannot be made up of lip service, rules, or ceremony. We will not experience the intimacy of the secret place by giving God intermittent worship on Sunday mornings. God knows the difference; He knows when we are offering Him our lips in worship or our whole heart. Matthew 5:8 says that only the pure of heart shall see God. Only a *pure* heart will commune with God. She is the one who shall come face-to-face with Him in intimate spiritual communion. Synonyms for the word *pure* are "clean; genuine; uncorrupted; spotless; undefiled;" and the word *heart* refers to the whole or entire person; the whole being, not just the organ within the body. David was a worshiper who sought the face of God with his whole heart—his entire being; and Psalm 63:3-5 gives us a wonderful example of that kind of whole hearted worship.

What do the following verses promise when we seek God's face with all our heart?

Deuteronomy 4:29:

_____

Proverbs 8:17:

_____

Jeremiah 29:13:

_____

If we are to enjoy the riches found only in the secret place, we must be willing to open our whole heart and submit to His love. In Revelation 3:20, Jesus tells His bride, "Here I am! I stand at the door and knock. If anyone hears my voice and opens the door, I will come in and eat with him, and he with me." The door that Jesus is speaking of is the door to the heart, the door to the bridal chamber. If we desire to commune with Jesus, to partake of Him and allow Him to partake of us, then we must be _willing_ to open the door and submit to Him. We must eagerly display our longing to go deeper in our relationship with Him. We must be _willing_ to seek His face with ardent worship.

The word _will (willing)_ means "the power of choosing what one will do; … determination; …wish; desire; …to be favorably inclined."[11] Synonyms are "eager; agreeable; ready; prepared." Christ greatly desires to communion with you in intimate fellowship, but you must first desire it; choose it; be eager for it; pursue it, and then be determined to submit to it.

I remember the first time that I expressed my desire to Jesus in wanting to draw closer to Him. As I read the verses in 1 John 1:1-4, I wept with spiritual jealousy over the Apostle John. He had the incredible privilege of hearing, seeing, and touching the living, breathing Word of Life. I wanted that, too. I wanted the same relationship that John and Jesus had—a cherished intimate relationship. My heart ached for it, and I longed for that same close-ness. And once I earnestly shared that desire of my heart with Jesus, He willingly came, prepared me to enter His chambers, and then revealed His intimate love to me.

Notice that He prepared me first. Prior to entering into the secret place for the first time, Christ prepared me to handle the holy. Look again at the synonyms for the word _willing_: "eager; agreeable; ready; prepared." If we desire to enter into the secret place, we must be willing to be prepared and made ready.

This doesn't mean that we need to have it all together in order to come. Not one person I know has entered the secret place because she is special, or because she has reached some heightened spiritual perfection. The fact is, none of us are perfect, and God knows that. We all need the love of Christ, and even in our weakness and immaturity He doesn't withhold it. You do, however, need a pure and willing heart, and an earnest desire to be near Him. I am emphasizing this point because if you are resisting, unwilling, fearful, skeptical, or harboring any unrepented sin, you will not enter into the secret place.

If you have not already experienced what I call the "honeymoon season" with your Betrothed, or if you have somehow drifted from the sacred romance with Christ, please ask for this time with Him and abandon yourself to His love. Close your eyes; center all your attention on Jesus. Fervently seek His face as you lay aside the distractions of the day. Worship with your whole heart. Remember, focused, passionate worship opens the door to the secret place, bringing the manifest presence of God near. Don't be in a hurry; relax and allow His Holy Spirit to draw deeper, closer (see Psalm 46:10), until you are wrapped in the warmth and tenderness of His love. One of the primary reasons most of us have never entered the secret place is because we are impatient. There will be times when you will seem to make that intimate connection with Christ immediately, but then there will be times when you will have to wait upon the Lord. Be patient; continue to worship, continue to seek His face, continue to pray "O God, you are my God, earnestly I seek; my soul thirsts for you, my body longs for you, in a dry and weary land where there is no water" (Psalm 63:1).

Oh, Bride of Christ, how I pray that you will receive a revelation of God's love. Not that you will ever understand it completely while on this earth, but I pray that the truth of His love will penetrate your heart. I have discovered that true spiritual intimacy with Christ does not begin on the day you realize you love Him, the day you claim salvation, or even grow in an appreciation of all He has done for you. True spiritual intimacy with Christ, the romance with your First Love, that heartfelt closeness with your Bridegroom and the Lover of your soul, does not begin until you receive the revelation of God's love for you. It is vital that your heart be awakened to the truth that God desires you, longs for you, dreams of you, and waits with great anticipation for the day you will be together forever. Until the astonishing truth of that revelation hits your heart, you are merely existing in the realm of salvation, and you have not begun to enter into the sacred romance with Christ.

Yearn for more because I guarantee you, no matter where you are right now in your journey with Jesus, it can be better. Christ is always calling His bride into deeper places of intimacy, continually encouraging her to take the next step in drawing closer to His heart. His desire is to pull you so close that it will feel like you are breathing the very air of heaven. This kind of fellowship is beyond measure, but how desperately does the willing desire of your heart yearn to be intimately acquainted with Christ? Is it the desire of your heart to enter into the secret place and know this love that surpasses knowledge? If so, then you must be willing to desire Him, submit to Him, and allow Him to prepare you.

If I can experience it with Christ, I want it. How about you? I have only begun to experience all of what God has in mind for me to experience with Him. Yet, at the same time, I feel that He has already taken me so far beyond my dreams and expectations that I don't know what could possibly be waiting for me in the near or distant future, but my heart cry is an enthusiastic, "Yes, I am willing!"

Won't you join me? Desire to draw near to God because He desires to draw near to you. Open the door to your heart and seek His face. Worship Him in purity, submit to His desires, and allow His Holy Spirit to lead you into the intimate chambers of the King.

If you are finding it difficult to come into the secret place, share your heart with Jesus. Ask Him to help you, by the power of His Spirit, to draw near.

_____

_____

_____

_____

_____

_____

_____

_____

_____

_____

_____

Day Four

God Desires to be Welcomed

Jesus replied, "If anyone loves me, he will obey my teaching. My Father will love him, and we will come to him and make our home with him"
(John 14:23).

Christ is longing for His bride to be excessive, wasteful, and unrestrained with Him. He loves to be extravagant with her, off the charts and without limit.

What is your home like? Is it inviting, warm and comfortable? Do people feel at ease when they come for a visit? Do you serve refreshments or light candles? Do you clean and prepare your house for company?

I have a dear friend; her name is Miriam. When I go to her house for fellowship and prayer, I always feel welcomed and invited every time I step through the door. A warm and friendly smile graces her face as cheerful greetings flow from her heart. She embraces me, making me feel loved and valued. The aroma from the lit candles fills the air and the Christ-honoring music delights me the moment it touches my ears. She is so enthusiastic about my arrival that it makes me feel as though she has been anticipating the meeting for days and could hardly wait for me to arrive. It is a wonderful feeling to be welcomed this affectionately and passionately into someone's home. It is such a joy that, I, too, greatly anticipate going to be with her. I just absolutely love being there; the atmosphere is so pleasing I immediately feel right at home.

We love it when someone goes out of her way to make us feel special, don't we? What a joy it is to feel loved and cherished. Words cannot describe the feeling, and our hearts just seem to soar. When this happens we want to visit again and again. This is exactly what God is longing for. He is looking for a place where He feels welcomed, cherished, treasured, and loved.

Think about this scenario: How would you feel if a friend invited you over for coffee, and then left you sitting in the kitchen while she went upstairs to make the beds? Whether we realize it or not, all too often, this is exactly how many of us treat Christ. We invite Him in, but then we ignore Him.

It is the goal of these next two lessons, to show you the importance of setting the atmosphere of your heart and making Jesus feel welcomed and loved. Christ is pursuing you with all of His heart; and, in turn, He delights in your efforts to make Him feel right at home.

Let's look at an example of this kind of cherished welcome from Scripture. Begin by praying Jesus will always be welcomed in your heart, and then read Matthew 26:6-10.

How does this scene from Scripture offer us an example of making Jesus feel welcomed?

_____

_____

List some of the specific ways Mary made Jesus feel cherished and loved.

_____

_____

_____

What are some of the ways you make Jesus feel loved and welcomed within your heart?

_____

_____

_____

In Matthew 26, Mary gives us a wonderful example of *extravagant* worship. Try to picture it. Mary enters the room with an alabaster jar filled with expensive perfume called Spikenard. As she walks over to where Jesus is reclining at the table, imagine with me the look of anticipation on His face as He patiently waits for her to come and sit at His side. She kneels down beside Him and breaks open the jar at His feet and begins anointing Him with the perfume. Envision the great love she displayed. In your mind, can you see Jesus' reaction? Can you picture Him thoroughly enjoying her extravagant affections, trying desperately to savor the moment, minus the aggravation dished out by His distraught disciples?

The word *extravagant* means "excessive; wasteful; unrestrained."[12] I love the word "wasteful" in this definition. Mary took her greatest earthly possession and she wasted it on Jesus. This jar of perfume was her earthly inheritance, but she had been given the revelation that there was something better, an even greater inheritance (see Matthew 6:21), and she did not hesitate to display her extravagance, despite the opinion of others (v. 9). The disciples saw her extravagance as wasteful alright, but Jesus saw the extravagance expressed in a different way as Mary poured out her excessive and unrestrained affection in an incredible act of abandoned worship.

This is the kind of loving welcome that Jesus is looking for from us. Christ is longing for His bride to be excessive, wasteful, and unrestrained with Him. He loves to be extravagant with her, off the charts and without limit. He longs to shower her with His unexplainable, unequivocal, unparalleled, supreme, matchless, and incomparable love and affection. This is the lavish romance that Christ desires to share with His bride, and this should also be the same kind of relationship that she desires to share with Him.

Like Mary, I want my worship of Jesus to be outrageous, too. How about you? Let's savor in the freedom to express our love for Him in true spirit-flying liberty—no hindrance, no obstacles, no fear, no condemnation, just pure unleashed outrageous worship. Allow me to challenge you, right now, to go and sit at His feet and pour out the sweet fragrance of your perfumed love all over Him. Prepare your heart for worship and then set the atmosphere, just like my friend Miriam. Create a mood for prayer and intimacy with Christ. Be expressive. Let the demonstration of your love reflect your personality. If you love candles, light them. If you enjoy music, play it softly in the background. Then, through intimate prayer, fill His heart with cherished words of praise and thanksgiving; express to Jesus how you feel about Him. Fill His ears with sweet terms of endearment. Invite His presence to come closer with praise and thanksgiving (see Psalm 100:4), shower Him with your gift of love, and offer up to Him the fragrant aroma of your adoration and affection.

If you like, use the space below to pen your extravagant prayer of worship to Jesus.

_____

_____

_____

_____

_____

_____

_____

_____

_____

_____

Day Five

God Desires Your Banquet of Love

"If it pleases the king," replied Esther, "let the king…come today to a banquet I have prepared for him" (Esther 5:4).

All this week we have been focusing on intimate fellowship with Christ. We have come to His banquet hall and feasted on the abundance of the love He offers. We have begun to understand the purpose of this intimate place and why it is so vital to our spiritual growth in becoming all of who we are meant to be in Christ. Then we examined our willingness to submit and our desire to enter in. Now it is time to continue setting the atmosphere of our hearts, to prepare a banquet of love for our King and worship Him in extravagance.

In our previous lesson we witnessed Mary's act of extravagance as she made Jesus feel welcomed and loved. Today we are going to focus our attention upon Esther. Now here is a gal who knows how to win favor with the king. Esther is a wonderful example to us of what it means both to prepare ourselves for our encounter with the king and lay a banquet before for him to feast upon.

Begin today by preparing to offer your banquet of worship to the King by preparing your heart through repentance then read Esther 4:1 through 5:8. If you are not familiar with the story of Esther, you may wish to begin your reading at Chapter 3 so that you can understand the context.

What did Mordecai ask Esther to do? (v. 4:8)

_____

What did Esther fear in doing what Mordecai asked? How long had it been since the king had requested her presence? (v. 4:11)

_____

What was the exception to this law?

_____

The king of Persia had great power and wealth, and according to the law, anyone who came before him without an invitation was put to death. Esther was scared for her life. If she approached the king unannounced, he had the authority to have her put to death. In our human response, the safe thing to do would be to avoid the conflict.

However, what did Mordecai tell Esther in verse 13? Check the correct response.

____ That she would be safe within the palace

____ That whatever she decided to do would be fine

____ That she would also be killed

Esther had no choice; she had to go before the king—either way she was at great risk of losing her life.

When she had made the decision to go before the king, she said, "If I perish, I perish," After she made this decision, what did she do? Place a one next to the first thing she did? (v. 4:16) Place a two next to the second? (v. 5:1)

____ She fasted and prayed

____ She took a nap, she would need her strength

____ She asked Mordecai for advice

____ She dressed for her encounter with the king

Isn't it wonderful to know that we do not take our life into our hands when we make the conscious decision to go before our King? Because of the atoning sacrifice of Jesus Christ, we have been given a way to come and share our heart with the King any time, day or night. However, there is something in Esther's approach that I would like to point out. Esther did not just come into the king's presence and announce what she had on her mind. First, she took the time to prepare her heart before presenting herself to the king; she even dressed for the occasion. She laid aside every distraction and fear and prepared her heart through fasting and prayer. I would like to suggest that our parallel to this sort of preparation is quietness of heart and mind. We do not need to fast for three days and nights before approaching our King, but prior to our offer of worship to the King, we must lay aside everything that is a distraction to us. This may be anything from worries to an overrun and hectic schedule. Ask the Holy Spirit to quiet your heart and mind. Be still and know that He is God (see Psalm 46:10), and then come before Him with a repentant and pure heart.

Continuing with our storyline, how did the king react when he saw Esther standing in the inner court? What did he say to her? (vv. 2-3)

_____

_____

We do not need to fast for three days and nights before approaching our King, but prior to our offer of worship to the King, we must lay aside everything that is a distraction to us.

Week Three: The Romance of New Love

How did Esther answer him? And how did the king respond to her? (vv. 4-5)

_____

_____

When the time had come to present herself, Esther stood in the inner court, at the entrance to the throne room and waited for the king to acknowledge her. Then, upon receiving the king's approval, she approached the throne. Notice that even though Esther thought she was risking her life to come before the king, he was pleased she had come, and he welcomed her into his presence. My heart floods to think we do not have to fear coming into the presence of our King—He is always pleased when we come into His courts and He delights in raising His gold scepter, giving us permission to approach His throne. Yet, even with this understanding, many of us often seem to stand in the distance.

When you desire to talk with Jesus, where do you see yourself in the palace of the King? Check the response that best fits you.

_____ The outer courtyard

_____ The inner court at the entrance to the throne room

_____ In the throne room, but standing off to the side with all the other people who have come to see the King

_____ Before the King, face-to-face

_____ Not in the palace at all

Do you understand that you do not need to stand in the outer courts shouting your prayer praises and requests to God. Do not be afraid to step over that threshold and draw closer to the Lord. And even though many others, elders, angels and the like, stand before and around the throne of grace, do not let this be a distraction in keeping you from coming before the King, face-to-face. Be like Esther, standing before the king, up close and personal.

Notice with me something special in Esther's encounter with the king. Esther begins her interaction with the king by offering him a banquet to honor him and express her desire to please him (v. 5:4). Even though the king opened the door for her to lay her requests before him, she does not begin the conversation with those requests; but instead offers him a gift. Do you see what Esther is doing? This is a very valuable lesson for us as the bride of Christ. Before you even hint that something is pressing your heart, come before your King and offer up your devoted worship prior to your request. The Lord desires to hear your petitions and requests. In fact, He already knows what they are before you utter a single word, but first offer Him your gift of love, devotion and heart-felt worship.

Before I learned this lesson from Esther, I would come before the King with no confession and very little praise and thanksgiving. If something was weighing on my mind I got right to it, dumping those prayer requests and petitions at His feet without even a greeting. It was like I was trying to walk straight into the Holy of Holies with my list of demands and mud on my shoes. I hope you understand what I am trying to share with you. Yes, we have complete and total access to our King because of the work done at Calvary, that curtain is torn in two. "It is finished" (John 19:30). And we can share with the King anything, anytime, but learn this lesson from Esther—prepare your heart and offer your banquet of worship first.

Let your fragrance of love fill the heart of the King first, then tenderly look up at Him and tell Him about your fears, worries, longings, and bad hair days.

Once at the banquet that Esther had prepared for the king what happened? What question did the king ask Esther? (v. 5:6)

_____

_____

_____

How did Esther respond to the king? (v. 5:7-8)

_____

_____

_____

Esther's gift had pleased and honored the king. She had touched his heart by her loving gesture of preparing this banquet for him, and he was delighted with her and her gift. Yet, when the king asked a second time what her petition was, Esther does not state her request at this time either. Instead, she offers up to the king another banquet, another offering of her honor, devotion, and love.

How do you think our King would react if we responded this way? What if we answered the King's acknowledgement with yet another offering of love? What if we said, "O Great King, I do desire to share my heart with you and to inform you of what is troubling me. I do have a matter to discuss with you, but, first, if it pleases you, allow me to continue worshiping you. Then I will offer you my requests, knowing that you will hear me and answer me with your wisdom and love."

These lessons from Esther are fundamental, yet extremely important. Learn to prepare prior to coming before the King. Come into His presence with thanksgiving, and offer up your banquet of love. Yes, we can share anything with Him. We can bring our burdens and lay them at His feet, because the Lord's compassionate heart is willing to listen to our needs and concerns; but learn to offer your banquet first. Shower Him with the sweetness of your affectionate praise. Let your fragrance of love fill the heart of the King first, then tenderly look up at Him and tell Him about your fears, worries, longings, and bad hair days.

End this week with a banquet of love. Christ is longing for you to be excessive, wasteful, and unrestrained with Him. Go, right now, sit together at the banquet table you have both prepared. He has taken you to the banquet hall and His banner over you is love (Song of Songs 2:4). Now, you too, offer your banquet and pour the sweet fragrance of your love all over Him in an act of extravagant worship.

God Desires You

"Come dance with me, my bride," He lovingly asks. "I will dance with you," she answers. In a grand ballroom, with a high graceful ceiling, he takes her hand. The walls are trimmed in gold relief patterns, displaying a charming design. And here in this stately room, their two elegant forms become one. The king, as if dressed for his wedding, is adorned in a white suit trimmed in gold. His bride is dressed in a white gown, interwoven with gold, which sways gracefully to the movement of their bodies. Warmly, he holds her in his arms, and together they dance timelessly to the flow of the music.

It is like a fairy tale as he moves her effortlessly across the ballroom floor, then lifts her high above his head and moving her in a circle. Her dress falls down around him, as he holds her in the air. With his eyes looking up at her face and his heart full of delight, he exclaims, "This is my bride." The moment is so exquisite, she can hardly breathe. Oh, how he has captured her heart. He is so pleased with her that he is enchanted by a single glance of her eyes. As the music comes to a close, he gently draws her close, so close that his heart is beating next to hers. And there they are, just the two of them, in this grand and glorious ballroom, inspired by new love.

Reflection and Response

Give Jesus every hurt, fear, and rejection and ask Him to restore you with His intimate love, so that, you, too, may pick up your tambourine and dance with the joyful.

_____

_____

_____

_____

The Lord does want to dance; and He longs to dance with you in beauty and grace. How does this offer of the sacred romance make you feel? Share your heart.

_____

_____

_____

_____

How do you think becoming one with Christ through intimate union and extravagant worship would transform your life?

_____

_____

_____

_____

Are you struggling to embrace the sacred romance? If so, express your heart to Jesus. Ask Him to give you the Spirit of wisdom and revelation so that you may know and understand what He desires to share with you.

_____

_____

_____

_____

Week Three

Lesson Three

Captured by Love

Song of Songs 1:9 to 2:7

1. God created _____, marriage and _____

2. The Song of Songs is a _____, a parallel, _____ of what God intended _____and _____ intimacy to be.

3. Jesus wants to reveal Himself as a _____ _____

4. You will not experience the sacred romance with Jesus until you _____ it.

5. How do we enter this place of intimacy with the King?

   a. _____ _____ your doubts, worries, distractions and fears (Esther 4:11-14).

   b. _____ for your encounter with the King through _____ (Esther 4:16).

   c. Dress: Wear the _____ of righteousness and _____ of salvation (Esther 5:1)

   d. _____ upon the King (Esther 5:2). _____ to the Holy Spirit.

6. This place of intimacy is found only through _____ in intimate _____

   a. Intimate prayer is a _____ form of _____

7. Great _____ is found in the King's chambers.

Gracefully the dawn awakens and peeks over the horizon, stretching its colors across the morning sky; gently kissing everything it touches. She opens her eyes to gaze upon the delicate hues of pink and yellow which fill her room. Slowly she sits up and gently lifts the blanket from her body. The soft sound of the bird's carefree song fills her ears. Quietly she moves toward the window, the breeze coming in through the open window blows her hair away from her face. As she sits at her window, she watches the trees as they sway with the wind; the rustling leaves dance so elegantly. A colorful butterfly rests its wings on the petals of a fragrant flower spreading its blossom to face the warmth of the sun. On mornings like these she could sit forever at her window watching nature come to life and listening to the joyful sound of creation awakening before her. Then something deep within her stirs her heart and she feels as alive as the world around her.

Week Four

The Awakening to Abundant Life

- Day One: *God Desires to Reveal Himself*

- Day Two: *God Desires to Display His Splendor*

- Day Three: *God Desires to Feed Your Soul*

- Day Four: *God Desires to Open Your Spiritual Eyes and Ears*

- Day Five: *God Desires Good Stewards*

- Reflection and Response: *God Desires You*

In this fourth week we are going to:

Define the glory of God
"Now show me your glory" (Exodus 33:18).

Witness the glory in Creation
"The whole earth is full of His glory" (Isaiah 6:3).

Know God in His Word
"Open my eyes that I may see wonderful things in your law" (Psalm 119:18).

Understand Him through Holy Spirit fellowship
"[For my determined purpose is] that I may know Him [that I may progressively become more deeply and intimately acquainted with Him, perceiving and recognizing and understanding the wonders of His Person more strongly and more clearly]" (Philippians 3:10, AMP).

Record the revelation of His glory
This is what the LORD, the God of Israel says, "Write in a book all the words I have spoken to you" (Jeremiah 30:2).

Day One

God Desires to Reveal Himself

"Arise, shine, for your light has come, and the glory of the LORD rises upon you. See, darkness covers the earth and thick darkness is over the peoples, but the LORD rises upon you and his glory appears over you. Nations will come to your light, and kings to the brightness of your dawn" (Isaiah 60:1-3).

In John 10:10, Jesus said, "I have come that they may have life, and have it to the full." The New Living Translation records Jesus' words this way: "My purpose is to give life in all its fullness." This is a wonderful promise, but do we truly know what it means to live an abundant life?

What do you think it means to live the abundant life?

Christ desires for you to live the abundant life in Him. He wants to take your life, at the point where you are right now, and awaken it by filling you with His life, love, and purpose.

Through this study you are in the process of discovering your heart's truest desires, the ones that God implanted and only Christ can fill. And whether or not the desires of your heart are being filled can be determined by one question: "Do you feel alive?" I don't mean simply breathing, but truly and expressively alive. Does your soul soar high above the clouds and feel the depth of the love you have been shown in Christ? Are you alive to where the very world around you dances and sings with life? Are you swept up in the joy of each new day? Beloved, the glory of the Lord is revealed in a person that is fully alive. If you feel alive, wonderful, I pray you will continue to open your heart to Jesus so that you may experience more than you could ask or imagine. If you don't, do not despair, desire is the beginning of an awakening that will stir your heart and inspire your soul.

Christ wants to give you a life full of abundance by giving you your truest desires. He desires to awaken your soul and stir your heart; because in Him you live and move and have your being (see Acts 17:28). Christ is alive, and He desires to be alive in you, not simply existing in your body. Beloved, "if the Spirit of him who raised Jesus from the dead is living in you, he who raised Christ from the dead will also give life to your mortal bodies through his Spirit, who lives in you" (Romans 8:11). Christ desires for you to live the abundant life in Him. He wants to take your life, at the point where you are right now, and awaken it by filling you with His life, love, and purpose.

The word awaken means "to rouse from sleep; to excite."[13] The awakening is a development; a beginning; a stirring of the heart; an arousing of the soul.

Often the romance of new love (that precious honeymoon season), and the awakening happen simultaneously. The miracle begins as the Wooer romances His beloved, and she delightfully loses herself in His love. His overwhelming approach in romance and love captures her heart, and she finds herself falling in love with Him. Suddenly, she begins to notice things she never noticed before; like the colors of the sky, or the fragrance of the flowers at the market, or the scent after a rain shower. She cannot explain it, but everything is just better. Joy floods her heart and she feels vibrant. Her senses are heightened with a keener sensitivity as her heart and soul come alive in new love. The world around her sings, coming to life with color and fragrance so alive she wonders how she ever missed it. Her life is awakened by love, and it is like she is breathing for the first time.

Through three key sources, God reveals His glory, longing for you to get to know Him through His creation, His Word, and fellowship with His Holy Spirit. Through all He has made, God has been wooing you from the beginning, inviting and arousing your desire. Starry nights, beautiful sunsets and fragrant flowers heighten and awaken the romance in your heart, telling you something about Eden, God's precious garden of love and beauty. Through His Word, God discloses His Person and personality, giving you a clear description of who He is, while romancing your heart through songs of love. And by His Spirit, He longs to fill you, without measure, of His life and purpose.

Reminders of His Person and love are everywhere, continually revealing His glory. According to Psalm 97:6, who will see the glory of the Lord?

    ___ No one

    ___ Only Christians

    ___ Everyone

Read Psalm 19:1-4, how will the glory of God be declared? Be specific.

_____

_____

_____

What language does the glory of the Lord speak? Where does it go?

_____

_____

_____

Once again—who will witness the glory of God?

____ No one

____ Only Christians

____ Everyone

What did Isaiah proclaim in Isaiah 6:3 about the glory of God?

_____

God desires to reveal His glory to the world. He wants the whole world to know Him firsthand. Therefore, be enthralled and in awe of the glory of the Lord. Stand in wonder and be amazed at all He desires to share with you. Seek His glory as Moses did when he told the Lord, "Now show me your glory" (Exodus 33:18).

Through His glory, God gives you the opportunity to see Him, hear Him, touch Him, smell Him, and taste Him, within the wonders of His creation, Word, and Spirit.

According to the *Vine's Concise Dictionary of Bible Words* the word *glory* means "beauty; ornament; distinction." In the New Testament the word *glory* is referenced to as the word *doxa*, which means "the manifested nature and acts of God; revealing and exhibiting the perfection of His character; righteousness; grace; divinity; everlasting power; His attributes; and eternal ways."[14] Through His glory, the Lord God reveals Himself; His true nature; making Himself recognizable, showing the world who He is.

His glory is the disclosure of His person. Through His glory, God gives you the opportunity to see Him, hear Him, touch Him, smell Him, and taste Him, within the wonders of His creation, Word, and Spirit. He desires for you to be aware of the fact that He is surrounding you all the time. He desires for you to know Him and recognize His nature, His character, and His worth; and He longs for you to savor in the fact that you know Him personally (see Jeremiah 9:24).

I am consistently asking God to reveal Himself to me, requesting for Him to show me and teach me something new about Himself. I want to know Him more. I want to love Him more. I desire for Him to transfigure Himself right before my eyes, as He did with Peter, James and John (see Matthew 17:1-8; Mark 9:2-8).

In what ways have you seen Jesus transfigure and reveal Himself before you? How have these revelations of His glory made you feel alive in Him?

_____

_____

_____

Through the prophet Jeremiah the Lord said: "Call to me and I will answer you and tell you great and unsearchable things you do not know" (Jeremiah 33:3). The Lord wants to *confide* in you, He wants to reveal His glory. The word *confide* means "to hand over to the charge of; to entrust to; to tell a secret; to put faith in; to rely on."[15] Synonyms for the word confide are "reveal; divulge; disclose; tell; open your heart to; unburden your heart to; and speak in confidence."

According to Psalm 25:14, who does the Lord confide in? What does He share with them?

_____

_____

Christ is desperate to talk with you through His creation, Word and Spirit. He greatly desires to confide in you and share the mysteries of His person and the secrets of His covenant. He wants to entrust His heart to you, and disclose the wonders that are now hidden (see Jeremiah 33:3). If you are willing, Christ will reveal Himself, giving you a glimpse of His glory here on earth.

God has given you senses; affording you the ability to know Him better. So, go ahead and dive in, use what God has given you to experience the wonders and beauty of the world around you. As the different seasons unfold, embrace each one. Go for walks, allow the Holy Spirit to open your spiritual eyes and see what God reveals to you. Dive deep into the living, breathing Word of God and taste for yourself the joy of finding the richness of His love for you. Come to the banquet hall and feast on what He has lovingly prepared. Come daily into the presence of the Lord and allow Him to pamper you with His sweet delights. Swim in His Holy Spirit and enjoy the wealth of His abundance and goodness.

In our next three lessons, we are going to ask God to share with us through His creation, His Word, and His Spirit, affording Him the opportunity to reveal Himself so that we may experience His glory. Pray for the Holy Spirit to open your heart and eyes wide, Beloved, because this week, we are going to take a deeper look at each of these three key sources in which God reveals Himself, in an attempt to witness the miracle of the awakening.

Share the desires of your heart with Jesus. In what ways would you like for Him to awaken your soul?

_____

_____

_____

Day Two

God Desires to Display His Splendor

"For since the creation of the world God's invisible qualities—his eternal power and divine nature—have been clearly seen, being understood from what has been made, so that men are without excuse" (Romans 1:20).

For me, new love was stirring my heart as passion gripped my soul. I went from what I would call a good relationship with God, to where I simply fell in love with Jesus. From that moment on I felt alive.

This week we are focusing on the awakening of our souls to the life of Christ within us. Therefore, let's ask the Holy Spirit to open our spiritual eyes and ears that we may witness the glory of His person in the world around us. As you do this lesson, weather permitting, go outside or sit by an open window, so that you may take in everything the Lord desires to reveal to you.

For me, the awakening happened in the spring of a very difficult year; and even though my future was uncertain and my life seemed to be falling apart, my soul soared to heights that I had never dreamed possible. At the start of this incredible season, God revealed Himself to me as my All-in-all when my husband became very ill and could not work.

At that time, I asked Christ to be my "husband." I desperately needed Him to step into that role. I needed Him to help me with caring for my ill husband and my children; to make decisions, provide finances and medical care; and to nurture my needs. Jesus faithfully and completely stepped into this role and filled my every need far beyond my expectations. When God said, "I AM WHO I AM" in Exodus 3:14, He was in essence saying: I Am the Everlasting; I Am the All-Powerful; I Am the Invincible; I Am the Great Supplier; I Am everything you will ever need. Look to me and I will fill those needs.

By God's healing grace, my husband did get better and is once again gainfully employed. But during that difficult year, because of the way Christ had revealed Himself to us and met our deepest needs and desires, He strengthened our marriage, and opened new doors of tenderness for us. Even though this was one of the most challenging times of our lives, it was also one of the most beautiful. Through the hardship and difficult struggles of that year, our relationship with Christ grew tremendously; differently, but we both drew closer to the Lord.

For my husband, he began to see Christ's care and concern when He graciously saved him from a terrible illness. He witnessed Christ's healing hand, and experienced His mercy as He placed his life on a new path. He went from having very little relationship with God, to a greater understanding of who God was as He began to deepen the revelation of His love in my husband's life.

For me, new love was stirring my heart as passion gripped my soul. I went from what I would call a good relationship with God, to where I simply fell in love with Jesus. From that moment on I felt alive. My heart and soul were flooded with life and love, and for the first time I knew what it meant to experience the abundant life. Suddenly, everything was better. I began to look at the world around me with the inquisitiveness of someone young at heart (see Matthew 18:3). Now, unrestricted in my new adventure, I began to see things I had never seen before. The whole earth simply came to life.

Throughout the psalms many mentions are made of the glory of God in His creation. According to the following verses, in what ways is creation coming to life before the psalmist's eyes?

Psalm 40:3:

_____

Psalm 96:12-13:

_____

Psalm 98:8:

_____

In Psalm 98:4, what does the psalmist instruct the whole earth to do before the Lord? Check all that apply:

____ Shout for joy

____ Burst into triumphant song

____ Celebrate

How is this jubilant celebration expressed in Isaiah 55:12?

_____

_____

Hopefully, you are outside for this question. Close your eyes and listen? What do you hear from God's creation? (Possibilities: birds, wind rustling the trees, water running along a stream). How is this joyful sound a praise offering to the glory of God?

_____

_____

Please read aloud Psalm 104. As you read, hear the voice of His creation and try to picture in your mind the wonders of the Lord. What do you witness in the interaction between God and all that He has created? How does He care for all He has made? How does it respond? How does each portion of His creation speak to you about who God is?

The heavens:

_____

_____

The earth:

_____

_____

The waters:

_____

_____

The mountains:

_____

_____

The beasts of the field:

_____

_____

The moon and sun:

_____

_____

Man:

_____

_____

In everything, see the wonder and majesty of who He is. With the curiosity of a child, enter in. Have you ever watched a small child enjoying the surprise of new things? She is so fascinated by the simplest things, tickled with delight over things that we, as adults, have long since stopped noticing. Go ahead, be a child again and watch the merriment of a butterfly as it dances on a breeze. Feel the gentle wind as it kisses your cheek and the warmth of the sun as it hugs and touches your skin. Smell the lilac in the spring, and the freshly cut grass in the summer. Splash in the colored leaves of fall and roll in the glittering sparkle of freshly fallen snow. Beloved, enjoy Him; He is all around you, and He longs for you to take Him in.

Take a walk this week and ask the Holy Spirit to awaken your soul to His creation. Go to a park, if possible, and embrace the wonder around you with the eyes of a child. Record any inspiration the Holy Spirit shares with you. Feel free to use a personal journal to record your heart if the space provided is not enough.

_____

_____

_____

_____

_____

_____

_____

_____

_____

_____

_____

_____

_____

_____

_____

_____

_____

_____

Day Three

God Desires to Feed Your Soul

"The eyes of all look to you, and you give them their food at the proper time. You open your hand and satisfy the desires of every living thing"
(Psalm 145:15-16).

Begin today with prayer, seeking to be filled by the bread of God's Word.

Yesterday we took a peek at the splendor and wonder of God in creation. As our souls are being awakened, creation seems to shout the praises of His Name, and we begin to bear witness to His glory. Today we will look at the second source through which God reveals Himself—His Word.

Nothing in creation is haphazard or unintentional. Everything God put on this earth—from the birds of the air, fish in the ocean, animals, and plants—is alive and/or sustains life. Soil, for example, nourishes the plants; the plants than feed the animals, and animals and plants produce for man. It is all intentional with the planned purpose of maintaining life. God's plan is perfect, and in His great mercy He cares for every living thing. At the time of their hunger, God opens His mighty hand and feeds all who look to Him, tenderly caring for their physical bodies and satisfying their needs.

The same is true of Scripture. Everything of God is either living or sustains life, and that includes His Word. Draw a line between the following verses and its function.

satisfies you	Deuteronomy 8:3
it's alive	
feeds your soul	Isaiah 58:11
strengthens your frame	
nurtures your spirit	Hebrews 4:12

It is not enough to eat only from the fruit of the earth; you must also dine on His Word. Physical food produced on this earth sustains our earthly bodies, but God's Word is the eternal food source that sustains our spirit and soul. When we look to Him, He opens His hand and gives us food to satisfy our needs and desires (see Psalm 145:15-16).

God has placed within your heart the desire to experience something bigger than yourself—the desire to experience Him. And God feeds this yearning by offering you His creation, Spirit and Word. Everything God does or creates is designed to draw you closer to Him. Everything in creation and in His Word points you right to Him, offering hidden treasures that beg you to be adventurous enough to take a peek. Through creation, His Word and His Spirit, God is presenting to you everything you need in order to help you discover His mysteries and beauty. What a glorious invitation!

Therefore, forge ahead, for blessed is the one who keeps His statutes and seeks Him with all her heart. She is the one who will see wonderful things in His law and find His words sweet to her taste (see Psalm 119:2, 10-11, 18, 103).

Open to Psalm 119. Pick up your knife and fork and indulge in this glorious feast. As you read, record some of the ways you witness the soul of the psalmist being fed by the Word of God.

_____   _____

_____   _____

_____   _____

_____   _____

Psalm 119 alone is a continual declaration proclaiming the richness, wisdom and joy of knowing and clinging to the Word of God. There is great value in knowing and understanding God's Word.

According to Psalm 19:7-11, what does the perfect Word of the Lord do for the soul?

_____

What does the trustworthy statute of the Lord do for the simple?

_____

What does His right precepts do for the heart?

_____

What do His radiant commands give to the eyes?

_____

What is more precious than gold and sweeter than honey?

_____

God has placed within your heart the desire to experience something bigger than yourself— the desire to experience Him.

What is given to those who keep the word of the Lord?

_____

What great rewards have you received by being obedient to His Word?

_____

The Bible is not just a book of history; it is a passionate love story.

Keep in mind, however, that knowing Scripture does not mean that you know God. You may be a Bible scholar. You may be able to quote Scripture and answer any Bible trivia question, but this does not mean you know God. The religious leaders of Jesus' day knew the letter of the law, but they did not know God when He stood right in front of them. You cannot divorce Scripture from a loving relationship with Christ. The Bible is not just a book of history; it is a passionate love story. In the same way, you cannot only seek after Holy Spirit encounters through prayer without partaking of His holy Word. You must seek the truth through God's Word and His Holy Spirit together, because zeal without knowledge is a dangerous thing (see Proverbs 19:2).

The bottom line, those who ardently desire to know, see, and understand God will find what they earnestly seek to discover when they pursue all of Him (see Jeremiah 29:13-14). Jesus spoke in parables to hide things from those who did not welcome him (Matthew 13:13). But He is more than eager to reveal Himself to those with seeking hearts.

I cannot encourage you enough; aspire to know His secrets. Let your heart be aroused by the wealth of opportunities within your grasp. Scripture is like a rose; it is fragrant and comes with many layers. As the warmth of the Son shines upon the rose it opens up, unfolding mysteries and giving off a fresh new aroma of awareness.

Therefore, open the Word of God and become acquainted with Him in a way you have never experienced before. Find out what His passions are. What are His joys? Discover what grieves Him and what raptures His heart. The Word of God is a vital key in knowing and understanding these things. Let me implore you to go back and take a deeper more intimate look at Scripture. As you read through the pages, witness the beauty of His love and hear His passionate heart's cry. Listen to the beating of His heart as you read His intimate love letters. Hear Him as He pours out His heart to His chosen, sharing His devotion and loyalty, longing, and desire. Experience the pain of His heartbreak, and the suffering He endured to win back the love of His cherished bride. Witness His tender care for her, His faithfulness to the covenant, and the sheer joy of His delight in her. Christ, in His words of wisdom and discernment, is generous to His bride. He is extravagant and lavish with the affections of His love toward those He loves. But don't take my word for it; read it for yourself. It is His story; it is her story; it is their story.

Share a time when the Wooer romanced you within the pages of His Word?

_____

_____

_____

_____

_____

_____

_____

_____

How did that portion of Scripture reveal His life and love to you?

_____

_____

_____

_____

_____

_____

_____

How did you respond to the awakening of that revelation?

_____

_____

_____

_____

_____

_____

_____

Day Four

God Desires to Open Your Spiritual Eyes and Ears

"He wakens me morning by morning, wakens my ear to listen like one being taught. The LORD has opened my ears, and I have not been rebellious; I have not drawn back" (Isaiah 50:4-5).

The third key source of the awakening is the revelation from God's Holy Spirit to know and understand God, who He is, and the ability to see Him in His Word and in the world around you. God speaks to you all the time, revealing Himself to you within His creation. His divine nature and invisible qualities are right before your eyes (see Romans 1:20); but in order to see them, you must look with your spiritual eyes and listen with your spiritual ears; because only in the Spirit are you able to see and hear beyond yourself. Only the Holy Spirit can reveal these insights to you, but you must be willing to see them and hear them. Then from your willing desire, God awakens your soul as He lifts the veil from your eyes (see 2 Corinthians 3:16). Your spirit moves in line with God's Spirit and heart, and your soul begins to respond to God's word and the world around you.

Pray for the invasion of the Holy Spirit in your life, and then turn with me to Matthew 16:13-20. What question did Jesus ask his disciples? (v 13)

_____

How did they answer Him in verse 14?

_____

What was the second question Jesus asked? (v 15)

_____

Who responded to this question? What was his response?

_____

_____

_____

Who did Jesus say revealed this revelation to him?

    ___ Man

    ___ The Pharisees and teachers of the Law

    ___ The Spirit of the Father

Peter knew the truth about Jesus' identity only because it was revealed to him by the Spirit of the Father. Never separate Scripture from the presence of the Holy Spirit. If you do, all you will have is a manual for right living. The awakening requires the Holy Spirit. There is no other way. In order to understand spiritual truths you must have the translation of the Holy Spirit. He is the One who brings creation and the word of God to life.

Please read 1 Corinthians 2:6-16. According to Paul, how can we know and understand the things and thoughts of God?

_____

_____

What has been given to those who know Christ? (vv. 10, 12, 16) Why does the man without the Spirit not understand the things of the Spirit?

_____

_____

The fellowship of the Holy Spirit is vital if you are to grasp and understand the world of God.

God reveals His heart and mind to us through the Holy Spirit. In order to have your spiritual eyes and ears opened, to have the veil removed, to experience the miracle of the awakening, you must receive a revelation from the Spirit of God (see Ephesians 1:17-18).

Now, this is not to say that you cannot appreciate creation or be amazed by the awesomeness of a sunset; be taken by the beauty of a landscape; enthralled by the power of the ocean; or be swept away by the fragrant aroma of the flowers. But when He, the Spirit of God, comes and shares His world with you from His perspective, you see a whole new world. He will take something as simple as a tree and make it dance with delight before you. He will show you the freedom of a soul as it comes to life through the delicateness of a butterfly. He will minister and speak to your heart about situations in your life and bring healing and strength through His word and creation. The fellowship of the Holy Spirit is vital if you are to grasp and understand the world of God.

The more we desire to yield, coming under His control, supremacy and authority, the more Christ will drench us in His Spirit, empowering us for His purposes.

Allow me to take you a step farther by asking you this question: "Are you living in the fullness of the Holy Spirit?" My Pastor says, "The receiving of the Holy Spirit is as foundationally critical for the believer as the receiving of Christ is to the non-believer." Allow me to explain.

When we receive Christ as our personal Savior, the Holy Spirit enters our vessels. God's word confirms this in Ephesians 1:13 when it said, "And you also were included in Christ when you heard the word of truth, the gospel of your salvation. Having believed, you were marked in him with a seal, the promised Holy Spirit." Therefore, those who receive Christ as their Savior and Lord, receiving salvation by grace through faith, they immediately receive the promised Holy Spirit within them, becoming the Holy Temple of God (see 1 Corinthians 3:16)—but—this does not automatically mean that they are walking in the fullness of the Holy Spirit.

If you are a believer who has received salvation by grace through faith, you have the Holy Spirit; but, the question is, does the Holy Spirit have you? Christ, through His Spirit, lives in us, resides in us, but that doesn't mean that we are all filled with the Spirit. Many believers today are walking in what the Bible calls "worldly" attitudes, still living as the world lives even though they have received Christ as their Savior. This hinders the flow of the Holy Spirit in their lives, hence, hindering the Spirit's power in them and through them.

What does 1 Corinthians 3:1-3 tell us about these worldly Christians? Check all that apply.

___ They remain infants in the Lord

___ They are unable to receive the solid food of the word of God

___ They still harbor a sinful nature

___ You cannot tell the difference between them and non-believers

We must not be satisfied with salvation alone. We cannot sit back, think we are content in our Christianity, and have no idea what it means to live the abundant life that Jesus talked about in John 10:10. The Spirit gives life (2 Corinthians 3:6); and the same Spirit that raised Christ from the dead lives in us (see Romans 8:11). Christ desires for each of us to live the abundant life in Him, but that takes complete surrender to the Holy Spirit.

Beloved, if you desire to walk daily in the fullness of the Holy Spirit, you must be submitted and yielded to Christ, putting to death the sinful nature, desiring to no longer look like the world, and desiring to be transformed into the likeness of Christ.

Fill in the blanks according to Ephesians 5:18, NIV:

Do not get drunk on wine, which leads to debauchery. Instead, _____

_____ with the _____ .

Ephesians 5:18 offers us a choice: Be drunk with wine (worldly things), or be filled with the Spirit. We must make the choice to no longer conform to the pattern of this world, but be transformed by the renewing of our minds (see Romans 12:1-2). Christ will not force us to surrender so that He may consume us with the power of His Spirit. But the more we desire to yield, coming under His control, supremacy and authority, the more Christ will drench us in His Spirit, empowering us for His purposes.

In Acts 1:4-5; 8, what did Jesus tell His disciples about the Holy Spirit? Check all that apply.

____ The Holy Spirit is a gift

____ The Holy Spirit is a promise from God the Father

____ You will receive power when the Holy Spirit comes upon you

____ You will be spiritually equipped to do kingdom work

Receiving the Holy Spirit is a precious and valuable gift, it is a promise from the Father and intended for all believers (see Acts 1:4-5; 2:38-39). And when He comes upon you, the Spirit will consume you, setting you on fire with the passions of Christ.

If you desire more of the Spirit's power in your life then ask. Luke 11:11-13 says, "Which of you fathers, if your son asks for a fish, will give him a snake instead? Or if he asks for an egg, will give him a scorpion? If you then, though you are evil, know how to give good gifts to your children, how much more will your Father in heaven give the Holy Spirit to those who ask him!" If you desire to walk in the fullness of the Holy Spirit, repent of all sin, surrender your life to the authority and control of Christ and ask for this incredible gift to flood your life.

Now, when we ask for something in prayer, what are we to then exhibit according to Mark 11:24?

____ Doubt

____ Faith

____ Peace

Stop right now and ask the Lord to empty you out of your sinful nature, and then pray in faith for the fullness of the Holy Spirit in your life. Also, praise God for the richness of His gifts.

_____

_____

_____

~❧~

As we grow and mature, no longer wanting to remain those "worldly" infants in 1 Corinthians 3:1-3, we must learn to come before the throne and ask God to empty us out of ourselves and be filled, consumed, and drenched with His Spirit. We must learn to pray, "Jesus, invade me!" Why? Because the more He invades us, the more He takes over and becomes active in our lives, revealing His glory to the world through us.

Now I understand that normally the word *invade* is an unpleasant word. It means to "attack or enter with hostile intentions."[16] But when the word *invade* is used to describe the advance of the Holy Spirit, it is a powerful and enormously immeasurable concept full of love, joy, peace, patience, kindness, goodness, faithfulness, gentleness and self-control (see Galatians 5:22-23), far beyond the reaches of our imagination. So, let's give it up. Let's give Him what He wants; what He desires; us, all of us.

Allow me to encourage you to connect with God daily. Dive in to all He has for you, and aspire for His Holy invasion. Allow the Holy Spirit to come and awaken your soul to a life of freedom, adventure, and joy that can only come from Him. Jesus desires to give you the abundant life, a life full and overflowing with His Spirit, Word, and glory. Let Him take over. Cry out, "Invade me, Jesus!"

In what ways has the Holy Spirit revealed His awakening power in your life?

_____

_____

In what ways do you desire to know Him better? Share with Jesus the desires of your heart?

_____

_____

_____

Day Five

God Desires Good Stewards

Then the LORD said to Moses, "Write this on a scroll as something to be remembered" (Exodus 17:14).

There are many ways in which God desires for us to be good stewards of all that He gives to us, but I would like to share with you one special way. Something that has helped me greatly during my journey with Jesus is keeping a personal spiritual journal. This is not an "I went here with the kids today" journal, but a journal of what I experience with God.

My journals are a gift. They are a gift to God from me because they contain the songs and praises of my heart expressing my love for Him. And they are His gift to me because what He teaches me, the inspirations of His heart, are captured within their pages. Through these journals we have talked and connected as we have journeyed together. The writing became a part of us, a reflection of the relationship we shared. And when I go back and reread the words that flowed from my heart, it is amazing how much of my journals He has used for my growth and His glory.

For this reason, I have given you journaling opportunities so you may record the wonders and adventures that you experience with the Lord as you grow more deeply and intimately acquainted with Him. Please take advantage of the "Journal Responses" in this study to capture any inspiration the Holy Spirit may graciously bestow upon you. Write down what He reveals to you; the wonders that He shows you, and the mysteries He unfolds for you.

Pray for the Holy Spirit to help you to be a good steward of all He desires to reveal to you, and then answer the following.

What instruction did the Lord give in each of the following verses?

Jeremiah 30:2:

_____

Jeremiah 36:2:

_____

Habakkuk 2:2:

_____

What was Moses instructed to do in Exodus 17:14? Why was Moses to do this, who else was to know about the scroll?

_____

_____

What took place in Malachi 3:16?

_____

_____

Why do you think the scroll was written in the presence of the Lord?

_____

_____

What do you think was the purpose of these scrolls? Do you think it is possible that these very scrolls of remembrance are the inspired Word of God you are reading today in what is known as the Bible? Why or why not? Read Luke 4:16-21 before considering your response.

_____

_____

According to Luke 4:17, who took the responsibility of writing down the revelation?

_____

Who is reading from the scroll of remembrance?

_____

What did Jesus tell the people in verse 21?

_____

Allow me to challenge and greatly encourage you to write down the revelation. I wrote my first book, _God's Heart: Drawing Close to the Heart of God_, through my cherished season of awakening. As the Holy Spirit inspired my heart, I began writing poetry. As He spoke to me through His word and creation, I wrote down the inspiration; and the more I wrote, the more God shared. It was like having an intense conversation in the company of a good friend. Have you ever noticed that the more inquisitive and interested you are as your friend shares her thoughts, dreams and life's happenings, the more she seems to keep right on talking? God does the same thing.

Before you get overwhelmed, allow me to share a little secret. There is a little tool that greatly helps me to capture the insight from the Holy Spirit. Are you ready? A tape recorder. Ah, the power of electronics. When the Lord and I go for walks, I take it with me. Then as the insights come to me from God's creation, I record them and later write them down in my journal. Then, of course, there are the times when the Lord shares things with me when it is not convenient to write; for example, when I am driving in my car. Because I also carry my recorder in my purse, I am ready for His inspired thoughts. The tape recorder, on many occasions, has proven to be quite a useful tool in documenting the treasures that God graciously sent my way. Plus, another added benefit to recording the inspirations is that you also capture the emotion and excitement of the revelation the moment that it happens.

I recall the time when two good friends and I went on a sabbatical retreat with the Lord. As we hiked through the nature park, we came upon a waterfall. As I watched the force of it move, spilling over, and falling to the ground, I was enthralled. I could not take my eyes off of it. There was something powerful and masterful about the waterfall. Then, suddenly, as I watched and pondered the sight before me, this revelation came to my heart: "Then the angel showed me the river of the water of life, as clear as crystal, flowing from the throne of God" (Revelation 22:1). "I will pour out my spirit on all people. I will pour out my Spirit in those days.... I will show wonders in the heavens and on the earth" (Joel 2:28, 30).

All at once I understood. God showed me that the waterfall represents His Holy Spirit being poured out onto the earth. The River of Life flows from the throne of God, pouring down into the hearts of the people. When this revelation came to my mind and heart, I was so excited that I started screaming and laughing and carrying on in such a way that the people observing me probably thought I was crazy; but I caught that enthusiasm and exhilaration on tape, and that is not something that can always be put on paper.

Another, and perhaps the most important reason we should keep a spiritual journal, is a powerful lesson God taught me when a friend passed away. Her family did not know God, and they did not have much of a relationship with each other. But my friend knew Jesus, and God had given her an incredible testimony of not only salvation, but deliverance, as He set her free from an addiction that plagued her life for many years. When she became ill as a result of her former lifestyle and was given little hope of

My journals are a gift. They are a gift to God from me because they contain the songs and praises of my heart expressing my love for Him.

pulling through, I refused to believe that God was finished with her. I went to her hospital bedside and prayed God's miracle over her; wanting with all my heart for this dear woman to get well and step into the mission I thought God clearly had for her. Shortly after that night, the Lord spoke within my spirit, revealing to me the inevitable. And as He shared His plans with me, my heart found peace and I knew that, above all else, God would be greatly glorified. A few days later she passed away.

As I spoke with my pastor about her memorial, he told me that the video of her testimony and water baptism would be shown at the service. And then, a little later that same day, another friend told me that before she died, she had penned her testimony, and that her written testimony, along with a copy of the baptism video, would be given to her family. At that moment, God showed me how He would be glorified. Even though this dear woman was no longer on this earth, her testimony would live on, proclaiming the works of His hands and how He had changed her life.

What an incredible opportunity we have to record what God gives us (see Revelation 1:19). What a legacy of testimony, encouragement and hope we can leave for our families and friends; precious experiences that we personally share with Jesus, captured in the pages of a special book, and filled with words of witness that will live on long after we have left this world.

I know that journaling is a time-consuming activity, and you may not even like to write, but it is worth it. Allow me to encourage you to record what you and Jesus share together. Take the time to stop and notice creation, indulge in God's word, and fellowship with His Holy Spirit, because the more you do, the more He will bring to life for you. Like a conductor of a symphony, He will orchestrate a personal concert just for you. As He does, He will want you to be a good steward by taking the time to write it down, because His words, the things He shares with you, are trustworthy and true (see Revelation 21:5).

If you already keep a journal, how has this practice blessed your life? How has it affected the lives of others around you? If you do not keep a journal—please start one today. God desires for you to write down His revelations. Use the space below to ask for His help in becoming a good steward of His revelation. Open your heart to the possibilities; you never know what the Lord might pen through you.

Record the wonders and adventures that you experience with the Lord as you grow more deeply and intimately acquainted with Him.

God Desires You

I sincerely hope that you have been inspired to make the connection with God through His creation, Word, and Spirit. Desire to know Him; He is like no other. No human, on the face of this earth, can compare to the richness of His beauty and splendor, the awesomeness of His majesty, the fruitfulness of His wisdom, and the friendship and love of His fellowship. If you are currently experiencing the awakening of your soul with Christ, dive deeper. This is just the beginning. If you had at one time tasted the joy of the awakening but somehow it lost its flavor, let me encourage you to begin again. And for those of you who have yet to embrace this glorious season with Christ, allow me to entice you to desire more than you could ever ask or imagine. Pursue, with everything that is in you, the abundant life that only Christ can offer.

Reflection and Response

As you have embraced knowing God through His creation, Word and Spirit, in what new ways have you witnessed Christ?

_____

_____

_____

_____

_____

_____

In what ways has the Holy Spirit awakened your soul, revealing the glory of God? How has this revelation changed your life?

_____

_____

_____

_____

_____

Week Four

Lesson Four

Awakening to New Life

Song of Songs 2:8-13

1. _____ brings everything to _____

2. The word *awaken* means, to _____ from sleep; to _____.
   The awakening is a development; a beginning; a stirring of the heart; an
   _____ of the _____

3. _____ _____ the soul.

4. When the soul is awakened, it witnesses the miracle of _____

5. As you join with Christ _____ _____ will be
   _____ in you.

She enters the garden so fresh and alive with color; a beautiful lavender field where the butterflies dance and the fragrance of the lavender captivates her senses, alluring her with its delicate bouquet. As her eyes search for him, she notices the great strength of the mountains as they stretch out their arms, creating a private fortress, secluding the garden from the world. A laughing stream sings with merriment as it dances along its way, and the trees planted along the water's edge offer abundant shade. Oh, how she loves being in this place—this place of peace and beauty where she finds him waiting patiently for her, perched high upon a rock in the center of the garden. She loves meeting him here; taking his hand she kneels down at his side; lifting her eyes she sings to him a song of love. He is sweet; so kind as he holds her hand and touches her cheek. How she delights in his gentle gestures of warmth and tenderness. For a long time now she has enjoyed the kindness of his company. She has come to know the charm of his voice, but she did not know the depth of his desire for her, until now. Slowly, yet with great intention, he moves from his place high upon the rock and into her hesitant arms. His love is beautiful; beckoning her to come closer; to draw near to his open and awaiting heart.

Oh, how she longs to let go, but his expression of love is far from what she was taught. Oh, how her soul aches to receive, but her mind says, "No! I know your love for me, but not your desire. I do not understand all of what your heart yearns for." Again and again his love reaches out for her. She could feel his tenderness awaken her soul. Yet, with each loving attempt she hesitates to receive his generous offer of affection, convinced that it is not meant to be this way.

Week Five

You'll Never Know Love Unless You Surrender to It

- Day One: *God Desires Surrendered Love*

- Day Two: *God Desires to Strengthen Your Love*

- Day Three: *God Desires Your Trust*

- Day Four: *God Desires the Fragrance of Your Love*

- Day Five: *God Desires to Set You Free*

- Reflection and Response: *God Desires You*

In this fifth week we are going to:

Surrender to the Desires of His heart
"Submit yourselves, then, to God" (James 4:7a).

Feel the earthquake
*"He alone is my rock and my salvation; he is my fortress,
I will never be shaken"* (Psalm 62:2).

Witness the miracle of His glory
"I am the resurrection and the life" (John 11:25).

Reflect on the transformation of His love
"For great is his love toward us" (Psalm 117:2).

Ask Jesus to set us free
*"It is for freedom that Christ has set us free. Stand firm, then, and
do not let yourselves be burdened again by a yoke so slavery"* (Galatians 5:1).

Day One

God Desires Surrendered Love

"Submit yourselves, then, to God" (James 4:7a).

In Week Three we saw how smitten the maiden became when she allowed herself to be taken to the banquet hall and fed by love.

Recall what season the beloved is sharing with her lover in Song of Songs 2:3-6.

___ The purification season

___ The Honeymoon season

___ The Betrothal season

We will not taste the fullness and richness of Christ's sweet love if we do not learn to surrender to Him, trust Him completely, and allow Him to set us free.

The pleasure of this glorious honeymoon season is wonderful; but, all too often, many of us don't want to leave. We often become absorbed in this season, unable or unwilling to move forward. We become just like the beloved in the Song of Songs who hides in the cleft of the rock, refusing to go when the lover calls, "Arise, my darling, my beautiful one, and come with me" (v. 2:10; 13b). If we are not careful we can become hindered in our relationship with Christ by holding back and clinging to what is comfortable and familiar when He is ready to move us forward.

The goal of this week is to understand that we will not taste the *fullness* and *richness* of Christ's sweet love if we do not learn to surrender to Him, trust Him completely, and allow Him to set us free. We may know and understand that Christ loves us—and that He loves us unconditionally, but have we learned to submit to His love? Have we learned to let go and surrender ourselves completely to all that He desires? Even when His desire brings a difficult season of growth?

Begin today's lesson by praying for His desires to be made manifest in you, and then read Song of Songs, chapters 2 through 4.

What does the lover ask the beloved to do in verses 2:10-13?

_____

What does the lover say to the beloved in verse 2:14?

_____

What do you think happened between verses 2:10-13 and 2:14? Why do you think the beloved is hiding?

_____

_____

What does the beloved proclaim in verse 2:16? Fill in the blanks according to the NIV:

"_____ lover is _____ and I am his…"

Why do you think she made this statement? How does this statement reflect the condition of her heart?

_____

_____

Look at verse 4:8; what does the lover call his beloved?

_____

What has his beloved become to him in verse 4:12?

_____

What do you think transpired in this story? How did the maiden move from being overwhelmed by his affections, faint with love (v. 2:3-5) and selfishly saying, "My lover is mine…" (v. 2:16) to where he is calling her *his bride* and *his lover*, his own private garden and a fountain that no one else can drink from?

_____

_____

To find the answer, let's walk back through today's reading:
Compare verse 2:10; 13b and verse 4:8a. What question does the lover ask of the beloved in each of these verses?

_____

_____

How does the beloved initially respond to his invitation to come with him in verse 2:14?

_____

The lover asked his beloved to arise and come with him; but, instead, she hides in the cleft of the rock. Basically she is saying that she is content with the relationship the way it is, and why not? She has, up until this point, been completely on the receiving end, and for good reason. She needed this time with him, but now he wants to move her into a higher place in their relationship.

Because of the beloved's unwillingness to submit to his desire and come with him, what does he do? (v. 3:1)

_____ He returns with her to the bed chamber

_____ He goes on without her

_____ He begs her to reconsider

All night long she waited for him to return. This was an agonizing time for the beloved. Stripped of his affectionate love, she finally came to the conclusion that it would be better to be with him, even if it meant that she had to arise from her place of comfort in order to pursue him (v. 3:2).

What happened in verse 3:4? How did she respond? Why do you think she reacted this way?

_____

_____

Now once they are reunited, according to Song of Songs 4:1-5, how does the lover respond to his beloved?

_____

The beloved took a step of faith. He had made such an impression on her soul that she had to be with him; so she left behind everything that was familiar in order to follow him, and when she found him he affectionately rewarded her.

Now, after being reunited with her, and once again displaying his love and affections, what statement does he make in verse 4:6?

_____

What the lover is telling his beloved is that he loves her so much he is willing to die for her. And as he continues to pour his affections upon her (v. 7), her heart melts. It must be at this point that the beloved agrees to leave behind the pleasures of the banquet hall and make the journey with him, because now, in verse 8, he calls her his *bride* for the first time.

What clues are given in verse 4:8 that tells us that this will not be an easy trip?

_____

_____

I know from experience that it is not easy to leave the honeymoon season and trust the Lord to lead you into new seasons. It is difficult to leave behind the contentment of His affectionate embrace and embrace a hard season that will challenge you to grow. During the Honeymoon season Christ wants to reveal many things. He wants to show you the wonders of Himself as He reveals His glory. He desires to shower you with His affections and mend your broken heart with His love; but, eventually, He wants to show you what He is beginning to produce in your life as a result of spending time with Him in the secret place.

But sometimes, when we resist the transition, when we refuse to surrender to His desires, He removes the awareness of His presence. This is not to torment us, although it can feel like torment when we lose the affectionate presence we have come to know. Rather it is because at this point we have two separate agendas. Our desire is to experience His presence; His desire is to mature our love.

Our desire is to experience His presence; His desire is to mature our love.

However once we decide to arise from our place of contentment and follow Him, when we make the choice to leave behind our own pleasures to pursue His, it sets His heart soaring and He begins to sing over us: "How sweet is your love, my treasure, my bride! How much better it is than wine! Your perfume is more fragrant than the richest of spices. Your lips, my bride, are as sweet as honey. You are like a private garden, my treasure, my bride! You are like a spring that no one else can drink from, a fountain of my own" (Song of Songs 4:9-12, NLT).

Hear Christ calling you, "Arise, come, my darling; my beautiful one, come with me (Song of Songs 2:13b). Come from your place of safety and comfort. Take my hand and ascend to the higher place. It will not be easy, but I will be with you. I will take great delight in you, I will quiet you with my love, and I will rejoice over you with singing" (see Zephaniah 3:17).

What is your response to His request? Share with Jesus the desires of your heart.

_____

_____

_____

Day Two

God Desires to Strengthen Your Love

*"Consider it pure joy…whenever you face trials of many kinds,
because you know that the testing of your faith develops perseverance.
Perseverance must finish its work so that you may be mature and
complete, not lacking anything"* (James 1:2-4).

I don't have the faintest idea why God loves me the way He does. I just know He does. I have long since stopped trying to figure it out. I just give way to it, allowing myself the joy of total surrender, falling helplessly into His loving embrace. And to my sheer amazement, He never gets tired of me; nor is He swayed by my attitudes, physical appearance, or emotional crises. His love is strong when I am weak. His love is faithful when I hesitate. His love reaches out for me when I am hurting, and His love touches my life with His healing. His love is constant, never rejecting me when I reach out for Him. And in His love I feel safe, treasured, and cherished beyond all words. It is here I find peace of mind and a freedom to be all that God intended for me to be.

It is not easy to totally surrender to the love of God. There are many obstacles, attitudes, and fears that keep us at bay, never allowing us the freedom to embrace all of what we were meant to experience with Jesus. Nonetheless, in an attempt to encourage women to reach for more, I enjoy presenting this question:

If you were totally surrendered to the love of God, completely submitted to the Alpha and the Omega, the Beginning and the End; the Creator of life, every day of your life, how differently do you think your life would look?

_____

_____

_____

As I am given the opportunity to minister to women, I am continually blessed by the testimonies of those who have learned to surrender their lives to the love of Jesus. Their stories are incredible, and sometimes, I even find myself filled with spiritual jealousy as I continue to yearn for more of His passion to overtake me. On the other hand, I am equally amazed at how many women carry burdens of fear, doubt, self-condemnation and feelings of unworthiness. As a result, they forsake their First Love, and miss out on the wonders of His love in their lives.

Christ desires to take you to the higher places and for your love to blossom and grow to new heights. He wants to strengthen your love so that your relationship will endure against all odds.

As we saw in our previous lesson, complete and total surrender takes a willingness to get out of our contentment, to let go of what is holding us back, and make a sacrifice of commitment. Beloved, this relationship with Jesus is a work in progress; a road to travel; a mountain to climb. And as you journey with Christ, He will teach you, guide you, and build the bonds of love between you. Christ desires to take you to the higher places and for your love to blossom and grow to new heights. He wants to strengthen your love so that your relationship will endure against all odds. But, in order to do this, He will need to lead you into difficult places, difficult seasons that will build your character, mature your faith and, hence, intensify the bonds of love. In these seasons the north winds blow and your faith is placed within the fiery furnace of God's love.

Pray for a revelation of Christ's love. Then let's begin our search today in the word of God by reading Hebrews 12:26-27. What has God promised to do in verse 26?

_____

What do the words "once more" indicate? What does this imply to you?

_____

_____

When the shaking stops, what will remain? (v. 27)

_____

God will shake your world to help you see and understand what you're trusting in, your Groom or temporal things. When the shaking stops, whatever is left standing will be from God. Embrace the trials, and understand that everything that can be shaken will be shaken. Learn to trust God through the trials, hardships, sorrows, testing, and sufferings of life; learn to rely on who He is when you do not understand what He is doing.

In what ways do you feel the earth shaking beneath your feet? Who or what are you clinging to for support?

_____

_____

_____

_____

Though these hardships and trials are difficult, ultimately, the place Christ desires to take you is to a level within your relationship where you are experiencing invincible, unshakable love. And in this place of deep committed love, the bonds between you and Christ will become so strong that no matter what you face in life, you will be convinced that the love you both share will never fail. Resolute and invincible love comes when you choose to accept whatever Christ has for you. Love wells up and overflows within your heart, and you surrender yourself because you know that He loves you in your best interest, and in His timing He will come through for you. Whether it is a miracle or the grace you need, He will carry you through the trial. And when you come to this revelation and understanding of God's love, you will not turn from Him when the going gets tough. You may not always realize what He is doing, but you will rest in the assurance of His incredible love. Those unbreakable bonds will withstand any trial, hardship, illness, or problem this world could muster up.

As we close today, take a minute and rest on the assurance of God's word. Fill in the blanks below according to Psalm 62:1-2, NIV:

My soul finds _____ in _____ _____; my salvation comes

from him. He alone is my rock and my salvation; he is my fortress, _____

_____ _____ _____ _____ (Psalm 62:1-2).

I know these seasons are hard, and I do not enjoy them any more than you do. But I must admit that it is through the hardest times that I have learned to trust Christ more as I experience greater depths of His unshakable and faithful love.

Share about a time when you experienced Christ's unshakable love during a season when everything around you was shaking.

_____

_____

_____

_____

_____

_____

_____

Day Three

God Desires Your Trust

"Trust in the LORD with all your heart and lean not on your own understanding; in all your ways acknowledge him, and he shall make your paths straight" (Proverbs 3:5-6).

Yesterday, we took stock in God's love when our lives seemed to be upside down from the turbulence of His promise to shake our world. Today, we are going to look at a wonderful example of Christ's unshakable love through a fiery trial as Jesus goes with Mary and Martha through a period of great suffering.

Whatever your circumstances are right now, pray for the Lord to increase your level of trust in Him, and then read John 11:1-44.

Here we are again, at the home of Mary and Martha. Only this time Martha is not serving her usual dinner party, even though the house is full of guests. No, this time the scene is quite somber as we see these two precious sisters beyond grief over the illness and death of their brother Lazarus.

Let's break down the text as we picture the scene together. Who sent word to Jesus that Lazarus was ill? (v. 3)

_____

How did Jesus respond when he got the news about Lazarus? (v. 6)

_____ He came immediately

_____ He ignored the request

_____ He stayed where He was for two more days

How do you think this made the siblings feel? Do you think they felt that Jesus didn't care, or that He had abandoned them? Take a look at verse 4; what is at stake?

_____

_____

Do you remember what we learned in Week Four about God's glory? The glory manifests the true character of God; revealing to us what God is really like; exposing the nature and attributes of God. Keep that in mind as we continue to look at Martha and Mary's situation.

Jump down to verse 17. Upon Jesus' arrival what had already happened?

___ Lazarus was well

___ Lazarus had died

___ Lazarus was upset that Jesus had not come sooner.

Sometimes in our grief we forget that the Lord is with us.

By the time Jesus finally arrived, the illness had taken its toll and Lazarus had been dead for four days. Yet, look at how Jesus interacts with each of the sisters in their time of grief. First, let's consider Martha.

When Martha heard that Jesus was coming she went out to meet Him (v. 20). Paraphrase what you think Martha is saying to Jesus in verse 21? Consider her state of emotion, tone of voice, expression.

_____

_____

How did Jesus respond to her? (v. 23)

_____

_____

Continue with their conversation: What did Martha say in verse 24 and how did Jesus answer her? (v. 25)

_____

_____

Continue down to verses 39 and 40. When Jesus had requested for the stone to be rolled away, what concern did Martha express?

_____

_____

What did Jesus remind her of in verse 40? Write His statement below:

_____

_____

The glory is the exposure of God's divine purpose. And life after death is God's ultimate display of glory. He loves to show us that He is a resurrection God. Amen! It is often, at our lowest point, when all appears to be lost, that Jesus comes to us and reveals His ultimate glory.

What can we learn from Martha's example? In what ways do you see her trusting Jesus even though she does not understand what He is doing?

_____

_____

How did Jesus reveal His unshakable love for Martha in this story?

_____

_____

Now let's consider Mary.

Beginning with John 11:28-29, how did Mary respond when she heard that Jesus was asking for her?

_____

When Mary reached the place where Jesus was and saw him (v. 32), what did she do? What did she say? Again consider the emotional climate, tone of voice, facial express.

_____

_____

Both of the sisters were heartbroken. They were beyond grief at the death of their brother, and maybe even feeling, in some way, that Jesus had let them down because He didn't come right away. When we are sitting in a hard situation, we can feel this same hurt. Sometimes in our grief we forget that the Lord is with us. We cry out to Him, but we do not hear Him answer. We ask for His presence, but He seems not to come. Beloved, in the midst of our pain, the Lord is ever present. Sometimes He withholds our awareness that He is present, but in His great compassion He is always right by our side, loving us. Be patient. When God is silent He is about to reveal a new part of His character. During a time of deep silence we must watch for the revelation where our understanding of Him deepens. At just the right moment Jesus arrived on the scene. At God's appointed time, the time He chose for His glory to be revealed, He came to Martha and Mary and comforted them with His great compassion.

According to verse 33-35, how did Jesus respond to Mary?

_____

It touches my heart to think that our Bridegroom is so moved when we grieve, bowed at His feet in humility, that He weeps with us. He does not sit up in heaven watching us suffer. He comes to us, and suffers right along with us. And we must always remember that if we allow God to work in us, the trial will bring hope and new life, even in the midst of devastation. The glory of the Lord is always revealed to an expectant and trusting heart; because the Lord's unfailing love surrounds the one who trusts in Him (see Psalm 32:10).

What can we learn from Mary's example? In what ways do you see her trusting Jesus even though she does not understand what He is doing?

_____

_____

How did Jesus reveal His unshakable love for Mary in this story?

_____

_____

The Lord was faithful in His actions. He is always faithful in love and in all He does. Jesus came through for Mary and Martha, and for Lazarus when He raised him from the dead, even though it was not done in their timing, or in the way they planned.

God always has a perfect plan; one that is beyond your natural vision. When you are suffering, cling to the promises of God's Word, humble yourself to His will, bow at His feet and give Him the opportunity to grieve with you, and then watch for the miracle He will raise up out of the devastation. He will be faithful. He will come through; and you will see the glory of the Lord.

In what way(s) is Jesus stretching your faith in order to get you to trust Him more?

_____

_____

_____

Share with Jesus the desire of your heart.

_____

_____

_____

_____

Day Four

God Desires the Fragrance of Your Love

"How delightful is your love, my sister, my bride! How much more pleasing is your love than wine, and the fragrance of your perfume than any spice!" (Song of Songs 4:10).

We have been looking at trusting God in the midst of His promise to shake our world; but, how do we respond when Christ leads us into difficult places in an attempt to grow our love and strengthen the relationship?

In John 11 we witnessed an example of testing as God shook Mary and Martha's world. Then, at the height of their fiery trial, Mary and Martha witnessed the glory of God as Jesus raised Lazarus from the dead. But what was the result of what they endured? What transformation took place during this time of suffering? Did Mary and Martha allow their love to grow to new heights? Were the bonds of their love intensified? Let's find out.

Begin by praying for a Spirit of wisdom and revelation, and then continue with their story by reading John 12:1-8. Describe the scene.

_____

_____

_____

I just love reading about Mary and Martha. They are interesting women, and we can learn much from them. Notice a couple of things with me as we once again consider their situation. Both of these women just went through the same trial; yet, look at how differently they each reacted after God displayed His awesome power and the family's grief instantly turned to joy.

As a result of the pain and suffering they just endured, coupled with the rush of enormous bliss from the events they just witnessed, how do you see these two very individual sisters responding to Jesus in John 12:1-8?

Martha	Mary
_____	_____
_____	_____
_____	_____
_____	_____

The goal is to embrace the trial and let it change us. The purpose of the trials we face are to move us from the place where we are right now, to a place where we move closer to Jesus.

First, we see Martha, again busy with the preparations and serving; she had learned nothing from the last dinner party (see Luke 10:38-42), and she seems to have learned nothing from the event she just endured. Dear One, we can move through a trial, feel the pain, rejoice when it is over, and even be grateful that we survived, but not grow. The goal is to embrace the trial and let it change us. The purpose of the trials we face are to move us from the place where we are right now, to a place where we move closer to Jesus.

Now look at Mary. She is also serving, but look at how she is serving. Mary took a pint of pure nard, an expensive perfume also called Spikenard, which in the original Greek means "genuine and pure," and she poured it on Jesus. As a result of the suffering she endured through the death of her brother and the exhilarating joy of witnessing his resurrection, Mary has undergone a transformation. Her trust level has skyrocketed and she has reached the place within her heart of invincible, unshakable love with Jesus. She just went to hell and back with Him, wouldn't you say? And now she has made the decision to completely surrender herself in love. This is what it means to move to the higher places with Jesus. Mary allowed Jesus to strengthen their bonds of love; making their relationship so strong that it will remain when all else fails.

In the midst of great trial, when your world is being shaken, allow Jesus to show you the power of His unshakable love. Call out for His miracles; send word that you are in need—but be patient. He wants to show you what real love is, and how to love unconditionally in return. He desires to be your *soul* source of edification, to fill all the voids that your soul so desperately seeks to find. Give Him the room to reveal His grace and mercy to you as you wait for His glory to be revealed in your life. Then allow it to transform you.

We can all experience a tender, passionate, mature, and unshakable love with Jesus. For that reason, let me encourage you to strive for deeper levels of this love every day the Lord gives to you on this earth. Make it your heart's greatest desire to grab hold of this invincible love, and savor it every moment you breathe. It is real, and it is offered to you right now, and for all eternity.

With Mary's example in mind, ask yourself this question again: How differently would my life look totally surrendered to the love of God; completely submitted to the Alpha and the Omega, the Beginning and the End, the Creator of life, every day of my life?

_____

_____

_____

Day Five
God Desires to Set You Free

"It is for freedom that Christ has set us free. Stand firm, then, and do not let yourselves be burdened again by a yoke of slavery" (Galatians 5:1).

Begin today by praying to be set free from whatever is holding you back in your relationship with Christ.

Allow Jesus to reprogram your thinking. He did mine. Ask God to help you to let go of fear, sin, disbelief, legalism, unforgiveness, and the lies of the enemy, and learn to embrace the most incredible truth you will ever know. Let go of anything that is holding you back; even hobbies, habits, television, careers, or money. If it is keeping you from Christ, let it go. This is not to say that you cannot have a career or develop a hobby or have money in your life. Just do not allow these things to take Christ's rightful place, making them the central focus of your life. Let go of the garbage and baggage that have weighed you down for years, and learn to spread your wings and fly to new heights of love. Let go to more!

What I have come to understand is that our hearts mean more to Christ than anything else. His greatest desire is for His bride (the church) to be completely and utterly taken with Him; burning with an intense fire of passion and love. And He longs for their relationship to mean more to her than any amount of service, ministry, or rules she could follow.

Christ wants to give us the richness and depth of His personal love; the problem is that many of us permit, even tolerate, the things that hinder the relationship. I suffered great setbacks in entering into intimacy with Christ; obstacles that hindered my relationship with Jesus and kept me from experiencing that close fellowship. For this reason, I would like to share my personal struggles in coming into intimacy with Christ. It is my hope that, as I share with you, the Holy Spirit will open your eyes to some of the pitfalls that can create distance between yourself and Jesus, cheating you both out of deeper levels of closeness.

For starters, one of the things that Jesus revealed to me is how I have missed out on love by not surrendering to it completely. He showed me how the fear of rejection and insecurities from my past had robbed us both of our precious romance, and that by not letting go of those hurts and fears, it had eaten away at the greatest and most perfect love I could ever know.

Plus those same hurts and rejections hindered my earthly relationships, as well. By holding onto the injuries of wronged relationships, I had unknow-ingly carried baggage into the relationships of those I dearly loved. In an attempt to protect myself, I built a wall which kept me from truly receiving love and giving my whole heart in any relationship.

The good news, though, is that nothing is wasted. In the past are life's lessons that strengthen us for the future; and bringing these attitudes and hurts before His throne of grace has been liberating. Through the wonders of His unconditional love, Christ gave me my first real look at what it means to love someone with all your heart and soul, regardless of what that person has done or not done. To love beyond reason; to love without hesitation or reservation; to love regardless of attitude or situation. To love beyond myself and just because.

Do not make the same mistake I did. Do not hesitate to receive the ardent love of Christ because of past relational hurts. Christ loves each of us with a deep abiding love just because we are His. We do not have to earn it; all we have to do is receive it. And once we allow His love to fill our hearts, we are then able to love, even when it is difficult to love.

Grab hold of the love of God in 1 John 3:1 and 4:19, NIV:

"How _____ is the _____ the Father has _____ on us."

"We _____ because He first _____ _____."

I also wrestled with pride, and still do. I must regularly pray for the Lord to guard my heart and rid me of all pride. Not that I think I am better than anyone else, but I do like recognition. In fact, what the Lord revealed to me is that pride is any form of self-focus. Anytime my eyes are on me instead of Him, regardless if I am beating myself up over little mistakes or puffing up my ego, it is pride. The good news is that the Spirit is also teaching me humility.

Grab hold of this safe-guard from 1 Peter 5:5-7, NIV:

"…clothe yourselves with _____ toward one another, because, "God opposes the _____ but gives grace to the _____." Humble yourselves, therefore, under God's mighty hand, that he may lift you up in due time. Cast all your anxiety on him because he _____ for you."

I cannot tell you how often my pride would close the door of my heart; not allowing others to see the real me. The Lord knew what I was trying to conceal, but that wall not only kept a distance between me and others, but between me and Christ.

This then led to my struggle with the perfectionist in me. For years my critical spirit enslaved me. Deep down I just wanted to be accepted, and I thought that by impressing people, they might respect me more. Even in my service to God—I so wanted to please God that I never grasped the fact that He was already pleased with me. Too many times I got caught up in serving and missed the whole message, caught in this cycle of trying to do the things that I thought God wanted me to do. My utmost goal, when my life was finished, was to stand before Him and hear the words: "Well done, good and faithful servant," and it still is; but what I didn't realize was what He really wanted. First and foremost, He wanted me to surrender completely into His love and to trust Him to do the rest. So often I would hear Him tell me, "Patty, let go." I believe now what He was saying was, "Patty, let go of it; everything. Take your death-grip off trying to control everything and let Me change you, heal you, and renew you. I will make you that pure, strong, and perfect bride. I will do it—not you."

Basically, I was trying too hard. I was so busy working for God that I missed being with God. In my effort to "do," I completely missed the point to simply "be." During the years of "my" service, I struggled to find fulfillment and a sense of purpose. I had no joy, no fruit, and no peace. And the enemy, of course, used these feelings against me, convincing me that I was not being a good Christian. Finally, I reached a point where I had had enough. At that time I totally emptied my plate and offered it up to Jesus to fill. Then, during this time of waiting to see what the Lord would have me do, a door swung wide open; an invitation came to draw near to His heart. My understanding now is that it is all about love. His love for me; a love that is greater than anything I could imagine. Plus, my love for Him; to surrender everything I have into His glorious love that surrounds me, woos me and leads me. From this point of surrender and committed love, everything else found its place. Like a set of dominos falling in sequence, the purposes of my life were gloriously revealed and my heart was transformed.

Another area that delayed me in the reprogramming process was believing the lies of the adversary. Be informed, and learn to recognize the tactics of the enemy. In the early stages of new love, the enemy will try to come into the picture by attempting to distort the relationship between the bride and Bridegroom by bringing confusion, fear, and doubt. There are many paths the enemy can take to cause the bride to feel unclean, but the following is the road he tried to take me on.

Soon after I began to experience the sweetness of the Lover of my soul, the enemy of my soul made every effort to tell me that what I was experiencing was wrong and even detestable. Thoughts began running through my mind that this kind of intimacy cannot possibly be of God. He is holy and pure, and ecstasy and pleasure is of the world. I began to feel ashamed that I could have even thought of Christ in this way because the accuser's logic sounded reasonable, justifiable and valid. Why? Because when we look at the world's idea of intimate pleasure it is perverse and permissive, exploiting the body and making physical intimacy appear ugly and at times vulgar. This is exactly the response Satan wants us to embrace, because his chief goal is to keep us from the One who loves us passionately and dearly.

Bride, again, let me be very clear here. As I stated in Week Three, this is not sex. The intimate touches of the sacred romance that I am sharing with you are not of a sexual nature. Please do not make that assumption. The intimacy Christ desires to share with His bride (the church) is a heightened spiritual pleasure you feel within your soul. You can also feel the warmth of His tender embrace and the refreshing touch of His grace as it revives your body. The caressing of your soul and spirit come only one way, through the power and love of the Holy Spirit of our Lord Jesus Christ. Earthly pleasure is the closest experience we have been given in which to compare this profound ecstasy. God will give us what is familiar to help us comprehend what is unfamiliar.

Christ wants to give us the richness and depth of His personal love; the problem is that many of us permit, even tolerate, the things that hinder the relationship.

Now when the attacks do come at you, and the enemy tries to make you feel unclean, hold fast to the Word of God. His Word is truth. Whenever you are in doubt of what you are experiencing, or even reading in this Bible study, ask God for wisdom (see James 1:5). Our God is not a God of confusion. He will always confirm what He is teaching you. He may use other people, other books or resources, but He will always back up His truth with His Word. His Word is the handle you need to help lift you from the pit of misconception, saving you from the fowler's snare, (see Psalm 91:3), and setting you high upon a rock (see Psalm 27:5).

Grab hold of this handle from God's Word and fill in the blanks to Psalm 40:1-3, NIV:

"I waited patiently for the LORD; he turned to me and heard my cry. He lifted me _____ of the _____ _____, _____ of the _____ and _____ He set my feet on a rock and gave me a firm place to stand. He put a new song in my mouth, a hymn of praise to our God. Many will see and fear and put their trust in the LORD."

Unfortunately, for me the attacks did not end there. When that approach was demolished, the enemy tried another tactic. His second course of deception was to attack the relationship and get me to doubt and question God's heart toward me. When God did not respond in a way I had predicted, or He was taking too long in fulfilling my desires, the enemy came in with an attack against God's heart. Placing an attitude within my mind that *"If God really loved me He would have done this for me…"* or *"How could a loving God have allowed that to happen…"* And while I was in this state of mind, the enemy came in and threw fuel on the fire, adding insult to the wounds and getting me to question God's love.

God is Sovereign, and we are not always going to understand His choices at the time. Some things may not even be answered until we stand before Him in glory. But, the bottom line, no matter the circumstance, Christ has already answered how He feels about you and about me. So, whenever you feel like questioning God's love for you, look to the cross. The place before the cross is the only place to stand, because it was here, at the cross, that Jesus proved His love for us.

Grab the handle of Romans 5:8, NIV:

"But God _____ his own _____ for _____ in this: While we were still sinners, Christ _____ for _____."

Another scheme the enemy used was to involve others, especially those whom I dearly loved and respected. They questioned some of my experiences because they had not experienced it for themselves. Let me remind you, this is an individual invitation to move together as one with your Bridegroom. Experiences will vary, but they are joined by a common thread —the love of Christ. Again, if you are in doubt that this is truly of the Bridegroom, then ask God to confirm your experience. Do not be afraid to ask. And do not be afraid to test the spirits.

What does the Apostle John tells us in 1 John 4:1-3? Check all that apply:

_____ Do not believe every spirit

_____ Test the spirits to see whether they are from God

_____ Many false prophets have gone out into the world.

A friend of mine says, "Not everything that glitters is from God." Be aware, the enemy is very deceptive. In everything of God, Satan has a counterfeit, and he can appear in the spiritual realm as an angel of light (see 2 Corinthians 11:14). If he can't get to you in the worldly realm, he will try and get you in the spiritual realm. Be alert! But make up your mind right now that no one will ever steal your passion. Never let anyone extinguish your fire!

Grab the handle of 1 Thessalonians 5:19, NIV:

"Do _____ put _____ the Spirit's _____."

Do not worry about what other people may think of you; trying to win the approval of others. Galatians 1:10 tells us that if we are trying to win the approval of men and not God, we are not a servant of Christ. We can become stifled or even paralyzed in our relationship with Jesus, because we are too concerned about what others may think of us. I hate to tell you, but this is pride, and, remember, I am an expert at pride.

Focus all your attention on Jesus and move out in spirit-flying liberty. Worship; praise; pray, and celebrate for your audience of One. Remember, "…there is now no condemnation for those who are in Christ Jesus" (Romans 8:1). And He desires to set you free, so come to Him with an open heart, willing to bare all before Him.

Grab the handle of Galatians 1:10, NIV:

"Am I now trying to _____ the _____ of _____, or of _____? Or am I trying to _____ men? If I were still trying to _____ men, I would _____ be a servant of Christ."

Be aware of the demons of bitterness, unforgiveness, doubt, fear, disapproval, impatience, gossip, slander, rejection, criticism, a condemning spirit, pride, jealousy, false doctrine and self-righteousness that will bring about confusion and division in the church, and will drive a wedge between Jesus and you.

Please indulge me for a minute; I need to vent. My heart aches because there are so many people today who are not experiencing freedom in their relationship with Christ. Thousands are suffering under the weight of oppression, depression, and other demons that have attached themselves to their precious lives. The enemy is stealing our freedom, and holding us captive; not allowing us to enjoy our God-given right to experience the life we were born again to live.

It is time to cry out for freedom! Enough is enough! It is time to draw the line and take a stand. The enemy is far too much for us. He devours and destroys everything in his wake, but victory is ours in Him who loves us. Bride of Christ, it is time to get a mental picture. The One who is in us is stronger than the one who is in the world (see 1 John 4:4). Christ came to proclaim freedom for the captives (see Isaiah 61:1). Hallelujah! So, let us not be mousy in spiritual warfare, lying down under the weight of oppression and wallowing in the attack of the enemy. Instead, let us take a stand against the devil's schemes (see Ephesians 6:11). The enemy of our souls does not mess around, so why should we. He spends countless hours, day and night, before the throne; asking for permission to attack (see Revelation 12:10).

If you desire to draw near to the heart of God you must allow Him to deal with the things that are trying to enslave you and hold you captive.

We, however, spend very little time asking for protection and praying on the armor of God (see Ephesians 6:10-20). What is wrong with this picture? If we are to have daily victory in our lives over the threat of the enemy, we have got to beat him to the throne, and we have got to be confident about it.

Grab the handle of Romans 8:37, NIV:

"No, in _____ things we are more than _____ through him who _____ us."

The bottom line: if you desire to draw near to the heart of God you must allow Him to deal with the things that are trying to enslave you and hold you captive. Christ desires with all His heart to set you free from the attitudes, fears, sins, legalistic views and hurts that have kept you from having close personal fellowship with Him; because these demons can shut the door of intimacy.

Yet, understand this, the door may be closed but it is never locked. *Seek* His face. *Knock* and the door will be opened. And *ask* the Holy Spirit to reveal to you what is keeping you from entering into close fellowship with Christ. Give Him permission to enter into all of the places of your heart and allow Him to tear down the strongholds that keep you in bondage. Then ask Him to show you how to love Him the way He desires to be loved.

Again grab the handle of our theme verse in this study, Matthew 7:7, NIV:

"_____ and it will be given to you; _____ and you will _____; _____ and the door will be opened to you."

If you have never experienced the sacred romance with Christ, do not be afraid. If you are willing, He will lead you, preparing you for this encounter with His Spirit. We will discuss the preparation of the bride in far more detail a little later, but the point here is that you will not be thrown into anything that you have not been graciously prepared for first. You may not always realize you are being prepared, but when you open your heart and surrender your life, Jesus will lovingly escort you to the secret place; to the vineyard; to the ripened harvest; to the valleys or mountain heights; anywhere He wishes to lead you.

Wherever you are in your relationship with Christ, let me encourage you to press on. Go deeper; surrender more to taste more. Never at any point should you take His love for granted, and never believe that you have reached some pinnacle point in your relationship. Keep asking. Keep desiring. There is more; so much more.

God Desires You

Listen—can you hear the heart of the Bridegroom: "Let go, My love, and let Me love you the way I desire to love you. Let Me reach out for you and hold you close. Allow Me to touch you and love you. Indulge in My love for you, and bask in the richness of My abundance. Smell the fragrance of My love as it washes over you. Do not hold back. Come with Me behind the veil and commune with Me. Feel the warmth of My embrace. My love for you is real. My love for you is strong. Oh, My darling, My heart races with anticipation. Do not keep your love from Me, it is what I long for; what I crave. So sweet is your love, My love, and I, too, desire to indulge in what you bring."

Reflection and Response

Share about a time when God shook your world in order to reveal His love and glory to you.

_____

_____

_____

What assurances of unshakable love has Christ revealed to you?

_____

_____

_____

What is the cost of the perfumed oil in your alabaster jar? How has your transformation through fiery trials made your love pure and genuine for Jesus?

_____

_____

_____

How have any attitudes and/or past hurts affected your relationship with Jesus?

_____

_____

_____

_____

_____

What setbacks are you suffering? List the pitfalls and obstacles that are still hindering your relationship with Christ, keeping you from experiencing deeper levels of intimate fellowship.

_____

_____

_____

_____

_____

_____

_____

_____

_____

Now give them to the Lord. Take every one of them and nail them to the cross and leave them there.

Week Five

Lesson Five

Lose it All to Gain it All

Song of Songs 2:10-3:1

1. Christ _____ your _____, and He _____ your
   _____. If you _____ to Him, He will help you to do what
   He is asking you to do.

2. The little foxes represent _____. If the little foxes are not dealt with, they can
   _____ and _____ what was planted.

3. We must allow the Lord to _____ our love so that we get past the
   _____ _____ _____. This is what the Bible calls _____.

4. When God doesn't do things the way I expect or want I
   _____

5. Christ wants to share an _____, _____ love with you.

6. Her goal is to _____ His _____. His goal is to make her a _____
   One who will not only join Him in _____, but will also join Him in _____

7. The purpose of our journey with Jesus is to become _____ _____

8. Christ is looking for a _____ who will _____ _____ _____
   and follow the passions of His heart.

9. We will not know the fullness of Christ's love until we _____ to Him—
   _____

In their private lush, green garden, a garden fragrant and overflowing with the wine of sensual love, the maiden falls into the arms of her love. She can no longer resist him; the fears and hindrances that once burdened her heart have melted away. His abundant love is strong, so strong that she is devoured by it. This is a garden of sheer delight; nothing else will do. Her heart is overcome by desire; yet, her human mind cannot conceive it. "My love," he whispers, "if only you knew how much I love you, you would never be afraid." How wonderful is his love, no one can compare. She is inspired, moved, completely undone.

Week Six

To Desire More

- Day One: *God Desires to Inspire Your View*

- Day Two: *God Desires Hunger*

- Day Three: *God Desires Awareness*

- Day Four: *God Desires to Reveal His Plan*

- Day Five: *God Desires to Do Great Things*

- Reflection and Response: *God Desires You*

In this sixth week we are going to:

Determine our perspective
"My lover is radiant and ruddy, outstanding among ten thousand"
(Song of Songs 5:10).

Pull a chair up to the banquet table
"He has taken me to the banquet hall and his banner over me is love"
(Song of Songs 2:4).

Pursue greater levels of His Presence
"My heart says of you, 'Seek his face!' Your face, LORD I will seek"
(Psalm 27:8).

Tap into God's plan
"Now to each one the manifestation of the Spirit is given for the common good"
(1 Corinthians 12:7).

Aspire to do great things in Christ's power
"I tell you the truth, anyone who has faith in me will do what I have been doing. He will do even greater things than these, because I am going to the Father" (John 14:12).

Day One

God Desires to Inspire Your View

"How is your beloved better than others, most beautiful of women?
How is your beloved better than others, that you charge us so?"
(Song of Songs 5:9).

Last week we took a look at trusting God, surrendering to His love and allowing Him to set us free from the lies, sins and traps that keep us from experiencing Christ in fullness. This week we are going to reach for more, learn to pursue greatness, and witness the Holy Spirit's power as He rests on the weaknesses of ordinary people like us. But before we dive into these concepts, let us lay some groundwork.

Our perspective of Christ, how we view Him, is important. It will not only make a difference in how we share Him with others, it will also make a difference in our level of hunger, our fullness, and our willingness to step into the plans He has for us. God has much in store; therefore, let's forge ahead and allow the Holy Spirit to inspire our view as we once again compare the allegory of the Song of Songs to the sacred romance. This time we will view the lover, in the Song of Songs, from the perspective of his beloved.

Begin by asking God the Father to enhance your perception of His Son. Then please turn with me to the Song of Songs and read all of Chapter 5.

In your own words, describe the scene in verses 5:1-9.

What similarities do you see between these verses in Chapter 5 to the scene in Chapter 3? In the margin, list some of the differences.

I don't want to get too far ahead in our study because we will take a deeper look at what is taking place here in this portion of Scripture in Week Seven, the Purification of the Bride, but for now it is important to understand that the beloved is being tested. Unlike the first time, when the lover leaves her because of her disobedience, she is now being taken through a test, a trial

136

because of her obedience. Remember in Song of Songs 4:6-8, when the lover invited her to go with him to the higher places? When she agreed to go he began to call her "his lover," "his bride." Through her act of surrender he is taken with her love and devotion, but now he is stretching her through an important process in developing her maturity.

The test begins with the lover coming up from the garden (v. 5:1). He comes to his beloved with dew drenched hair and knocks at the door, asking her to open the door. Notice in verse 5:5, as opposed to verse 3:1, how quickly the beloved responds in willingness to arise from her bed, her place of comfort and safety, to open the door and respond to the call of her lover.

What happened, however, when she opened the door for her lover? (v. 6)

_____

_____

What was the response of the beloved? Where did she look for him?

_____

_____

As she searches, who does she come in contact with? How do they respond to her? (v. 7). Why do you think they abused her?

_____

_____

In verse 5:8 what does the beloved instruct the daughters of Jerusalem to do? Why do you think she told them of her love for him?

_____

_____

How do the daughters of Jerusalem respond to her statement? (v. 9)

_____

All through the night she searched, but she did not find him. Again and again she called out, but he did not answer. The watchmen approached her, and beat her, yet this did not end, or even delay, her desperate search. She was determined to be with him no matter the cost.

Why do think she was tenacious in her pursuit? Why do you think she willingly endured such abuse?

_____

_____

This is the hunger and thirst that Christ Jesus desires for you to have for Him. Just like the beloved in the Song of Songs, He desires for you to be so taken with Him, so focused on His Person, that you cannot, and will not, live without Him.

I believe she is hungry. She is hungry for what she longs for; thirsting for the water she has tasted. Her lover has made an impression on her soul. He has placed his seal upon her heart. She is utterly in love and nothing will stop her from being with the one she loves. Her lover has so captured her heart that she cannot live without him. He is everything to her. He has become the very air that she breathes.

Then, during her search, she approaches the daughters of Jerusalem and asks them for a favor. "Please tell him," she says, "if you see him, tell him that I love him and desire to be with him." (v. 8)

"Why should we do this," they reply. "Who is your lover? What makes him so special?" And her reply is priceless, as the exquisite words pour from her heart, revealing her complete abandonment of self to the one she loves.

Please read verse 5:10-16 again, this time aloud. As you read, try to picture yourself as the beloved in this scene. What are you feeling? Let the tone of your voice reflect your heart.

What stands out to you the most in the beloved's description of her lover?

_____

I love the response of the daughters of Jerusalem recorded in verse 6:1. Write their words below:

_____

_____

They go from, "How is your lover better than anyone else?" To, "Where is he? Where has he gone? We will help you look for him" Now what do you think made them change their attitude when all the beloved did was describe his appearance? I believe there was something special in the way she described him. Her eyes lit-up, full of longing and love. Her smile drew them in as she explained her lover. I believe their hearts melted right along with hers as she told them about her lover. By the time she finished, they wanted to know this lover for themselves.

How do you share Jesus with the daughters of Jerusalem that you know? Is He outstanding among all others? Has He become the love of your life to the point that you are desperately in love and hungry for Him?

This is the hunger and thirst that Christ Jesus desires for you to have for Him. Just like the beloved in the Song of Songs, He desires for you to be so taken with Him, so focused on His Person, that you cannot, and will not, live without Him. Yes, the Lover woos His bride, initiates and invites her into the relationship. He is constantly pursuing her, desiring for her to be by His side in love and service; but, and let this next remark go down deep within your heart, the bride must respond.

I implore you, be like the beloved in the Song of Songs and desire to know Christ. Pursue Him regardless of what others say about you or do to you. Desire to know who He is and what He desires to accomplish in your life. Make the choice to receive His love and return His love. Then, from this outpouring of love, others will be drawn in. They, too, will desire to know this One whom you so desperately hunger for and crave.

How has Jesus become outstanding among ten thousand in your life?

_____

_____

_____

_____

_____

_____

Share about a time of separation that increased your level of hunger for Jesus.

_____

_____

_____

_____

_____

_____

_____

Day Two

God Desires Hunger

"As the deer pants for streams of water, so my soul pants for you, O God. My soul thirsts for God, for the living God. When can I go and meet with God?" (Psalm 42:1-2).

I hope you brought your appetite today; our text will have two main courses. Therefore, let us come and partake of the Lord.

Begin today by asking God the Father to increase your hunger for Christ, and then read Isaiah 55:1-3.

In verse one, what does the Word repeatedly tell us to do?

_____

In your own words, describe what we are to partake of. What is being offered, and what is the spiritual significance?

_____

_____

What should we *not* partake of? What is the spiritual significance?

_____

_____

The word *come* is a very significant word. It is the initial invitation Christ offers His bride to *come* and partake of Him. When Jesus invites His bride to come to Him, He is inviting her to join with Him in spiritual intimacy.

Every day Jesus offers us the opportunity to *come* and partake of His goodness, richness, and mercy, to be our sole source of satisfaction. We don't need money; in fact, we don't need to bring anything at all, just ourselves. When we are hungry and thirsty for more of Him, all we need to do is come to Him and eat and drink.

What does each of the following verses instruct us to do? What is the reward for obedience?

Revelation 22:17:

_____

Matthew 11:28:

_____

Mark 6:31:

_____

Matthew 4:19:

_____

The primary invitation to *come* and receive salvation by grace through faith is offered to everyone—no matter who you are, or where you come from, the invitation is yours. Come to Him and ask, and you will receive salvation. But don't stop there. Come and seek out satisfaction with your whole heart.

It breaks my heart to think that there are many who have been Christians for numerous years; yet, have still not found satisfaction in Christ. Why? What is the problem if we know that Christ yearns to fill us with His love and power from His Holy Spirit? The problem is due to a lack of hunger.

What about you? Are you hungry for Christ? Do you thirst for His Person like parched ground crying out for rain? (Psalm 63:1). Do you crave the sweetness of His presence more than life itself? Are you like the deer in Psalm 42:1-2, whose soul pants for God, who thirsts for the Living God? If not, then get hungry for Him, because hungry people get fed (see Matthew 5:6).

The word *hunger* means "any strong desire."[17] Synonyms for *hunger* are *desire, need, wish* and *appetite*. What is it you hunger for? Because "where your treasure is, there your heart will be also" (Matthew 6:21). What means the most to you is what you will crave.

We all hunger for something. Whether the things of this world or the things of God, our souls continually search for what we think will fill us, and that is what will consume us. If we desire things, things are what our minds will dwell on, and things are what our hearts will hunger for. We get one thing, we want another. We buy this; but then we want that. It is an unrelenting cycle of want, pulling us into an endless pit of chasing after things that will never satisfy us (see Ecclesiastes 2:10-11).

If God is our treasure (see Job 22:24-25), then bringing glory to God will be our ever-waking thought, and our deepest desire will be to be with Him. We will hunger for His Spirit to take us in. We will joyfully surrender under His influence, addicted to the power that has invaded us. We will long to linger

We all hunger for something. Whether the things of this world or the things of God, our souls continually search for what we think will fill us, and that is what will consume us.

Let His love surround you. Let it stir your heart and soul. Permit the aroma of Christ's love to intensify your longing, intensify your hunger, and increase your desire.

on His river banks, filled, overflowing with grace, joy, peace, and love. We simply will not be able to get enough of Him.

Absorb this concept: Christ wants you to eat and drink of Him; He doesn't want you to *snack* on Him (see Haggai 1:6). He wants you to feast on what He has permitted you to indulge in now; to taste His abundance and drink your fill from His River of Joy. Bride, hear what your Bridegroom is saying to you: "Oh, beloved, eat and drink! Yes, drink deeply of this love!" (Song of Songs 5:1, NLT). "Like sweet nectar from the vine, partake of Me. Dine on tenderness and enter into a place of fulfillment and joy."

The word *eat* means "to consume or devour; to dine on; savor."[18] The divine Bridegroom freely offers to you Himself, His Spirit, and His heart. Desire Him; yearn for Him, and hunger for a life that will bring you satisfaction in Christ. The word drink means "to swallow; …to breathe in, as air."[19] The Lover of your soul desires for you to drink Him in as if you were breathing in the very air around you; to be drunk on Him; intoxicated by inhaling His life and love.

In this life, prior to heaven, Christ's love whets your appetite. It is like the appetizer before the meal, or the sample taste before the feast. But, instead of taking the edge off your hunger, as appetizers tend to do, His love increases it so that you will crave more, desire more, and hunger for more.

Let His love surround you. Let it stir your heart and soul. Permit the aroma of Christ's love to intensify your longing, intensify your hunger, and increase your desire. Because once you have breathed in the sweetness of His presence and love, you will not be satisfied with a whiff alone, you must partake.

Allow your hunger to become ravenous, because the size of your appetite will make a difference in the speed of your growth and your level of closeness. No longer settle for a half-hearted or casual desire, go after Him with an intense desperation. Seek to make Christ your heart's greatest desire, because when you begin to desire Him more than your next breath, it will tremendously increase your level of commitment. And it is through commitment to the Bridegroom that you bring glory and honor to God (see John 15:8). Go ahead, eat and drink of Him because "He does satisfy the thirsty and fills the hungry with good things" (Psalm 107:9).

Fill in the blanks below according to Psalm 84:2, NIV:

"My soul _____, even _____, for the courts of the LORD; my heart and my flesh _____ _____ for the living God" (Psalm 84:2).

What do you think it means to have your soul faint with yearning and desire for God? What do you think it feels like to be so overwhelmed with hunger and longing that you simply cannot live unless you have the very One you crave? What is it to have your heart, and every ounce of soul and flesh cry out with intense passion for the living God? Do you know? Are you desperate for Christ? How badly do you crave the Lord your God? Is your soul faint with desire? Are your heart and flesh panting, crying out in sheer desperation for Him?

Share the desire(s) of your heart with Jesus.

_____

_____

_____

For our second main course, let's consider the desperate cry of a hungry heart.

God gives us many examples of this kind of hunger. King David understood it; the beloved in the Song of Songs experienced it, and the Canaanite women in Matthew 15:21-28 and the blind beggar in Luke 18:35-42 give us incredible examples of this kind of intense desperation.

Please read Mathew 15:21-28 and Luke 18:35-42: What common cry did both the Canaanite woman and the blind beggar have? Record their words below:

_____

_____

How did Jesus respond to the Canaanite woman in Matthew 15:24; 26?

_____

_____

How did He respond to the blind beggar in Luke 18:40-41?

_____

_____

Why do you think Jesus initially responded differently? What do you think He was looking for in the hearts of those who cried out to Him?

_____

_____

The Canaanite woman cried out. Yet, Jesus does not respond to her right away. So, again she cries out, her heart begging, "Lord, help me!" The disciples hear her and try to discourage Jesus, telling Him to send her away. Jesus silences their complaints and keeps on walking.

In Luke 18:35-43 the blind beggar beside the road is like the Canaanite woman when he shouts out, "Jesus, Son of David, have mercy on me!" But unlike Jesus' response to the Canaanite woman, He stops and orders the man to be brought to Him (v. 40). Bride of Christ, Jesus stopped, immediately and without hesitation; stopped. Now this may imply that Jesus was more willing to help the blind beggar than the Canaanite woman, but I think something else was happening here. I think that in His heart Jesus did stop at the sound of the Canaanite woman's voice, but He was waiting for more from her; He was looking for a heart full of hunger.

Let's look at her story again. Matthew 15:25 says that the woman came and knelt before Him and cried, "Lord, help me!" See the exclamation point? She is shouting here, and I will bet that she pushed a few of those unwilling disciples out of the way in order to get to Jesus and throw herself at His feet. Now look again at the Lord's response to her distress in verse 26, "It is not right to take the children's bread and toss it to their dogs." Okay, be honest here. If Jesus came to you in your hour of need and said this to you, would you continue in your pursuit of Him? Or would you, at this point, be so greatly discouraged that you would give up, or even be angry? Would you be struck dumb that He seemed unwilling to help; thinking that God was not answering your prayers?

Nevertheless, let's put our feelings aside for a moment and look at the precious response of the Canaanite woman in Matthew 15:27. Pen her words below:

_____

Can you believe it; she agreed with Him. "Yes," she says, "I am undeserving, but I am so hungry that I am willing to eat the crumbs that fall from your table. I will eat anything you give me, because I need you. I am helpless, utterly dependent; therefore I am willing to fall at your feet and beg for the leftovers."

Week Six: To Desire More

How did Jesus response to her in Matthew 15:28?

_____

_____

Overjoyed at her hungry heart, He filled her need. He granted her full request, and He did not give her the crumbs. He gave her the whole meal!

Not for one minute do I believe that Jesus ever intended not to help this woman. He was simply fueling her hunger, desiring for her to understand her desperation for Him, her desire for Him. The Lord will at times allow you to struggle as you reach out for Him. He hears you, but He wants you to come to a deeper understanding of your need. You need Him!

Bride of Christ—get hungry! Never be satisfied with the crumbs that fall from the Master's table. Stand up and see the abundance of the banquet table (see Song of Songs 2:3), because once you have seen and tasted this great source of life, nothing else will fill your heart and life the way He can— nothing!

Oh how do I express my heart to you; there are no words adequate enough to describe this relationship. And, yet, my heart is heavy, because I know that there are so many, right now, struggling in their lives. They are searching and finding nothing, weary with longing in their hearts, and finding a void. Cry out to Him. He is able, and He is waiting to fill your hunger. Christ is longing to shine His love into your life and fill the emptiness.

It is not enough just to have salvation, as wonderful as that is, but it is not enough. So, go ahead and discover the treasures and glorious satisfaction of being intimately in love with Jesus. Go after it; all of it. Pursue it with all your heart. Love Him more than anyone or anything else in this entire world, and crave the satisfaction that only comes from tasting the richness of Christ (see Psalm 36:7-8; Psalm 34:8).

Share with Jesus the desire of your heart to partake of Him at the banquet table.

_____

_____

_____

_____

_____

Day Three

God Desires Awareness

"Be still and know that I am God" (Psalm 46:10).

In our hungry pursuit we must develop a more vivid awareness of God's presence. The omnipresence of His Holy Spirit perpetually surrounds us all of the time, but we are not always aware of it. We must learn to abide in His presence continually, going through the course of our day with the indulgent thought that He is with us. Understand, however, that only those who greatly hunger for His manifest presence will experience it on a persistent basis.

Pray for an increased awareness of God's manifest presence, and then please read Psalm 139:1-18. According to this Psalm where can we go to escape God's presence?

_____

What does it mean to you to know that God's eyes are always upon you, His presence is continually with you and that His thoughts concerning you are as numerous as the grains of sand?

_____

_____

What name is recorded in Matthew 1:23? What does this name mean?

_____

God's Word assures us that He is with us—now and forever—He will not leave us or forsake us (see Hebrews 13:5). Scripture has given us a clear picture of His omnipresence, the presence that continually surrounds, leads, guides, guards, and protects. This is wonderful to ponder. It gives us a sense of security and hope. Yet, as wonderful as God's omnipresence is, there is more—His manifest presence. Throughout this Bible study, thus far, I have been sharing with you glimpses, little peeks into the power and joy of being in the Lord's manifest presence.

The manifest presence is an awareness of the focused and intentional increase of God's omnipresence. It is the awareness of a presence so potent and consuming that the moment you experience it, it is like He has reached down from heaven, picked you up and cradled your feeble body in His arms. It was God's manifest presence that Moses cried out for in

Exodus 33:18 when he said, "Now show me your glory." And it is this same manifest presence of God that we will be focusing on in today's lesson.

Never, for one minute, be content to stay where you are. Desire more of Him at all costs. Never be complacent in your journey. I guarantee you, no matter where you are, you have not yet reached the fullness of relationship that Jesus desires to share with you. Be careful never to take His glorious presence for granted. Don't let the magnificence of His Holy presence become common or casual to you. Supernatural encounters with God's manifest Spirit are astounding, extremely profound, and enormously powerful; but in order to experience it, you must be willing to pay the price of utter submission.

One of the greatest setbacks to coming into His presence is that, all too often, most of us are unwilling to come under His control. We cling tightly to the things that cannot truly satisfy us, and we often refuse to yield to the control of the Spirit.

Another hindrance is fear. I ministered to a woman who was terrified about the thought of coming into the manifest presence of God. She had assumed that it would be painful; as a result, she completely resisted the idea. Also, many of us fear change. For years our church services have been conducted in the same manner, and when any part of "the program" is altered it upsets those that have become accustomed to the schedule. We do not serve a stereo-typical God. He wants to come into our assemblies and reign, but many are too afraid to give Him the freedom to move into our congregations.

Bride, can we not trust the Holy Spirit to come into our lives and guide us? Do we not want the manifested presence of Christ to come into our churches? A presence-driven church is fueled by presence-driven individuals. We must learn to rely on the Spirit. We must learn to be presence-driven. We must, as individuals, get past our self-absorbed agendas and quiet our hearts before God, allowing His presence to fully consume our lives.

What would happen if the Lord God Almighty descended in a cloud upon our churches? What would happen if we made God feel so welcomed in our midst, so delighted to come among us, that He would choose to show up in all His glory?

Please read 2 Chronicles 5:11-14. In your own words, describe the scene.

_____

_____

_____

Supernatural encounters with God's manifest Spirit are astounding, extremely profound, and enormously powerful; but in order to experience it, you must be willing to pay the price of utter submission.

What specifically happened in verse 14? Check all that apply:

   ___ All the people stood up and shouted

   ___ The musicians and singers continued to worship the Lord in song

   ___ The glory of God filled the Temple

   ___ The priests could no longer perform their tasks because of the glory

What do you see happening in verse 13 that created the atmosphere for God's presence to descend upon them?

_____

Unity sang the heart of praise that day, and the glory of the Lord filled the temple, consuming it to the point that the priests could not function, could not perform, totally paralyzing them to the point that they were unable to move.

When the glory comes there are no options. At this point, you are wholly surrendered before the Lord, helpless, and completely at His mercy. Does this thought scare you? Or are you ecstatic over the prospect of this kind of encounter actually happening among our congregations?

Explain your feelings.

_____

One of the reasons we find the manifest presence of God's glory so scary is that with each new level of closeness, as we dare to step more and more into the light of His magnificent presence, we become weaker and He becomes more powerful (see John 3:30).

Now, let's consider another day when the glory of the Lord appeared. Please turn to Exodus 19 and 20. Scan through these verses to once again familiarize yourself with the scene. As you review, pay special attention to verses 19:9, 16, 18-19; 20:18-19. What did the Israelites witness on the morning of the third day? Be specific:

_____

_____

_____

Gauge your level of excitement:

Ecstatic

↑

↓

Scared to death

How did the Israelites respond to the glory of God? (vv. 20:18-19)

_____

Even today many of us are exactly like the Israelites who stayed at a distance, not hungering for the Presence of Life to come near. Why? Because He is too loud; He smokes too much; and He makes the sanctuary tremble. The heat from His fire is too powerful, and the thunder and lightning are too much like stormy weather conditions. All too often, the heart of the matter is, many of us are simply too content to stay in our places of comfort, believing it is safer to stand back. Many are absent of the desire to draw closer and step into God's omnipotent presence; and, as a result, they miss out on the greatness of what God desires to do in and through their lives.

In Exodus 20:20, how did Moses respond? What did he tell the people who were standing at a distance?

_____

Moses was unafraid to step into the glory of God. And even though the Israelites did not listen to his words of encouragement, he, himself entered in and approached the place where God was (v.21). Moses knew the significance and recognized the value of the Lord's presence, and He cried out for it regularly.

To emphasize this point, let's consider a conversation between Moses and the Lord in Exodus 33:12-18. In your own words, record the dialogue between Moses and God.

Moses said… (vv. 12-13)

" _____

_____ "

God said… (v. 14)

" _____

_____ "

Moses said… (vv. 15-16)

" _____

_____ "

When the glory comes there are no options. At this point, you are wholly surrendered before the Lord, helpless, and completely at His mercy.

God said … (v. 17)

"_____

_____"

Moses said… (v. 18)

"_____

_____"

What was Moses' specific request? What was it that he refused to live without?

_____

_____

My heart does back flips at just the thought of being in the tangible, manifest presence of God. Jesus desires for you to seek Him, all of Him, the manifested glory of His presence, just like Moses, with all your heart. If you are tired of the status quo and desire to see revelation come into your life, for revival to overtake you, then agree with me in prayer.

Lord God, we cannot fathom the love you have for us, but, Lord, how we pray to hunger for Your presence in our lives. Come in and blow the door off of our hearts. We need you! Do not let us settle for complacency or be content to stay where we are. Help us, Lord, to look past our fears and draw near to Your heart. Enable us to let go completely of anything that is keeping us from you, surrendering everything into Your hands, and offering You our ardent worship. Move among us, Lord God, and stir the passion in our hearts. Fill us with an exhilaration of desire to be close to you, overwhelmed with love and devotion. Fan the flame, Lord, and increase our fervor in seeking Your presence. In Jesus' marvelous Name we pray. Amen!

Share with Jesus the desire of your heart to experience greater levels of His manifest presence.

_____

_____

_____

_____

_____

Day Four

God Desires to Reveal His Plan

"For I know the plans I have for you," declares the LORD,
"plans to prosper you and not to harm you, plans to give
you a hope and a future" (Jeremiah 29:11).

Do you desire to know your purpose in life? If the answer is "yes," then seek God's manifest presence. No one who is intimately acquainted with Christ is at a complete loss as to what He desires to do in and through him or her. This, however, does not mean that you will have all the answers or that you automatically will know what will happen in your life tomorrow. And it does not mean that you will always act in wisdom. We are human, after all, and we will make wrong choices; but, as we connect with Christ through His Holy Presence, we will learn where we fit into the Master's plan. Just as each part of creation instinctively knows its purpose on this planet, each member of the bride will also understand her place. She will learn her gifts; her God-given abilities and talents will become more evident. The tasks, the service, the ministry will all become clearer as she draws closer to her Groom's heart.

Pray that God would fill you with His Spirit and increase your focus on Him so that He may reveal His plans and purpose for your life.

Please read 1 Corinthians 12. What is the main message of these verses?

_____

_____

Paraphrase 1 Corinthians 12:4-6. From Whom do we receive our spiritual gifts?

_____

_____

In 1 Corinthians 12, what ways do you see relationship at work between Christ and his church?

_____

_____

If you know what your spiritual gifts are, record them below. If you are unaware of your spiritual gifts, ask the Lord to reveal them to you. Speak with your pastor or someone in leadership at your church. There are wonderful aids and tools available to determine your spiritual gifting.

_____

_____

_____

List as many of the gifts of the Spirit as you can as they are recorded in 1 Corinthians 12:8-10; 12:28; Romans 12:6-8 and Ephesians 4:11.

_____

_____

_____

_____

_____

_____

_____

_____

_____

_____

_____

_____

_____

_____

_____

_____

Christ desires for you to join Him in His work, and He longs to share with you the purposes and plans He has for your life. But in order to function fully in these plans and purposes, you must be intimately connected to the Lover of your soul. If I have not already made myself clear on this point, absorb it now. The relationship is the most important thing and must come before anything else. The relationship you share with Christ through His Word and His Holy Spirit is the key to everything, because without the relationship, you are simply going through religious motions.

To emphasize this, let me ask you a question the Lord once asked me: "If it was all stripped away; if I removed your gifts, talents, and abilities; if it all stopped and all you had was our relationship, would you still love me?" This is a profound question and one which took me by surprise. If I never wrote again and all I had was my relationship with God, would that be enough? If I lost all of the talents and gifts which He had given me to serve Him; if I were to be stripped of everything but my relationship with Him, would I still love Him? Desperately I wanted to say yes; but something inside of me made me stop and think first. What is our relationship based on? Did I love the books or the idea of writing the books, more than I loved God? I began to think: *What am I doing this for? What is my motivation?* I love to share Jesus with others, but was I writing these books for Him or for me?

Then one day, in order to help me better understand where my focus was, God erased the manuscript for this book from my computer. I truthfully don't know exactly what happened. I somehow hit a wrong key, and poof, it vanished—all of it. It was gone. My initial reaction was to panic, but to my surprise I didn't. My mind raced as I tried to think of what to do next, but I did not get angry or upset. I simply contemplated my next move before I touched any other keys on the keyboard. And as I weighed of my options, I heard the Lord speak to my heart, "What do we do now?"

Immediately John 6:5-6 came to mind, so I opened my Bible and read: "When Jesus looked up and saw a great crowd coming toward him, he said to Phillip, 'Where shall we buy bread for these people to eat?' He asked this only to test him, for he already had in mind what he was going to do." It was a test. Christ was testing me to see where my loyalty lay. "Well," I said to Him as my heart sank, "I guess we start over." Though I was heartbroken at the thought of beginning again, I trusted God in what He had in mind. If it was His desire to start over, then that was what we would have to do. It was not what I wanted. Hours of work and research had just vanished. Time and energy went right out the window, but I had come to realize at that moment that God was more important to me than the book.

The good news is that the book was not lost. God had it under control, and with one simple touch of the keyboard it was all back, complete, and fully intact. So as a result of this experience, I came to this conclusion. Yes, my relationship with the Lord would be enough. It has to be, because without the relationship I have nothing. If He did take away everything, if I had completely lost the book that day, I would have still had Him, the greatest treasure in heaven and on earth. But if I lost Him and had everything this world had to offer, I would have nothing.

And once I came to that place in my heart, when I came to that realization, that is when the real story began; when the real commitment of love began. You see, His desire is for me to stay focused on Him and not on the task. The relationship is everything. From there everything else is given its life.

In light of what I just shared with you, paraphrase what you think the writer of Habakkuk 3:17-18 is trying to communicate.

_____

_____

The relationship is the most important thing and must come before anything else.

Focusing on Christ is essential. It keeps our heads on correctly and our hearts in the right place. When I am focused, I am not anxious and worried. And when my thoughts and heart are on Christ, as He promises in His Word, He guards me and showers me with His peace, helping me to remain in His presence and stay on track. When my focus is off and my flesh has a say in the matter, my mind becomes confused and peace evades my heart.

Fill in the blanks according to Philippians 4:6-7, NIV.

"Do not be _____ about anything, but in _____, by prayer and petition, with _____, bring your requests to God. And the _____ of God, which transcends all understanding, will _____ your hearts and your minds in Christ Jesus" (Philippians 4:6-7).

In what circumstances of your life do you need the peace of God that transcends all understanding? In what areas and attitudes do you need Him to guard your heart and mind?

_____

_____

_____

There is nothing on this earth more effective or powerful than a life that is focused on the Lord Jesus Christ

Often, when our focus is off, it is because we either have too many things on our plate or we are trying to run between two agendas: God's and ours. When we continually have a list of things to do running through our minds, we can feel tired and frustrated, and we run the risk of burning out. We're wearing too many hats if we cannot place our focus where it needs to be. When we meet with Jesus for that intimate time in the secret place and what is going through our minds is what we need to do, then we have an overloaded schedule.

Let's pray and ask God to help us unload some of what we're trying to carry. Let's jump off these treadmills and get refocused, because there is nothing on this earth more effective or powerful than a life that is focused on the Lord Jesus Christ, believing He will do what He has promised. People who are focused, listening carefully, walking in obedience and are completely yielded to God's desires, are the ones Christ powerfully manifests Himself in. And when Jesus is firmly evident in a person's life, that person ceases to function in the natural, because she is operating in the supernatural. It is God's desire to fill each of us with His Holy Spirit so that we may be filled to the measure of all the fullness of God (see Ephesians 3:19), to His glory and the growth and enrichment of His body—His bride.

End today's study by reading Ephesians 4:11-13. What are the purposes of the gifting He has given us by our relationship with Him through His Spirit?

_____

_____

In what ways is the Holy Spirit accomplishing His purposes in your life? Thank God for His faithfulness in giving you gifts to accomplish His purposes. Thank Him for the plans He has for you.

_____

_____

_____

_____

Day Five

God Desires to Do Great Things

"I have raised you up for this very purpose, that I might display my power in you and that my name might be proclaimed in all the earth" (Romans 9:17).

If our desire is to know God's purpose for our lives, if we are to step into the plans that Christ has for us, we must set aside our self-seeking agendas and seek His. If we truly desire to embrace all of what God has in mind, we must be willing to surrender all areas of our lives for a better life—His.

The word *surrender* means "to yield or hand over power to another; to cease resistance; to give oneself up into the power (control, authority, and influence) of another."[20] In Chapter Four we talked about how Christ offers each of us the abundant life, but in order to experience it, we must surrender ourselves to His love, His work, and His plans, allowing the Holy Spirit to live through us unhindered.

Pray to have a surrendered life and then begin our Scripture reading today with Luke 9:23-27. What is the cost of following Jesus?

_____

_____

What must a follower of Christ surrender before he will gain life? (vv. 24-25)

_____

Christ desires your life, and He desires mine. Christ desires for our whole life to belong to Him, not what is left over. In Luke 9:23 Jesus told His disciples, "If anyone would come after me, he must deny himself and take up his cross daily and follow me." Jesus desires for us to daily deny ourselves, take up our cross and follow Him. I do not believe, however, that this means that we are to deny our God-given dreams and desires. Our self-promoting dreams and desires, yes, but not our God-given dreams and desires. Let me explain.

God has planted dreams and desires within my heart, as He did in everyone's heart when He created them, and He has every intention of using those dreams and desires for His glory. These implanted dreams and desires are what connect us to Christ. When we open the door of our heart to Jesus, He begins bringing those dreams and desires to life for His glory, and that brings us great joy and fulfillment. It gives us a sense of purpose because we are connecting to Christ through these desires. God is the dream-Giver and the dream-Creator. He is the One who makes it all happen. His will is for each of us to become the person He intended us to be in Christ. When we are surrendered (taking up our cross) and focused on His will (denying ourselves), He is able to bring those implanted dreams and desires to life.

When we truly surrender our hearts and say, "Show me, Lord, your plans for this life," He will transform us through our dreams and desires, revealing to us His intended purpose for our lives. Even dreams and desires that have become buried throughout the years will be renewed as the Lord digs them up and brings them out into His light. When we accurately tap into the heart of God, He reveals the greatest dreams and desires of all, and the wonderful thing is that these dreams and desires are already a part of who we are.

How does Psalm 139:13-16 tell us that God created all of who we are complete with God-given dreams and desires?

_____

_____

God desires what is best for you, and He greatly desires to reveal to you those unique desires that only He can bring to life

Before you were born, God knew you, filled your innermost being, and ordained every day of your life—knowing full well all of the dreams and desires that He had in mind for you. And, if that were not enough, He wrote down all of those plans, dreams and desires.

God desires what is best for you, and He greatly desires to reveal to you those unique desires that only He can bring to life. Beloved, do not let fear keep you from plunging into your deepest dreams and desires. Do not back away from what intimidates you, retreating back into a place of safety because you're afraid of the unknown.

Too many times in life we run back to the familiar security of our comfort zones where we feel safe. But Christ is calling us to greatness, not mediocrity. Greatness may mean different things to different people. You may think of someone who is famous or someone who has experienced success as achieving greatness. *Webster's Dictionary* defines *great(ness)* as "admirable; important; uncommonly gifted; of high rank."[21] But God has something even grander in mind. He interprets greatness as living beyond oneself. Christ wants us to go beyond anything we think we are capable of doing.

In Acts 4:1-22 we see an example of greatness. Briefly describe the scene.

_____

_____

After Peter and John were arrested, the next day they were brought in and questioned before the elders and the teachers of the law (v. 5). What question were they asked? (v. 7) What answer did Peter give? (v. 10)

_____

_____

How does Acts 4:8 support the promise of the Lord in Matthew 10:19-20?

_____

What astonished the elders and teachers of the law about Peter and John? (v. 13)

_____

God chooses the ordinary to do the extraordinary. Jesus chose unschooled, ordinary men to teach, train, and join with Him in His work. But the thing that set them apart was that they were filled with the Holy Spirit, and, as a result, they exemplified great courage, they spoke with authority, and the religious leaders took note.

According to 2 Corinthians 4:7, how do we know that this all-surpassing power was from God and not from their efforts or natural capabilities?

_____

_____

God delights in using weak, common, everyday people like you and me. That way we know beyond a doubt that it is the work of the Holy Spirit. God created you and me just the way He intended, including all of our weaknesses, and He designed us for a purpose. To tell you the truth, when I discovered that God uses weaknesses, I became very excited. For a long time I had been trying very hard to get this whole thing right. But the pressure really came off when I realized that God is looking for weaknesses.

If you are willing to indulge me, I will share with you a few of those weaknesses that frankly I saw only as hindrances. I have gone much of my life with my temper getting the better of me. Thank goodness, I can see the Lord changing that one. Low self-esteem and insecurities are huge for me. Feelings of inadequacy pierce my heart almost daily—anytime I think about what God desires to do in my life. My insecurities keep me coming frequently to the Lord looking for affirmation. And, as I shared earlier, there is the issue of perfectionism.

Surrender your life, desires, plans, and weaknesses to His life, desires, plans, and strengths.

But then one day my Savior saved me again when He showed me something else. All throughout Scripture, God used weak people to do His work: plain, simple, ordinary people, who in the Holy Spirit's power, did amazing things, revealing the glory of the Lord. Moses had a temper. His hot-headed behavior caused him to murder an Egyptian (see Exodus 2:12) and smash the tablets of the Ten Commandments (see Exodus 32:19). Yet, God worked in Moses' life, changing him into a man of humility (see Numbers 12:3). Gideon had a tremendous lack of self-confidence and huge insecurities, but God converted him into a mighty warrior (see Judges 6 and 7). Impetuous Peter (see Matthew 26:69-75) became the rock upon which the Church was built (see Matthew 16:18). The adulterer, David, we all know, became a man after God's own heart (see 1 Samuel 13:14). The conceited disciple John (see Luke 9:51-56 and Mark 10:35-40) became the Apostle of Love (see 1 John). Not one of these men was perfect or capable; yet, God used them in spite of their weaknesses and shortcomings.

Please do not misunderstand. I do not for a minute put myself in the same category as any of these men, but I can relate to weaknesses: theirs and mine. The fact is if God can use them despite their weaknesses, then He can use me. He can use you. When I came to the realization that I didn't have to have it altogether, that I didn't have to be strong or perfect, and that God was looking for weakness, I was liberated. The very thing I was ashamed of and desperate to overcome, He would transform and use for His glory. Hallelujah!

According to 2 Corinthians 12:9, what was Paul more than happy to boast about and why?

_____

_____

Surrender your life, desires, plans, and weaknesses to His life, desires, plans, and strengths. Allow Him to raise you above mediocrity. Cease resisting, and hand over complete control and authority to the Holy Spirit so that He may fill you with His power. And as He releases the supernatural filling of His power and anointing in your life, you will reflect and bring forth the glorious proclamation of His Name. Now, that's living in greatness!

Share with Jesus the desires of your heart to let go and embrace the plans, dreams, and desires that He ordained for you.

_____

_____

God Desires You

Know He is with you: "I love you, My darling, and I will never leave you. We are partners, and I will in My great power help you and support you in every endeavor. I have filled you with My Holy Spirit. I have given you gifts, talents, and desires in order to bring our dreams to life. I have chosen you, My bride. The Father has given you to Me, and I have chosen you to be with Me forever. Open your heart to greatness, My love, and follow Me into the plans I have for you; for us. Stay focused on Me, and do not be afraid. I am with you always, and together we will do great things."

Reflection and Response

As you have taken this journey, thus far, how has your perspective of Christ changed?

_____

_____

_____

_____

_____

_____

What scares you the most about experiencing the manifest presence of God in your life?

_____

_____

_____

_____

_____

_____

What excites you the most about experiencing the manifest presence of God in your life?

_____

_____

_____

_____

_____

_____

Reflect on the desire of God's heart to do great things in you and through you. How do His desires inspire you to hunger for more of His plans and purposes, more of His manifested presence, and more of His love in your life?

_____

_____

_____

_____

_____

_____

_____

_____

_____

_____

_____

_____

_____

_____

_____

Week Six

Lesson Six

Hungry for More

Song of Songs 3:2-4; 4:1

1. We are _____ when we come regularly into the manifest presence of God. And once we begin to hunger for Him _____ else will do.

2. Jesus is continually watching us, waiting for us to leave behind our _____ _____ and take _____ _____ _____ into the plans He has for us.

3. Receiving a revelation of God's love is _____

4. Once you allow Christ's love to touch you, you are _____ _____ _____

5. His goal, at this point, is to _____ and _____ our love.

6. Each of us must eventually answer the question: "Am I in this for _____ or for _____?"

7. The significance of this season has powerful ramifications; and its sole purpose is to _____ your _____ and _____ your level of _____ for the Bridegroom.

A bride typically spends days, months, even years preparing for the big day, spending countless hours and dollars on what she believes will be the most memorable day of her life. She will select the place; she'll make all decisions concerning food, drinks, flowers, cake, décor and theme, music, colors, attire, and photographer. In some cases, as it was with my wedding, the groom will make the arrangements for the car. "It's a guy thing." I am certain there are exceptions, but, nevertheless, the burden rests primarily on the bride.

Now for the gown. This is a big deal and normally the bride will make her best effort to select the perfect gown. For hours, and store after store, she will try on so many dresses that by the end of the day they will have all blended together. But finally she will make her choice and the alterations will begin, transforming the dress into the gown of her dreams, reshaping it until it fits perfectly. And as the special day arrives, the bride will attend all necessary salon appointments to make her look complete. Her hair will be like silk—not at all the way it normally looks. Her nails will be manicured, her body perfumed and her makeup meticulously applied. Usually, a woman never looks more radiant than on her wedding day.

The wedding ceremony and celebration itself typically can last, depending on her background, anywhere from several hours to several days. Guests arrive from near and far. Some the bride has never seen or heard of before, but she smiles with grace and elegance, greeting all of those who have come to share her special day. In her heart she is overjoyed to be united with her husband, yet her eyes are ever watching and her heart anxious, waiting for the flaw, for that one mishap or imperfection that everyone will surely notice. The pressure, if she allows it, can be overwhelming.

Isn't it wonderful though to realize that the pressure has been taken off of us as the Bride of Christ? Our Groom and His Father are making all of the arrangements for the grand affair, and all we need to focus on is getting dressed. Yet, even though all the formalities will be handled, it will still take some effort on our part to get ready and a willingness to be helped into the dress. We have to show up for the fittings, stand still for the alterations, and bear the report that the dress is still too tight, and we have to lose a few pounds of excess baggage. Yes, it is work, and not always easy, but Bride, we are not being prepared for a wedding but for our Groom. Therefore, let us focus of the joy ahead, that grand and glorious day when our Groom will return for us, and we, as His bride, will be pure, perfect, spotless, and beautifully dressed.

Week Seven

Prepared as a Bride

- Day One: *God Desires to Bless His Bride*

- Day Two: *God Desires a Purified Bride*

- Day Three: *God Desires to Purify Your Love*

- Day Four: *God Desires to Cleanse You*

- Day Five: *God Desires to Anoint and Clothe You*

- Reflection and Response: *God Desires You*

In this seventh week we are going to:

Embrace the blessings of God
"See, I am setting before you today a blessing…" (Deuteronomy 11:26).

Understand that suffering means partnership
"For them I sanctify myself, that they too may be truly sanctified"
(John 17:19).

Ask God to purify our love
"The crucible for silver and the furnace for gold, but the LORD tests the heart"
(Proverbs 17:3).

Ask for the power to grasp the fullness of Christ
"And I pray that you…may have power…to grasp…the love of Christ…
that you may be filled to the measure of all the fullness of God"
(Ephesians 3:17-19).

Look forward to our completion
"For the wedding of the Lamb has come, and his bride has made herself ready"
(Revelation 19:7).

Day One

God Desires to Bless His Bride

"…prepared as a bride beautifully dressed for her husband"
(Revelation 21:2).

Begin today's lesson by praying for the blessing of the Lord in your life.

As grand and glorious as the affair will be, and with all my heart I look forward to that celebrated day when I will see my True Love face-to-face, but there is more, much more. As the bride, we, the church, are being prepared for eternity with our Groom. Think about it—a match made in heaven and a marriage that will last for all eternity. Does this not remind you of the fairytale ending "and they lived happily ever after?" Only this time it will be true. But in the meantime there is much to be done and we had best get to work if we are to be prepared as a bride.

I have been anticipating this week but not looking forward to it. It is fun to record the favor and what we fondly think are the blessings of God, capturing these delights and precious moments on paper, breathing them in and feeling like a princess. But there is another side of the equation: seasons of struggle and testing that we all, as the bride, must go through in order to be made ready for our Groom. Personally, I would like to pass by this week and stick with the romance of the sacred courtship, but in order to be a fully rounded and mature bride, we, too, like Jesus, must be perfected in our suffering.

This portion is entitled, "God Desires to Bless His Bride." This is true, but do you realize what the word *bless* really means? Some might say that it means an outpouring of God's love or gifts that He is willing to bestow upon His own. Well, essentially this is true. A blessing is an outpouring of God's love and gifts, but it is given in a way we might not always appreciate. To better understand, let's look up the word *bless* or *blessing*.

The word *bless* means "to consecrate; glorify; sanctify; set apart; praise; to give thanks to; to approve."[22] Therefore, to be blessed or to be a blessing is to be consecrated; set apart and made holy; to be sanctified; made sacred; and purified. Ouch! Not quite what we had in mind is it? But when we are set apart for the work of the Lord, and we follow through in obedience, we are a blessing to others and God is greatly glorified. God blesses us so that we can be a blessing to others. Now, also keep in mind that the word *bless* means "to praise and give thanks to; to glorify; and approve." Bride, we are to thank God for His blessings and praise Him for His acts of helping us to prepare for the day when we will be with Him. And as He continues to bless us He will be greatly glorified in our lives, smiling on us with His grace; and

164   Week Seven: Prepared as a Bride

we, in turn, will be a blessing to Him, a blessing for which He will give thanks and praise. Amen!

Quite likely for most of us, what we thought was God's blessing was actually His favor smiling upon us. The word *favor* means "a gracious act; kind regard; goodwill; partiality; a token of generosity or esteem."[23] For fun, let's take a look at some synonyms for the words in the definition of *favor*. Other words for *goodwill*, for example, are "kindness; friendliness; concern; care; and helpfulness." For *partiality* they are "bias and favoritism." For *generosity* synonyms are "bigheartedness; openhandedness; liberality; and bounty." And for *esteem*, they are "respect; admiration; value; prize; high regard; good opinion; and appreciate." I love digging into words, it opens up many new doors of understanding.

Now, since we are having fun with our word definitions, let's put them all together. To receive the blessing of the Lord is to be set apart and made holy for Him; to be made sacred; to become a purified bride of whom He greatly approves and enjoys; one whom He can shower His favor upon and lavish with His kindness, care and concern; in bigheartedness He can rain on her His bounty with openhandedness, value her; prize her with high regard; and hold her in good opinion and admiration. Wow!

Probably like me, you originally thought that receiving blessing from the Lord was an enjoyable thing, but when I saw the words "consecrate" and "sanctify" in the definition, initially I felt dread. However, as I come to know the true heart of God, what is at stake, and the ultimate goal, I have also come to realize that going through the process of being sanctified, consecrated and purified for the Lord truly is a blessing. Perhaps not always the blessing we would like because it can mean suffering, tests and trials, but a blessing to Him; not because He enjoys watching us suffer, but because we are being prepared for Him, which in the end will also be the ultimate blessing for us.

I know that this week may not be easy for you who may have endured so much already, and this is not easy for me to say, but don't pray your way out of trials and times of testing. Daily, God is working out your purification and maturity, making you complete, so that you will lack nothing and will be perfected to the glory and honor of God (see 1 Peter 1:6-7). You are being prepared as a bride; adorned, dressed and made beautiful for Christ. I know it can hurt when you are at the hairdresser and getting those tangles combed out of your hair, but the combing is necessary if you don't want a bad hair day when you stand by your Groom's side. Okay, so the wedding dress embroidered in gold is a little snug right now. By the time the trumpet blows, announcing the grand affair, it will fit perfectly. Rise to the challenge. Embrace and endure whatever season God has you in and always remember that you are His beloved. You are on a journey of becoming who you were created to be.

When we are set apart for the work of the Lord, and we follow through in obedience, we are a blessing to others and God is greatly glorified.

Day One: God Desires to Bless His Bride

According to Colossians 3:1-17 verses 5-9 what are we to take off and put to death? Check all that apply:

____ **Everything belonging to your earthly nature**

____ **All sin and unrighteousness**

____ **Whatever does not fit our lifestyle**

Pray for the Lord to help you to submit to the preparation process, and then please turn with me to Colossians 3:1-17. As you read, inhale the life of His words. According to verse 2 what are we to do?

_____

I love verse 4; it is like air to me. Ponder this verse. What is Christ meant to be to you?

_____

The word *become* means "to pass from one state to another; to be suitable; appropriate; fit."[24] Beloved, we are being transformed from one state of being, "old self," to a new state of being, "new self." It is by His grace and mercy that He lovingly prepares us; shaping us into the persons He created us to be. We are made in His image and we were predestined to be a pure, strong, virgin; spotless, bride beautifully dressed for her husband (see Revelation 21:2).

How does 2 Corinthians 3:18 confirm this transformation of becoming in Christ?

_____

_____

According to verses 10-14, what are we to dress in? Check all that apply:

____ **Love**
____ **Forgiveness**
____ **Pride**
____ **Compassion**
____ **Humility**
____ **Gentleness**
____ **Slander**
____ **Patience**
____ **Anger**
____ **Kindness**
____ **Greed**
____ **Impurity**

When I first began to understand this transformation process, something delicate and very special came to my mind. This is a process of beauty given to us by the Lord's grace. The purification and preparation process of becoming should be a joy, not a hardship, as it says in James 1:2: "Consider it pure joy…whenever you face trials of many kinds…." Bride, our self-image is very important. And as we go through these seasons, we must develop a stronger understanding of who we are and a vivid awareness of Who we belong to, because this perspective will help us to not only endure, but to overcome.

How do you see the blessing of the Lord in your life?

_____

_____

How is He revealing His favor to you?

_____

_____

Day Two

God Desires a Purified Bride

"I promised you to one husband, to Christ, so that I might present you as a pure virgin to him" (2 Corinthians 11:2).

Yesterday we began to grasp the reality of God's blessing; that He desires to sanctify, consecrate and set us apart. Today we are going to continue to look at our time of preparation through suffering, understanding more profoundly that this process of sanctification and preparation is a joint effort.

Let's begin by asking Jesus to become strong in us and help us to endure. Then ponder Hebrews 2:17-18 and 4:14-16. What do these verses tell us about our compassionate High Priest?

_____

_____

This process of *becoming* is not an easy one, but we must remember that we are not alone in our journey of becoming the purified bride. Jesus is able to identify with our limitations and struggles in preparing for Him because He already endured for His bride.

How does John 17:19 tell us that the sanctification process is a partnership, a joint effort?

_____

_____

Compare John 17:19 with Isaiah 61:10. In what way do these verses parallel in the preparation process? How do you see the bride and the bridegroom getting ready for each other in Isaiah 61:10? In the margin, remind yourself of what Hebrew 4:14-15 called our Groom.

_____

_____

In Isaiah 61:10, what has the Lord clothed his bride in? What do you think is the spiritual significance to these garments?

_____

_____

In our process of being made ready for Jesus, we will never suffer as greatly as He did when He was being sanctified for us.

Do you see the beauty of getting ready, being prepared as a bride with garments of salvation, robes of righteousness, and adorned with jewels? The finished work as recorded in Isaiah 61:10 will be a glorious sight to behold, indeed, but John 17:19, which also speaks of being prepared and made ready through sanctification, also tells us that it will not be easy. And we see in both of these verses a joint effort was made to prepare for the other. Jesus was already perfect but He was perfected in His suffering (see Hebrews 2:10; 5:8-9) which He endured for us, His bride, per the will of His Father. We then, in turn, are to be like Him, sanctified and set apart, being made perfect through suffering for Him.

The word *suffer* means "to endure; to undergo; to allow."[25] Synonyms are "to experience; to go through; and to bear." *For the Love of the Bride*, Jesus "endured" the heartache and loss of His beloved. For her He had "undergone" flogging and beatings. He "allowed" mock trials and Roman soldiers to mock Him and spit on Him. And *For the Love of the Bride* He "experienced" the shame of a criminal's death, "bearing" His cross on the hill of Calvary and in agony "went through" the pain of being nailed to that cross.

In our process of being made ready for Jesus, we will never suffer as greatly as He did when He was being sanctified for us. And we must remember that He promised to walk our personal road of suffering with us. We are not on this journey alone, He is with us, and Jesus is no stranger to suffering.

Fill in the blanks according to Isaiah 53:3a, NIV.

"He was despised and rejected by men, a man of _____, and familiar with _____."

I know that suffering is not easy; I know because I've been there, more times than I would like to count. If you will permit me, though, I would like to share with you a valuable lesson I learned during one of those periods of immense anguish. In this time of preparation, something happened that brought my heart into an even deeper understanding and love for Jesus. In the midst of the greatest pain I have experienced to date, I began to grab hold of a small glimpse of the possible suffering Christ went through in the Garden of Gethsemane.

The agony I felt was unthinkable as tremendous grief gripped my soul. Not even the depression I experienced or the loss of my baby due to miscarriage compared to the agony that stirred in my heart that first night. I could not go to bed. I was up until 4:00 a.m., crying out to God in pain and prayer. I was tired; weary in my own sorrow, and I struggled with whether or not I could even do this. Yet, to my amazement I found myself praying, "Lord, Your will be done." Please understand, this, in no way, was a trial and a test that I wanted to go through, but if it was what God the Father wanted to use to prepare me for His Son, then, "Lord, Your will be done."

I can't fully explain it but something happened during that season within the chambers of my heart. I was more concerned about what was best for Christ than I was for myself. A revelation came to my heart that I had not known before. Something was different. I had passed through a fire—a consuming fire that purged my heart; moving it into a whole new understanding of what it meant to love in another's best interest. I am beside myself with awe of what God produced during that time of suffering. And as I ponder these things, I lay hold of the fact that my trust level for the Lord's hand in my life took a huge leap.

During that time, I believe three things were indispensable in this process of sanctification. First, I clung to Him, desperately, passionately crying out to Him. I kept the lines of communication open. I did not shut Him out. Secondly, I relied on the Word of God instead of my emotions. Beloved, the more we trust Him and claim the promises of His Word, the less we will suffer emotionally. And thirdly, I kept saying, "Lord, Your will be done." Even though it was painful, and I greatly struggled at times with what was happening, I had His best interest at heart above my own. I was more concerned about being made perfect for Christ than I was about my own personal pain. And from this, God produced something beautiful that I would have never known absent this season of suffering.

How does Romans 8:17-18 bring comfort to you during your time of preparation for your Groom?

_____

_____

The goal is to become the purified bride for the Lord Jesus Christ (see 2 Corinthians 11:2). Daily we are being perfected as His partner; a partner who will run with Him in intimacy and servanthood. But in order for the purification to take place we must pass through the all-consuming fire of God's love. We must endure the heat of His fiery furnace, being brought forth as pure gold; a blemish-free, virgin bride for God the Son.

How does the desire of Paul's heart, in Philippians 3:10-14, to know Christ and be made ready for Him, inspire you to want to press on toward perfection?

_____

_____

Something was different. I had passed through a fire —a consuming fire that purged my heart; moving it into a whole new understanding of what it meant to love in another's best interest.

That night, when all this began, when I experienced the agony of my own personal little garden, I shared in the fellowship of His suffering. Suddenly, I understood Him better. I drew closer to His heart. Jesus and I now, through this experience, shared a common bond. No one understands pain better than Jesus, and He desires a bride who can relate to Him; one who can identify with Him in both joy and suffering.

We are the bride "of" Christ; His inheritance; His eternal reward; and we are being prepared for Him. The suffering that we endure on behalf of our Bridegroom is not for nothing, because it is in these times that we receive the revelation of who we are in Christ. It is through this revelation that we begin to understand the blessings that are placed on our lives. We are the bride *of* Christ; His treasure; His possession; His co-partner; and His lover. We are blessed, called, chosen, selected, set apart, consecrated, sanctified, and made holy for Him and Him alone.

When my personal journey with Jesus began, I did not understand the price I would have to pay in drinking from His cup. It can be painful and not at all easy. Yet, the love He has shown is incomparable to anything that I have ever known, and I cannot forsake Him. Oh, how I hope you agree with me. If you do, please pray with me: "Purify our hearts, oh, God, and make us ready because we desire to be that perfected bride for Your precious Son. Oh, Father, we do not want to know a halfhearted lukewarm love. We choose to be on fire. Father, throw us into the fire; prepare us because we desire to be the bride of Christ."

If you are struggling with the purification process, it's okay. Share your heart with your Bridegroom. Don't be afraid to ask Him for help.

_____

_____

_____

_____

Share the desire of your heart to be made ready for Jesus as His inheritance.

_____

_____

_____

_____

Day Three

God Desires to Purify Your Love

"There is no fear in love. But perfect love drives out fear, because fear has to do with punishment. The one who fears is not made perfect in love" (1 John 4:18).

Before you begin, pray for an extra measure of God's mercy and love to be made known to you through today's lesson.

In this process of *becoming*, being sanctified and made ready for our Groom, we cannot allow ourselves to be ruled by fear. Fear is a terrible feeling; and we must comprehend the barrier that fear can cause. It's a driving energy that can paralyze us; it can stop us cold in our tracks if we let it. It consumes us with a mighty force, gripping us so tightly that we can feel crushed under the weight of it. When we misunderstand what God is doing in our lives, fear can overtake us. If we are not nestled in the peace and comfort of His love, grounded in who we are in Christ, the fear of the fiery furnace can send us running. God desires to purify our love, and He does it through fire.

What does Proverbs 17:3 compare the concept of purification to?

_____

What does this tell you about the purification process?

_____

Pure love is revealed when we no longer fear God's fire. A deep grace and tender mercy touches our lives when we are placed in the Refiner's fire. We may not see it as we struggle through the suffering, but in Christ's infinite love He is taking us through a progression where we will be able to trust Him completely, no matter the cost. He is igniting a flame of love within our hearts that will burn brighter than the sun. This process may take months or even years, but, what a precious moment it is when we can face the fire and embrace it instead of running in the opposite direction. What freedom we will experience when we can come to a place where we can say, "Fire of purification, burn within me; consume my life, until the only thing that is left is love."

You are being perfected in love when Jesus has become your Magnificent Obsession for His sake; when your soul's greatest purpose is to love Him for His benefit and not your own. Maturing love is when everything in your life has been surrendered to the passions of Christ, and you find yourself awestruck in a love so pure that you completely abandon yourself to His love and the pleasure of doing His will.

Read Song of Songs 4:16, what do you think is the spiritual significance of the north and south winds?

_____

_____

Why do you think the beloved is calling for these winds to blow on her garden (to come into her life)?

_____

_____

What does the beloved invite her lover to do? What do you think is the divine significance of this invitation?

_____

_____

Pure love is revealed when we no longer fear God's fire.

Although the words sound quite sensual and lovely in this portion of Scripture, the beloved is embracing something here that is not obvious. As her love matures and blossoms in her lover's hands, she opens her life, her garden to him. She now understands that her garden (life) belongs to him, and she invites into the garden the blistering suffering of the north winds. She is actually inviting the fire, desiring for it to come into the garden and purify her of everything that does not beautify the garden. Yet, at the same time, she is requesting that the gentle south winds also blow past the garden gate, bringing with it the refreshing breeze that will help her sustain the trial. This is serious praying! The maiden in this allegory is demonstrating for us the spiritual significance of asking God to come into our lives and burn up the debris that is cluttering our garden so that its fresh fragrance of life will come forth for Him and, hence, for the world to smell and enjoy (see 2 Corinthians 2:14-15).

As promised in Week Six, Day one, let's revisit Song of Songs 5. This time we will look a little more deeply into this particular test of the beloved. In verse 4:16, the beloved just prayed and asked for the north and south winds to come and blow into the garden.

In Song of Songs 5:2-6, how do you see her prayer being answered?

_____

_____

Some scholars say that this portion of Scripture can be seen as Jesus coming up from the Garden of Gethsemane with dew drenched hair, coming to His beloved and inviting her to share in His suffering. In obedience we see in verse 5:5 that the beloved arose much faster from her bed than she did back in verse 3:1. But when she opened the door—he was gone. This is the ultimate test. Hebrews 13:5b tells us that Jesus never leaves us nor forsakes us, but there are times of testing, even when we are obedient, where the Lord strengthens our love for Him by removing from us the awareness of His presence.

It is by the power of the Holy Spirit that you can invite the north winds, and it is by the grace of His refreshing south winds that you will survive them. Our natural response is to try to find a way out of trials and suffering, not wanting the pain of the hardship; so, why does the beloved pray in obedience this way? Simple. She is hooked.

How does Song of Songs 5:7-16 convey this type of passion for her lover who has captured her heart? Check all that apply:

    ____ She was willing to suffer just to be near him.

    ____ She was willing to share her love for him no matter the cost.

    ____ She was willing to hold onto the hope of his love in the midst of suffering.

At this point in their relationship, the beloved has come into a place where the love she feels for her lover goes far beyond any price she will have to pay. Her love for him far outweighs any suffering that she may endure. His desire has now become her greatest desire, because nothing will bring her more pleasure than to embrace what touches his heart. The beloved is not being naïve. She has come to realize that there is nothing better in life than his love, and she would rather be standing in the fiery furnace with Him, than be in a place of comfort without Him.

Consider the heart cry of the psalmist in Psalm 63:2-3? What has he seen?

_____

What did he say was better than life?

_____

How does the psalmist's attitude compare to that of the beloved in the Song of Songs?

_____

Both have seen and tasted the beauty and love of the one their heart loves. They have beheld splendor. They know firsthand. They have witnessed, they have basked, and now they both sing out from the overflow of their hearts, "Your love is better than life!"

In what ways have you seen and tasted the beauty and love of the One your heart loves? How has His love become better than life?

_____

_____

Be like the beloved in the Song of Songs. Pray: "Whatever it takes! North winds blow! Purify my life! I am Yours. Place me in the fire of Your love and consume me until my heart, soul, mind and spirit melt into one with Yours. Amen!"

I understand that prayers for purification can be scary, but remember that perfect love drives out all fear. If you are led by the Spirit, step out in faith right now…use the space below and pray for the north winds to blow in your life, but also pray for the Holy Spirit to bring His refreshing south winds to comfort you as He purifies your love for Him. This is not easy, I know, but it will be worth it!

_____

_____

_____

_____

_____

_____

_____

_____

_____

_____

Day Four
God Desires to Cleanse You

"I will sprinkle clean water on you, and you will be clean; I will cleanse you from all your impurities and from all your idols. And I will put my Spirit in you and move you to follow my decrees and be careful to keep my laws" (Ezekiel 36:25, 27).

Let's continue with our preparation for our Bridegroom by first asking Christ to help us keep our eyes on Him so that through this process we may, by His grace, remain faithful. Then dive into today's Scripture reading, Ezekiel 16:4-14.

Make it personal: Let's picture that the "you" mentioned in this portion of Scripture is literally you. With this in mind, answer the following questions.

Describe how you were found on the day you were born in verse 4, and how others had treated you, verse 5.

_____

_____

Who found you? What is the spiritual significance in being found?

_____

Describe all the ways in which you were prepared, (bathed, anointed, clothed and adorned) in verses 9-13. What do you see as the spiritual significance in this elaborate preparation from birth to completion?

_____

_____

Compare Psalm 45:13-14 with Ezekiel 16:9-13. What connection is evident between these two portions of Scripture?

_____

_____

Hold onto what we have discovered in these Scriptures. It may not seem obvious at first where we are going with all of this, but as we journey together over the next two days, we will piece this cleansing/preparation process together like a glorious puzzle.

To begin our transformation process, I would like to suggest that this allegory found in Ezekiel 16:4-14 can be seen as a parallel to the journey of the bride of Christ, taken from her uncleanness to where she is redeemed, bathed, anointed, clothed and adorned just for Him. With this in mind, let's look at each of these preparation steps in an attempt to better understand our own cleansing/preparation process in being made ready for our Bridegroom.

Salvation—the first step in *becoming* the prepared bride of Christ. At the time of our salvation our crimson sins are made as white as snow, they are removed from us as far as the east is from the west (see Psalm 103:12). But although our sins are atoned for, there are still impurities, like wrong attitudes and bad habits that block or hinder the flow of the Holy Spirit in our lives. Therefore, it is imperative that we be cleaned out and washed daily.

Depending on our life's happenings, each of us is carrying within our souls roots of infectious weeds that need to be pulled up completely. If not, the weeds keep coming back. Jesus said, "Every plant that my heavenly Father has not planted will be pulled up by the roots" (Matthew 15:13). It's the same concept as putting the silver or gold into the fire causing the impurities to rise to the surface so that the imperfections can be removed.

For me, immediately after salvation I went through a season of joy and liberation from my sins, and I enjoyed this season tremendously and was even used by God. But then I entered a season, my first of many, where the Lord began to clean me out; a time where I was scrubbed, rubbed and scoured. There were moments when I felt like the Lord was using an SOS pad and a lot of elbow grease.

During those early years, God put His finger on so many issues that needed His touch that I thought I would not make it through the process. It was not fun, and there were many times when I wanted to give up. Then one day, after many seasons of cleansing, I realized what He was doing. He was cleaning out my vessel, making room for Himself. Every chance He got, He would lovingly clean house preparing me to receive His Holiness; arranging it just the way He wanted; making more and more room so He could fill me to capacity.

The house of the Lord is no longer the tent of meeting (see Exodus 33:7-11), or a man-built tabernacle (see 1 Kings 6). It is not a church or synagogue. God's dwelling place is in the hearts of His people, and God has chosen you and me to dwell in forever.

How does 1 Corinthians 3:16-17 confirm this?

So, how does Christ get us to make the sacrifice, to surrender, to take up our cross daily and follow Him? The answer: with love; tremendous amounts of love.

And God desires to bless His dwelling place, *cleaning* it out and *consecrating* it in order to fill the house with His glory.

Fill in the blanks according to 2 Chronicles 7:16, NIV:

"I have _____ and _____ this _____ that my name may be there forever. My eyes and my heart will always be there."

The word *cleanse* or *clean* means "to make free from dirt, stain, or any defilement; pure; guiltless."[26] The word *consecrate* means "to set apart for sacred use; to dedicate; to make holy."[27] Christ desires to clean us out, to sanctify our vessel, to make us holy so that we may be dedicated to His purposes and for the desires of His heart. He desires for us to be His pure bride, cleansed and ready to contain the fullness of His Holiness.

Share one specific way, during your journey with Jesus, in which the Lord has cleansed and prepared you for Himself.

_____

Do we truly understand this? Can we truly begin to fathom the significance of what the Lord has done for us? Can we see that He desires to clean us out and prepare us to house the fullness of His Holy Spirit? Bride of Christ, do we realize that our Bridegroom desires to dwell inside each of us to the point that we are walking in the fullness of the Godhead.

Try to grasp this if you haven't already. He redeems us for Himself. He cleans and empties us out of self, desiring to bring each of us into a place of spiritual maturity to where we are *dead to self* and fully alive in Christ (see Galatians 2:20).

I realize that for most of us, *death* is not a pleasant word. It implies an end or loss. And when Jesus tells us in Luke 9:23 to take up our cross daily and follow Him, He is implying a one-way ticket; placing us on a road of no return. Yet, He desires for us to make the decision to take this road with Him and not to look back; but, understand that death by way of the cross brings life. We must see the joy of the end result and get a glimpse of the eternal glory found in Christ. Understand that nothing compares to knowing Him and the hope of eternal glory with Him (see Romans 8:18). The *death of self* is utterly important and must be done daily, because then and only then, with complete sacrificial surrender, total submission, and with absolute abandonment of self, will we "be filled to the measure of all the fullness of God" (Ephesians 3:19).

According to Ezekiel 36:25-27, in what ways has the Lord promised to clean and prepare us for Himself? Check all that apply:

___ **Give us a new heart and spirit**

___ **Help us to follow his decrees and laws**

___ **Save us from all uncleanness**

___ **Wash away all of our impurities**

Gage your response: How do you feel about embracing the possibility of you becoming one with God and walking in the fullness of the Godhead?

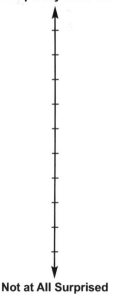

Completely Shocked

Not at All Surprised

So, how does Christ get us to make the sacrifice, to surrender, to take up our cross daily and follow Him? The answer: with love; tremendous amounts of love. Turn with me to Ephesians 3:14-21 and listen to Paul's words and passionate heart cry as he intercedes for the Ephesians that they may grasp this extraordinary concept.

What is the one thing that Paul prayed will be a powerful revelation to them? (v. 18)

_____

Why was this revelation vital? (v. 19)

_____

_____

On his knees before God the Father, Paul prayed that the Ephesians would be strengthened in their inner being to be able to grasp and hold on to the revelation that they are loved beyond any reasonable amount of thinking. That they, only by the power of the Holy Spirit, can grasp the fact that they are loved beyond anything they could imagine; and through this incredible love there comes an awakening, a virtual arousal of the heart that will completely captivate them, compelling them to the depths of total surrender (see 2 Corinthians 5:14).

This unfathomable love is powerful, and only by the revelation of the Holy Spirit can we begin to grasp it. And once we do, once we allow the revelation of Christ's love to penetrate our hearts, we will be overcome to absolute abandonment of self. Oh, Beloved, to know this love that surpasses knowledge is to be captivated by it, held prisoner and taken so completely by it, that you may receive the fullness of God, unhindered, filled to capacity, and overflowing without measure (v. 3:19-20).

End today by sharing the desires of your heart with Jesus. Pray for Him, through His Holy Spirit, to grant you the power to grasp how wide and long and high and deep is His love for you. Pray that you may know, first hand, this love that surpasses knowledge, that you may be filled without measure of all the fullness of God.

_____

_____

_____

_____

_____

Day Five

God Desires to Anoint and Clothe You

*"I delight greatly in the LORD; my soul rejoices in my God.
For he has clothed me with garments of salvation and arrayed me
in a robe of righteousness, as a bridegroom adorns his head like
a priest, and as a bride adorns herself with her jewels"* (Isaiah 61:10).

Yesterday we looked at the cleaning out process by understanding that it first begins with salvation. After we are atoned for, the cleaning process continued with a thorough cleaning of the vessel, which God now dwells in. We looked at the importance of complete death to self and learned that the cross is embraced only one way—in Christ's love. Then, finally, we prayed to receive the power to grasp this all-surpassing love that we may be filled without measure of all the fullness of God.

If you are still not convinced of this awesome revelation, of becoming the fullness of the Godhead, pray for the Spirit of revelation, and then look again at the Word of God. Compare Mark 10:7-9 and Ephesians 5:31-32. What is the common denominator between these verses? What parallel is God drawing for us?

_____

_____

Scripture tells us that we are to be one with Christ, just as a husband and wife become one through the bonds of holy matrimony. God desires to be joined with you, to become one with you, forever.

Even on the night He was betrayed, Jesus prayed, "Make us one!" In John 17:20-21, Jesus asked His Father for oneness with His bride. Just as the Father is in Him and Jesus is in the Father, she, too, will be one with Him, so that through her He will reveal His glory to the world. Like Jesus, she, too, is to be the fullness of the Godhead.

At this point you may be thinking that I am placing the bride in a position of being equal to Jesus. This could not be farther from the truth. Jesus was The Word who became flesh and made his dwelling among us (see John 1:14). Jesus was fully God, as well as fully man. And we are fully wo(man), but we are in no way God; however, we do house the fullness of God when we, like Jesus, make the choice to surrender to the complete will of the Father. Christ is the fullness of God, and we are to be in the fullness of Christ.

What was the prayer Jesus prayed according to John 17:20-21?

What specifically did He ask the Father for? Check all that apply:

___ **Unity in the church**

___ **That the church would be one with the Godhead**

___ **For the world to see Jesus in us**

How does Colossians 2:9-11 confirm this concept of fullness with the Godhead?

_____

_____

I love the way the *Amplified Bible* says it: "For in Him the whole fullness of Deity (the Godhead) continues to dwell in bodily form [giving complete expression of the divine nature]. And you are in Him, made full *and* having come to fullness of life [in Christ you too are filled with the Godhead—Father, Son and Holy Spirit—and reach full spiritual stature]" (Colossians 2:9-10, AMP).

The word *full* means "to be filled to capacity; crowded; abundant."[28] Another word for *fullness* is "completeness." The Lord Jesus Christ made His bride a special promise in John 14:16-18 when He said that He would send the Spirit of Truth to dwell in her. And it is His unyielding desire to fill each of us to absolute capacity, making Himself one with us; the fullness of the Godhead in you and me, forever.

Oh how I pray that we would all seize the magnitude of this revelation. All of us need to "reach unity in the faith and in the knowledge of the Son of God and become mature, attaining to the whole measure of the fullness of Christ" (Ephesians 4:13). We must allow Christ the opportunities to cleanse us from all impurities that clog the flow of His Holy Spirit, and to bring each of us into a place of spiritual maturity to where we are dead to self and fully alive in Christ.

Stop! Take a minute to express your gratitude to Christ that He desires to be one with you, filling you to complete fullness, and without measure with Himself.

Now, if we are ready to move forward, let's continue with the next aspect of the cleansing/preparation process.

Glance back to yesterday's lesson and refresh your memory by rereading Ezekiel 16:4-14 and the answers you recorded. After being found and restored to life (v. 6)—representing salvation (atonement). Then being bathed and washed—representing being cleaned out; what is the next step in the preparation process? (v. 9)

___ Clothed in fine linen

___ Adorned with jewels

___ Anointed with ointments

According to Esther 2:12, what were the beauty treatments prescribed for the women prior to going into the king?

_____

_____

_____

Whether we realize it or not, just like the maidens in Esther, we, too, are going through a prescribed series of beauty treatments prior to coming face-to-face with our King. As part of our cleansing process it is essential that we bathe in the Holy Spirit and be anointed with the sacred oils (see Leviticus 8:12 and I Samuel 16:13) from the bride's garden (see Song of Songs 4:13-14).

This part of *becoming* the prepared bride of Christ is vital; unfortunately, it is also one of the most neglected parts of the process. Christ wants us to take the time to regularly come into the beauty of His presence and spend time soaking in His Spirit. He wants us to take our time and indulge, because the more time we spend bathing and soaking in the Holy Spirit, allowing Him to anoint us with the sacred oils, the more our hearts will be transformed and made new.

Let's take a stroll through the bride's garden. Read Song of Songs 4:13-14, list the different plants, spices and fragrances of this beautiful garden.

Let me urge you to never miss one of these prescribed treatments. Never re-schedule or cancel your appointment because life simply got too busy. Through intimate fellowship in private prayer, allow Christ to lavish His care on you. Soak in the richness of His Spirit. Take your time as the sweet spices of myrrh, calamus and cinnamon are massaged into your spirit and soul. Be still, breathe in His sacred oils and afford Him the opportunity to anoint and prepare you.

_____

_____

_____

_____

_____

_____

I like to come first thing in the morning for this special time. Before I do anything else, I come into the sweetness of His presence, allowing Him to bathe me with His love and mercy. Ah, and right then, heaven opens before my very soul, arousing my spirit and leading me to a special place in the garden, a place where I am surrendered before Him and His hand is upon me.

_____

_____

_____

The bride's garden, a fragrant blend of aromas to prepare the bride and stir the heart of the Bridegroom. Henna, with its small white blossoms, so fragrant and delicate. The rich purple-colored plant of Saffron is so vibrant, it is used for coloring and dyeing. Cinnamon, a sweet brown aromatic spice, as precious as gold. Calamus/cane, a strong, spicy, aromatic scent has the taste of ginger. Myrrh, a spice used as medicine, a cosmetic or perfume. And nard, spikenard, is a rose-red fragrant ointment, inviting intimacy.[29]

Now cross reference the bride's garden with Exodus 30:22-25 and circle the spices from the garden that are used in making the sacred anointing oil.

Now, let's look once again at our guide for the cleansing/preparation process found in Ezekiel 16:4-14. After being found and restored to life (v. 6)—representing salvation. Then being bathed and washed—representing being cleaned out; filled, and anointed with oils and sacred ointments (v.9). What is the final step of the preparation? (v. 10-13). Check all that apply:

___ Clothed in fine linen

___ Arrayed in an embroidered dress

___ Adorned with jewels

___ Bestowed with a crown

Finally, we have reached the point in our cleansing/preparation where the bride is ready for the wedding gown. Traditionally, on that special day when the bride takes the hand of her groom, she is beautifully dressed in a gown of white, symbolizing her purity and long-awaited anticipation of being united with her husband. And we, who are the bride of Christ, also wait with great anticipation for the return of our Groom; eagerly awaiting the announcement that will ring out in the heavenly realm: "Let us rejoice and be glad and give him glory! For the wedding of the Lamb has come, and his bride has made herself ready. Fine linen, bright and clean, was given her to wear" (Revelation 19:7-8).

Fill in blanks according to Ezekiel 16:10 and Psalm 45:13-15, NIV:

"I _____ you with an _____ _____ and put leather sandals on you. I _____ you in _____ _____ and covered you with costly garments" (Ezekiel 16:10). "All glorious is the princess within her chamber; her _____ is interwoven with gold. In _____ _____ she is led to the king…" (Psalm 45:13-15).

And, oh, how our Groom also waits with great anticipation for that long-awaited day when He will finally be physically face-to-face with His beloved bride. I believe every day He leans over and quietly whispers to the Father, "Is today the day, Father?" And one day it will happen. That celebrated time will come when the Father will smile warmly at His Son and say, "Yes, My Son, today is the day. Go get Your bride!" Can you picture it? And we, His bride, will be prepared and ready for Him: atoned, washed and scrubbed, perfumed and anointed with oils, transformed in His Spirit, and filled with all the fullness of His love and person; clothed with a garment of salvation and a robe of righteousness (Isaiah 61:10), an embroidered garment of fine linen. And this wedding gown will be beyond all wedding gowns; a gown lovingly prepared just for us—and, like us, it will be perfect.

Christ wants us to take the time to regularly come into the beauty of His presence and spend time soaking in His Spirit.

Share with the Bridegroom your personal anticipation of the day you will be with Him in glory. Also, ask the Father to help you to remain steadfast during this, your time, of cleaning and preparation for His Son.

_____

_____

_____

_____

God Desires You

Embrace the fire of My love, My bride. Don't be afraid of the word *fire*; rather, concentrate on the word *love* in the same sentence. The word *fire* tells you how hot My love is for you, My bride. My love burns within My heart like a blazing torch. When you stand near a fire, you feel its heat rising, and the heat from My love is consuming, burning within Me with a great passion, and I am consumed by love for you. Oh, My darling, do not be afraid of the fire. If you only knew how much I love you, you wouldn't be afraid. You are safe, My love, in the center of the fire; it's the center of My will, because there you are in the center of My love. And when you pass through the fire, the love within your heart for Me will grow, intensify with passion and desire, because the fire burns up everything but love. Allow the fire of My love to consume you, My bride. I desire to move you forward, to draw you closer. There is much I long to share with you. Step into the fire of My love and allow it to overcome everything in your life but love.

Reflection and Response

In what way(s) are you in the process of becoming like Jesus right now? Share how you are in fellowship with Christ through suffering?

_____

_____

_____

_____

When your personal journey with Jesus began, did you understand the price you would have to pay in drinking from His cup? Explain.

_____

_____

_____

_____

Does the fire of His love frighten you? Are you resisting any part of the cleansing/preparation process? If so, which part scares you the most and why?

_____

_____

_____

_____

_____

In what way(s) have you seen God at work purifying your love for Him? How has this purification process increased your love for Jesus? How has His incomparable love helped you to prepare and endure during this time of preparation?

_____

_____

_____

_____

_____

Thank the Father for His efforts in preparing you for His Son, so that upon His return you will be prepared and beautifully dressed for Christ.

_____

_____

_____

_____

_____

Week Seven

Lesson Seven

The Ultimate Test of Love

Song of Songs 5:1-8

1. The season the beloved is about to enter is the _____ _____. And this test comes with at least one of two parts:

   a.) the loss of His _____

   b.) the loss of _____

This season often begins with north wind, south wind prayers:

2. Giving God permission to come and test you is profoundly _____, unless you have an equally profound revelation of His _____

3. God removes the awareness of His presence because He wants to determine our _____ and our _____

4. Christ wants a bride who has been purified of all motives and ambitions but one—_____ _____ _____ _____ _____

5. It's a lifelong journey that will, if you let it, completely _____ _____ _____ and _____ _____ to be the purified bride of Christ.

6. There comes a point where the focus shifts and He becomes outstanding among ten thousand, simply because of _____ _____ _____, not because of what _____ _____ _____ you.

7. The Lord Jesus desires to draw you into a passionate love that is _____ than anything else on this earth.

   "Fire of purification burn with me, consume me, until the only thing that is left is love."

*W*eary and blood-stained from the wounds of agony, the maiden comes into the presence of the king. With tears in her eyes, she hides her face from him thinking, *How could he receive me now?* The clothes on her back are torn, rags hanging limp on her frail body, so battered and worn from the suffering. She feels weak, completely at the end of herself, totally unable to go on. Her hair is tangled and dirty. The sweat mixes with her tears to streak her soiled face. *What must he think of me?* The thought plays in her mind. *How could he love me now? There is nothing left of me. I cannot even look at him. He is so beautiful and I am so....ugly.* The sobs rack her withered body; yet, her broken heart is full of love for him.

"Look at me." The king's words pierce her heart.

Somehow she finds the courage to turn her unsightly face so he can look at her; her heart beats fast as she braces herself for his harsh and rejecting words. Gently, he takes her hand and stares into her fearful eyes. *"How beautiful you are my darling,"* the king states. *"Oh, how beautiful. Turn your eyes from me. They overwhelm me"* (see Song of Songs 6:5). Lovingly, the king touches the face of the maiden. Affirmation of his loving affection touches her lips. Suddenly, the tattered rags which hung limp on her body turn into a glorious dress made of fine white linen embroidered in gold, which now graces her form. Clean and radiant, she stands before him a breathtaking beauty, elegant and fair.

Week Eight

Beauty is in the Eyes of the Beholder

- **Day One:** *God Desires to Reveal Beauty (part one)*

- **Day Two:** *God Desires to Reveal Beauty (part two)*

- **Day Three:** *God Desires to Paint Your Wedding Portrait*

- **Day Four:** *God Desires a Warrior Bride*

- **Day Five:** *God Desires to Prepare You*

- **Reflection and Response:** *God Desires You*

In this eighth week we are going to:

See beauty through Christ's eyes
"How beautiful you are, my darling! Oh, how beautiful!"
(Song of Songs 4:1).

Witness true beauty
*"Carrying his own cross, he went out to the place of the Skull
(which in Aramaic is called Golgotha)"* (John 19:17).

Reveal the beauty secret
"Then you will look and be radiant, your heart will throb and swell with joy"
(Isaiah 60:5).

Take a stand
"They are brought to their knees and fall, but we rise up and stand firm"
(Psalm 20:8).

Stand on the promises
"The LORD is faithful to all his promises and loving toward all he has made"
(Psalm 145:13b).

Day One

God Desires to Reveal Beauty

Part One

"You have made my heart beat faster, my sister, my bride; you have made my heart beat faster with a single glance of your eyes, with a single strand of your necklace" (Song of Songs 4:9, AS).

Imagine with me the beauty of the bride of Christ (see Song of Songs 4:1). She is His treasure (see Deuteronomy 7:6), and He values her more than anything He possesses (see Isaiah 43:3-4). His love for her is so overwhelming that He cannot stop thinking of her (see Psalm 139:17). He is so taken with her affections (see Song of Songs 4:10); and so enthralled by her beauty (see Psalm 45:11) He is taken captive from just one glance from her in His direction, so taken that it sets His heart pounding with great anticipation (see Song of Songs 4:9), arousing His delight (see Psalm 16:3), and increasing His desire for her (see Song of Songs 7:10).

I love Jesus so much that it is overwhelming. Yet, even with all of the love that I carry in my heart for Him, His love for me is greater, so much greater that I can only begin to feel the magnitude of it. And as I ponder our opening verse from Songs of Songs 4:9, how His heart beats faster and faster with just a single glance, I think of how great His anticipation must be. I know that I love Him; dwell on Him and long to be with Him, yet, even with the depth of my longing, anticipation, and desire, His is multiplied to the maximum degree. And when I come before Him, quiet and still, it is if I can hear His sweet song of love singing over me, "You have ravished my heart, my treasure, my bride; I am overcome by one glance of your eyes" (Song of Songs 4:9, NLT).

When Christ looks into the eyes of His precious one, He is hooked. He is taken by her; smitten to the point that His heart beats with delight and He is ravished with just a single glance from her; so overcome and captivated that He melts. So, what is it that makes Christ respond this way? As we know, God's love is unconditional; the bride does not have to earn His love. No matter what, His love remains steadfast, the same yesterday, today and forever (Hebrews 13:8). But something special is taking place within her heart. He has willingly given her His love, but now the bride is responding, she is willing; willing to open her heart before Him in true repentance; willing to worship Him the way He longs for, and she is willing to embrace His cross.

Let's begin by asking the Spirit of Revelation to help us understand what ravishes the heart of our Groom, and then read Luke 7:36-50:

While Jesus was reclining at the table, who came and stood behind Him?

_____

According to verses 37-38, what did she do? Be specific.

_____

_____

How did Jesus respond to the actions of her heart?

_____

_____

If I could have one opportunity to go back in time and be any woman mentioned in Scripture, I would choose this one. Why? Because I can relate to her. Like her, I, too, am a sinful woman who found acceptance and forgiveness at the feet of my Savior. What a privilege she was given to represent the heart of true repentance, bestowing upon the Bridegroom love in an act of penitence. In spite of everything, any humiliation she might experience, any ridicule she might endure, this precious woman makes the willing choice to return and cry out in repentance, to be forgiven. She comes to Jesus, expresses her love, and finds forgiveness for her many sins.

In this account from Luke, we see godly sorrow and grief of sin expressed from a woman who has wandered from true love. She is returning to Jesus and asking for forgiveness as she breaks open the jar of her heart and pours its contents on His feet. And in that moment He finds her irresistible.

True Repentance—the first step toward infinite beauty.

◦❧

What was the second "willingness" I mentioned at the start of our lesson that the Lord finds irresistible?

_____

Continuing with our original text in Luke Chapter 7, what did the sinful woman bring with her? (v. 37)

_____

Do you think that perhaps, like Mary of Bethany, her alabaster jar was also filled with spikenard; the fragrance of the bride?

Please read John 12:1-8 and compare it with Luke 7:36-50: List all the connections in these scenes that you see between these two women.

Mary of Bethany	Sinful Woman
_____	_____
_____	_____
_____	_____
_____	_____
_____	_____
_____	_____
_____	_____

As we compare these two women, we can automatically see a few differences, but look deeper within their hearts and see what they have in common. Both women broke open the jar of their hearts, allowing Jesus entrance into the innermost parts, offering Him their worship. Both women are in an intimate exchange with the Bridegroom. They both are expressing intimacy; abandoning themselves in worship, affection and love; desiring relationship; and they are both humble, showing devotion and serving.

The only difference is the motive for their approach to Jesus. The sinful woman has come to repent, desiring for her heart to be mended, healed, and forgiven. She is receiving from Jesus as she pours out her regret and love because she is in need. Mary, on the other hand, is offering up to Jesus love from the overflow of her heart.

True worship—the second step toward infinite beauty.

Compare something else in Luke 7:39 and John 12:4-5. When these beautiful women came forward to express their worship to Jesus, what was the response from those who witnessed their expression? Who objected, what did they say?

Sinful Woman

_____

Mary of Bethany

_____

Understand, when you break open your heart and begin pouring out your extravagant worship upon Jesus, there will be people observing you who will not understand, and will, at times, object; even dearly loved brothers and sisters in Christ. Why? Perhaps, like the Pharisee, they are caught up in the legalism and rituals and do not see the love that is expressed from a repentant heart. Or maybe, they are more like Judas, someone who is walking with Jesus but has not experienced, for himself, the richness of Christ. Dear One, allow me the privilege of inviting you to dare to be different. Do not be afraid of what others might think of you or say about you. Keep your focus on Jesus, and He will guard you.

How did Jesus respond to the complaints and opinions of those who did not understand the beauty of His beloved?

_____

_____

When you humbly come to the feet of Jesus, loving Him the way He longs to be loved, you are never rejected, no matter the condition of your heart. When you come before Him honestly, expressing what is truly in your heart, you are never turned away or criticized. Whether you are hurting or rejoicing, you must come and bow at the feet of the Bridegroom, because He will always look upon you with love. In His eyes you are beautiful, no matter if you have been crying for days or celebrating His goodness.

Take a minute right now and share with Jesus. If you need forgiveness and acceptance, pour out your heart; weep at His feet with tears of repentance. If you are overflowing in your heart, break it open and pour your favor and fragrant affection upon Him.

_____

_____

_____

_____

_____

_____

_____

_____

_____

_____

Day Two

God Desires to Reveal Beauty

Part Two

"You are beautiful, my darling, as Tirzah, lovely as Jerusalem, majestic as troops with banners. Turn your eyes from me; they overwhelm me" (Song of Songs 6:4-5a).

Yesterday we began looking at the beauty of the bride through the eyes of Christ. The beauty He sees in her humble repentance. How stunning she is to Him when she comes to bow at His feet in abandoned worship and love, breaking open the alabaster jar of her heart and pouring her affections upon Him. Yet, even with all this devotion, she is never more beautiful to Him than when she expresses her willing desire to embrace His cross.

Please invite the Spirit of Revelation to show you the beauty found in our Savior's crucifixion, then read John 19:1-3; 16-18; 28-37.

When you look at what Jesus did for you, what do you see? When you ponder the brutality of all Jesus went through for you and His suffering upon the cross, what do you see?

_____

_____

_____

_____

I'll never forget the night when the images of the Lord's bloody and beaten face weighted on my heart. As I thought about His sacrifice and all that He had done for me, to my amazement, all I could think of was how beautiful He was.

How beautiful His heart was toward me as He surrendered on my behalf. How beautiful His love was as He walked the road of suffering for me; a suffering beyond anything I could hope to endure for Him. Through the Holy Spirit, I began to see the beauty of the suffering my Savior went through because of His love for me, for all of us. Words cannot begin to explain the cultivated fire that grew within my heart at that moment. When I recognized the beauty of the willing sacrifice He endured just because He loved me, something happened within my heart. My love for Him grew, intensified. Suddenly a great love flooded my heart; I was so overcome that my heart could not contain it.

Then, in that same moment, I began to realize that the beauty I saw during His time of suffering is the same beauty He sees in His bride when she willingly suffers purification, persecution, or offers up her life to Him as a willing sacrifice out of the love in her heart. Suddenly, I began to understand how His heart bursts with love, how overtaken and besieged His heart is over His beloved.

Do you realize how beautiful you are when you suffer for Christ? Do you truly grasp how radiant you are when you endure for Jesus in the process of becoming His purified bride? When you suffer persecution, hardship, trials and tests, all for Him, He finds you breathtaking. And when you, as His beloved, lay down your life for Him, or even give Him your willing desire to embrace the cross for Him, offering your life as a pleasing sacrifice, His heart is ravished. Can you fathom His heart and the look in His eyes as He exclaims, "How beautiful you are, my darling! Oh, how beautiful! You have stolen my heart, my sister, my bride; you have stolen my heart with one glance of your eyes…. Turn your eyes from me; they overwhelm me" (Song of Songs 4:1, 9 and 6:5).

Please turn again to Song of Songs 4:6-10. We looked at this portion of Scripture in Week Five, Day One, but this is such an important concept that we are going to look at it again with a little more depth of insight.

According to verse 4:6, where is the Lover going?

_____

When you leave behind your old ways, and embrace His life by way of the cross, you will come forth with a beauty that is beyond measure—a true beauty that raptures the heart of Christ.

The Mountain of Myrrh is symbolic of death. This represents the sacrifice that the Bridegroom made for His bride at Calvary. Then in verse 4:8 He invites her to go with Him to the higher places, representing the invitation for the bride to die to self by embracing His cross.

Putting to death the sinful nature and throwing off "everything" that hinders is not easy nor is it something we can do for ourselves. This is why we must allow God to crucify these things in us.

What is the Lord putting to death in you during this season of your journey with Him? You may be asked to share in your small group. Please do not feel condemned or that you are alone. We all, no matter how long we have been walking with Jesus, have things in us that need His hand.

According to Hebrews 12:1, what are we to throw off, or put to death? Check all that apply:

____ Old clothes that no longer fit

____ Every pattern of life that hinders us

____ All sin

____ All bad attitudes, habits and harmful desires

Beloved, it is not the bloody brutality and the agony of pain that is beautiful. The beauty lies in the sacrifice; the complete giving of oneself for the benefit of the one that is loved. Just as it says in John 15:13: "Greater love has no one than this, that He lay down His life for His friends."

Take heart, Dear One, and re-read (aloud) Song of Songs 4:9-10. How do you see the heart of Christ responding to His beloved who is willing to go with Him to the Mountain of Myrrh?

_____

_____

_____

_____

_____

_____

_____

_____

_____

_____

_____

_____

I know anguish and suffering are not easy, but please know that Jesus sees your weaknesses, and He knows your fears. He knows all your shortcomings and not one of these things hinders His love for you. Oh, Treasured One, hold fast to the fact that Christ finds you irresistible. The fervency in your heart for Him and sincere willingness to walk with Him every day in surrendered obedience and sacrificial love sends His heart soaring, and He is completely taken captive by your beauty.

When you lay all other things that hinder aside and lay down your life just for Him, in that moment He exclaims, "You are beautiful, my darling, as Tirzah, lovely as Jerusalem, majestic as troops with banners. Turn your eyes from me; they overwhelm me" (Song of Songs 6:4-5a). Like a troop returning in victory from battle with their banners waving, you, too, are beautiful because you are victorious! You have overcome the calling of the world. You have left all other things behind and surrendered your life so that He may live through you.

Fill in the blanks according to Galatians 2:20, NIV.

"I have been _____ with Christ and I no longer _____, but Christ _____ in me. The _____ I live in the body, I live by faith in the _____ _____ _____, who _____ me and gave _____ for me."

Only through being crucified with Christ can you truly live. When you leave behind your old ways, and embrace His life by way of the cross, you will come forth with a beauty that is beyond measure—a true beauty that raptures the heart of Christ.

True Sacrifice—the third step toward infinite beauty.

Beloved, willingly choose to rapture the heart of the Bridegroom. Set out to capture His heart to the point that He becomes overwhelmed by just a single glance of your eyes. And, as you endure just for Him, remember that your royal Husband delights in your beauty; therefore, honor Him, for He is your Lord" (see Psalm 45:11).

Share with Jesus the beauty you see in His sacrifice for you; then share with Him your desire to rapture His heart by being crucified with Him.

_____

_____

_____

_____

_____

Day Three

God Desires to Paint Your Wedding Portrait

"You're beautiful with God's beauty, Beautiful inside and out!"
(Luke 1:28, Msg).

Bride of Christ, to the Bridegroom you are a most beautiful creature as you steadily make yourself ready for Him. As you yield day after day to the purifying love of the Father as He prepares you for His beloved Son. Daily He paints your portrait; skillfully working; creating you into the masterpiece that He knows you will be. You are a work of art in the Master's hands, and when your portrait is complete, it will be beyond imagination. Allow Him to create in you. His desire is to make you as beautiful on the inside as the beauty your countenance will display on the outside in eternity.

Right now you may not think you are beautiful. You may hate your body and a number of other features, but Jesus does not see you the way you see you. When I come in the morning for my quiet time with the Lord, I am looking nothing short of atrocious. But there I am, coming before His throne of grace in my pajamas, no make-up and serious bed-head. I do at least brush my teeth, which I am certain He appreciates. But even with my disheveled appearance, He tenderly meets with me, touches me, and loves me affectionately, and I cannot tell you how beautifully radiant this makes me feel.

Allow me to let you in on a secret: The more time you spend dwelling in His temple gazing upon His beauty, the more beautiful you will become, and the more your life will radiate His. And when you radiate Christ's beauty, you display the splendor of the Lord (see Isaiah 60:5).

Begin by asking Christ to reveal His true beauty in you; then look up the following verses. What does each verse say about Christ's beauty and how His beauty is reflected in you?

Psalm 27:4:

_____

Isaiah 33:17:

_____

Isaiah 60:5:

_____

As you gaze upon Him, you will become the light of His glory, an oak of righteousness, a planting of the Lord for the display of His splendor (see Isaiah 61:3; 2 Corinthians 3:18). Synonyms for the word *display* are "to present; to show; to exhibit." For the word *splendor* they are "magnificence; grandeur and majesty." When you display Christ's magnificence, grandeur and majesty, you are glorifying Him. You are bringing Him honor and renown; revealing to the world His life and love; displaying His splendor in a transformed life; a visible living portrait of beauty.

The ultimate goal is to become the likeness of Christ in every way, and Christ is perfect in beauty (see Psalm 50:2). The All-Powerful Creator of heaven and earth has selected you as His beloved. He desires that your life offer evidence that He has been talking with you, spending time with you, and that you have been spending time with Him.

In Exodus 34:29-35 we see the radiance of the Lord as it reflected off the face of a man who knew how to spend time gazing upon His beauty.

According to Exodus 34:29, when Moses descended from Mount Sinai, what was his appearance like?

_____

In verse 34 and 35, when Moses entered the Lord's presence again what was his appearance when he came out?

_____

Intimacy with Christ is evident upon the one who enters in. When Moses spent time in the Lord's glorious presence, gazing upon His beauty, a change took place in his own appearance. And when you, like Moses, climb God's holy hill to spend time in His presence, to look to Him and seek His face daily (see 1 Chronicles 16:11), lingering in the beauty of His splendor and majesty (see Psalm 96:6), you, too, will come down off the mountain with a face of radiance.

How does Psalm 34:5 confirm this truth?

_____

Exodus 34:29 tells us that Moses was unaware that his face was radiant. According to Exodus 34:30, who was acutely aware of the radiance?

_____

Just like Moses, you yourself may not see the light that shines from your face but others will. And there is no makeup or beauty cream in the world that can duplicate it.

How protective God is that He would allow others the privilege of seeing His glory shine upon our faces, but not allow us to witness the miracle of the holy makeover. He guards our hearts from arrogance so that our beauty will not make us prideful. He ensures this by the simple method of shining His light. Light is revealing. The closer you get to the light of His presence, the more awesome and beautiful He becomes; the more vivid He becomes. But, at the same time, you are able to see yourself more clearly, and in the light of His radiance you begin to realize just how unpleasant and corrupt you would be without Him.

Dwelling in God's presence is beyond words of expression. It is so wonderful, in fact, that you may desire to stay there and never come down from your mountaintop experience. But Moses had to come down off the mountain in order for others to witness the glory of God; only then was the change evident to the world. Moses shared with the people, both the words of the covenant written on the stone tablets and his experiences, only after he came down off the mountain. Only then could the people see the transformation.

Look again at Exodus 34:30. What initial reaction did the Israelites have when they saw Moses as he came down off the mountain?

_____

After Moses had finished speaking to the people, giving them the commands the Lord had given him, what did Moses do in verse 33?

_____

It saddens me greatly to think that Moses felt for their sake that he had to hide his radiance behind a veil. Oh, Beloved, go ahead and "let your light shine before men, that they may see your good deeds and praise your Father in heaven" (Matthew 5:16). I know it is not always easy because there will be people, even dearly loved brothers and sisters in Christ, who may react disapprovingly at the changes they see in you. Forgive them and pray for them. People, who have not witnessed for themselves true intimacy with Christ, will not understand, and they may even take offence at you because the light of radiance is convicting. But take heart, because there will be others who will be drawn and attracted to the light they see in you. They are seeing the changes in you that they desire, the relationship they hunger for and these, Beloved, are the true seekers of intimacy.

You yourself may not see the light that shines from your face but others will. And there is no makeup or beauty cream in the world that can duplicate it.

Therefore, go to Him, gaze upon His beauty, and let the light imparted into you shine brightly. Do not allow the rejections of others to keep you from entering into all that Christ has in mind for you. Allow His beauty to rip through the old rags that have kept your light hidden for years. Let His Spirit ignite the fire that has been extinguished because of heartbreak and rejection. I am living proof that nothing is lost if you allow it to be redeemed by His saving grace. Every humiliation, failure, mistake, hardship, and sorrow in my life has been redeemed by God, changed into joys, victories and successes by His infinite beauty.

Beloved, seize the fact that nothing is lost if you allow it to be redeemed by grace. Until you believe that, you will not be completely set free from what is holding you back. Ecclesiastes 3:11 says, "He has made everything beautiful in its time." Praise God for His faithfulness to complete the work He has begun in you (see Philippians 1:6), and hold tight to the knowledge that He is painting your portrait, transforming you into the radiate beauty He knows you will be.

What are you still holding on to that you have not allowed the Lord to redeem by His saving grace? Give it to Jesus, and ask Him to change it into something beautiful.

_____

_____

_____

_____

_____

Pray and ask Jesus to give you the eyes of His heart, so you may see yourself as He sees you.

_____

_____

_____

_____

_____

_____

_____

_____

Day Four
God Desires a Warrior Bride

"It is God who arms me with strength and makes my way perfect. He makes my feet like the feet of a deer; he enables me to stand on the heights. He trains my hands for battle; my arms can bend a bow of bronze. You give me your shield of victory; you stoop down to make me great" (2 Samuel 22:33-36).

The spiritual realm is in continual motion all around us, and we, as the bride of Christ, cannot be found relaxing on the side lines or pretending that spiritual warfare does not exist. Ignoring it, or hoping it will pass us by, will not keep us from coming up against the enemy of our souls. We cannot afford to be caught sleeping on the job. We cannot, under any circumstance, sleepwalk through our journey with Jesus, blinded to the enemy's schemes and unaware of his tactics. Where Satan is concerned, there are no safe zones, so our only option is to engage in the battle.

One day we will be clothed in fine linen bright and clean, but right now our attire needs to be the spiritual armor of God. God desires for us to be dressed everyday in battle gear, equipped and prepared as a soldier, ready to stand our ground.

This is an important topic. Therefore, our focus for the next two days will be on Ephesians 6:10-20. Please pray for the mind and heart of Christ and read this portion of Scripture.

Every day you are under attack by the enemy of your soul. Your flesh, your mind, your will and emotions are all areas of attack, and one of his tricks is to get you to think that you can fight him on your own.

Ephesians 6:10-20, however, does not tell us to fight. Along with putting on the full armor of God, what are we told to do? (vv. 11; 13-14). Check one.

___ Run and hide   ___ Fight with courage   ___ Stand firm

According to 2 Chronicles 20:14-17, what was King Jehoshaphat and the people of Jerusalem and Judah told to do through the power of the Holy Spirit when faced with the threat of war? Record the specific instruction in verse 17:

_____

_____

The trouble is, when faced with an attack or circumstances, we do not do this. We are a self-reliant society, and when we fail in our own strength and lose control, the enemy then tries to convince us that we are not good Christians.

Look again at Ephesians 6:10, what is the first thing this verse tells us?

_____

The Amplified Bible says, "…be strong in the Lord (be empowered through your union with Him); draw your strength from Him (that strength which His boundless might provides)."

If you are not completely dependent upon the strength and aid of the Lord in the battle, united with Him, you are operating in the flesh and the enemy will devour you. Do not give the adversary a foothold in your life, because footholds will become strongholds if they are not demolished by spiritual weapons. And, be advised, those areas of stronghold are the areas of weakness that Satan will attack the most. Please understand, everyone who is a believer in Christ is a threat to the enemy. He will attack; no one is exempt, and he often attacks hardest at those who do not believe they are susceptible, so be ready.

Now also understand that just because we are not told to fight the enemy, this does not mean that we do nothing. It is vital that you pray every morning, before you begin your day, to be equipped with the armor of God so that you may "stand firm with the belt of truth buckled around your waist" (v. 14), undergirded with God's holy truth, guarding the seat of your emotions. The more you trust in the truth of God, the less you will suffer emotionally. The more you cling to the truth of the Spirit, the less likely you will be to take the bait of the enemy's lies. Then ask for the Lord to protect the work He has begun in you with "the breastplate of righteousness" (v. 14). Put it in place over your heart, so that you may be sheltered by His uprightness and shielded from sinful desires.

Have your "feet fitted with the readiness that comes from the gospel of peace" (v. 15), that you may be ready to reveal the hope to which you have been called; "continue in your faith, established and firm, not moved from the hope held out in the gospel. This is the gospel that you heard and that has been proclaimed to every creature under heaven" (Colossians 1:23). And each day pray for the "helmet of salvation" (v. 17) to be put in place, thanking God daily for your precious redemption in Him.

You are the beloved of Christ and a child of the Most High God. Never for a moment forget who you are in the eyes of your Creator. The helmet of salvation protects your mind from the lies of the enemy who tries to convince his victim that he or she is worthless; useless in the sight of God. He even goes so far as to try to convince God's own children that they are not really saved. If you have received Christ as your personal Savior, praying that gracious merciful prayer of salvation with sincere conviction, making Jesus Lord of your life, I assure you, you are saved. Claim it daily; speak the truth out loud and remind the enemy to whom you belong.

And while you are at it, ask for the mind of Christ to reign within you so that you may dwell on the things of God and not on the things of man (see Isaiah 55:9). "For though we live in the world, we do not wage war as the world does. The weapons we fight with are not the weapons of the world. On the contrary, they have divine power to demolish strongholds. We demolish arguments and every pretension that sets itself up against the knowledge of God, and we take captive every thought to make it obedient to Christ" (2 Corinthians 10:3-5). By surrendering your mind to the Lord Jesus Christ, He gives you the power to demolish strongholds and break through the chains that hold you captive. Also ask for the heart of Christ to have supremacy within you, so that you may grow in the passions of Christ, making room for His love to increase in you, both for Him and for others.

And "In addition to all this, take up the shield of faith, with which you can extinguish all the flaming arrows of the evil one" (v. 16), and will enable you to advance in the battle and leave you standing tall behind the victory that is yours in Christ Jesus. Then, at the same time, lift high and hold fast to "the sword of the Spirit, which is the Word of God" (v. 17). May the praise of God be in your mouth and a double-edged sword in your hand (see Psalm 149:6), that you may be strengthened according to His word (see Psalm 119:28).

The Word of God is your best offensive spiritual weapon. The enemy cannot stand against the power of the Holy Spirit, which is in you, and against the Word of God. Therefore, surrender every day; be totally dependent on Christ, stand firm behind the shield of faith, and assert the authority of God's Word over your flesh. Daily, take in your hands the sword of the Spirit, the very source of truth, and verbally and expressively acknowledge that truth above the enemy's lies.

What did Jesus tell His disciples in John 8:31-32? Why was holding to what He taught them so important?

_____

_____

_____

The more you trust in the truth of God, the less you will suffer emotionally. The more you cling to the truth of the Spirit, the less likely you will be to take the bait of the enemy's lies.

Hold firmly to what Jesus instills in you and allow the truth of His Word to set you free from the lies, temptations, and strongholds that hold you bound to a life of slavery. Stand firm upon the promises of Christ, and His truth will blanket you in such a way that you will break free from the torments and traps the enemy sets for you.

First Thessalonians 5:8 tells us to be self-controlled and put on what?

_____

_____

Every day, and without fail put on the full armor of God. Daily ask God to search your heart and cleanse you as He covers you with His breastplate. Do not let loose of, or even undo, a notch on that belt of truth. Never for one second slip out of those gospel shoes of readiness to put on a pair of relaxing slippers. Keep the helmet of salvation squarely placed upon your head as you continually praise God for His precious gift of eternal life given to you through His glorious Son. And, always remember, even in battle gear, you are the most beautiful of creatures.

Is there an area of your life where you are being oppressed by the enemy? If so, hand it over to the Lord, and share with Him the desire of your heart for victory in this area.

_____

_____

_____

_____

_____

_____

_____

_____

_____

_____

_____

What does Psalm 119:89 tell us about God's Word?

___ **It is powerful**

___ **It stands firm**

___ **It is ceaseless**

You are the beloved of Christ and a child of the Most High God. Never for a moment forget who you are in the eyes of your Creator.

Day Five
God Desires to Prepare You

"For in the day of trouble he will keep me safe in his dwelling; he will hide me in the shelter of his tabernacle and set me high upon a rock"
(Psalm 27:5).

I cannot stress to you enough how important the topic of spiritual warfare is, but right now you may be asking, "What does spiritual warfare have to do with the beauty of the bride?" Incredible as it may sound, Christ prepares you for spiritual warfare in very much the same way He prepares you for intimacy, service, and ministry; by affirming you and pouring out His affection upon you; telling you all of the wonderful things He sees in you; lavishly sharing His tender heart toward you and calling forth the qualities He sees in you, even though they are just beginning to take shape in your life. So, again we find ourselves in the secret place gazing upon the beauty of the Lord. Why? Because this place is not only a place of relational closeness and a place of restoration and healing, it is also a place of becoming strong in the Lord.

To show you what I am talking about, turn with me to Psalm 27. Pray for His power to be made manifest in you, and read verses 1-6.

Who is the writer of these verses up against? (vv. 2-3)

_____

Why do you think the psalmist is so confident? What did he say would happen to those who came against him?

_____

_____

What was the psalmist's one request of the Lord? (v. 4) Why did he make this request?

_____

_____

What was the benefit he saw in being near the Lord? (vv. 5-6)

_____

_____

We must draw our strength from the Lord and the Lord alone. Even though great opposition is threatening our lives, we must be convinced that we are secure in our Lover's embrace, being strong in the Lord (empowered through our union with Him); drawing our strength from Him (see Ephesians 6:10, AMP), daily dwelling in His glorious temple and gazing upon His beauty.

Remember, your best offensive weapon is the Word of God, but your best defense against the schemes of the enemy is found in Psalm 27:4; when you come daily into the manifest presence of the Lord, to worship Him and gaze upon His beauty.

Look again at verse 4 and fill in the spaces.

"One thing I ask of the LORD, this is what I seek; that _____ may _____ in the _____ of the LORD _____ the _____ of my _____, to _____ upon the _____ of the LORD and to _____ him in his temple" (Psalm 27:4, NIV).

David knew and understood the importance of dwelling (living, abiding, basking, lingering, staying put), in the house of the Lord. David desired to live every day of his life in the manifest presence of God.

In God's manifest presence He will prepare, fill, transform, renew, equip, protect, train, guide, and heal you; He'll shower you with His extravagant love and renovate your appearance. And the more you rest in the Holy of Holies and learn to see yourself through the eyes of Christ, the more whole you will become. You will feel so beautiful and so loved that you will begin to believe, and that belief is what will make you become powerful enough to stand in the battle. Satan cannot stand against one who knows who she is in her Lover's eyes. And when she is utterly connected to Him in intimacy, resting in His promises, and sheltered in the shadow of His powerful love and holiness, the enemy cannot destroy her. She will be able to take up her position against his attacks and resist his temptations.

I hope by now you see the beauty and understand the importance of intimacy with Christ. The secret place behind the veil is critical to your spiritual growth and your becoming in Christ all you were meant to be. It is imperative, for your own sanity, that you become spiritually equipped through intimacy with Christ to stand against the lies and schemes of the enemy. I cannot express this enough; the defense and fortification you need are consummated in the intimacy of prayer. Therefore, "pray in the Spirit on all occasions" (Ephesians 6:18 NIV), shielded and protected by his mighty armor; standing firm and secure in the power and knowledge of His incredible love.

Learn to see yourself through the eyes of Christ. You will feel so beautiful and so loved that you will begin to believe, and that belief is what will make you become powerful enough to stand in the battle.

Week Eight: Beauty is in the Eyes of the Beholder

Now, does this mean that you will never fall prey to the enemy's temptations or be captured in the clutches of a stonghold again? No! Even a strong, devoted lover of the Lord Jesus Christ can still be had by the enemy. So, be on guard at all times. The enemy is dangerous. Therefore, as you faithfully stand in the battle, allow the Lord to give you some assurances; promises from His Word to cling to in times of overwhelming attack and temptation.

Please read each Scripture portion and answer the question(s).

1 Corinthians 10:13

What is the promise?

_____

_____

Claim this guarantee with all your heart. God will not allow (permit) you to be tempted beyond what you can bear. Plus, every time you are tempted by the enemy, God is faithful to provide a way out. You are not at the mercy of the enemy but the mercy of the Most High God. Even though Satan would love every opportunity to devour you, Christ, who knows you intimately, will never allow you to be attacked or tempted beyond what He has equipped you for. Hallelujah!

Revelation 19:11-16: (As you read these verses try to get a strong mental picture.) What is the promise? (Also see Exodus 15:3.)

_____

What is the Warrior's name according to verse 13? What does His name mean?

(v. 11)

_____

Describe His appearance.

_____

Who is riding with the Warrior on the white horse? (v. 14)

_____

Christ is an Almighty Warrior who is prepared at all times; and He is ready and waiting to come to the aid of His beautiful bride. He has given you the promise that when you call on His name, the very Word of God (v. 13), the mountains will crumble. He is Faithful and True; and He will always be there for you, but also remember that this Mighty Warrior, this Rider on the white horse, greatly desires for you to become His partner. Christ is putting together a spiritual army of prayer warriors, and He greatly yearns for each of us to stand in the battle with Him as His warrior bride; a fellow soldier of the cross (see Philemon 1:2), riding by His side in behalf of truth and righteousness.

Now do not worry, thinking, *I can't do this. I'm not a warrior. I don't even like conflict.* In His great and infinite mercy you can count on this assurance:

2 Timothy 3:16-17:

What is the promise?

_____

_____

God promises that through His "Self-breathed" Word, He will equip you. He will carefully make you ready for the work set before you and for the daily battles you will face. I call this preparation "mercy" because if He didn't take this time to prepare you, you would be crushed under the weight of the task and/or ministry; and if He did not take the time to train you for the battle, you would not stand for a minute.

And, when the battle does get too rough, always remember the assurance of these promises.

James 4:7-8a:

What is the promise?

_____

_____

Psalm 91

What is the promise?

_____

_____

Draw near to God at all times, because the enemy does not stand a chance in the presence of the Almighty. Turn away from all evil and turn toward the Lord. Submit to His authority over your circumstances, temptations, and fears and watch the enemy flee from you. Come daily and camp out in the shelter of His wings and draw near to His side. Do not resist the protection of the Lord's mighty wings. Draw near to Him, and you will not fear the terror of the night, nor the arrow that flies by day (v. 5). Focus completely on Christ. Worship Him, and the enemy will run.

Warrior Bride, the stakes are high and the closer you get to God in an intimate relationship the more of an effect you will have for His Kingdom.

Week Eight: Beauty is in the Eyes of the Beholder

Warrior Bride, the stakes are high and the closer you get to God in an intimate relationship the more of an effect you will have for His Kingdom. And the more effective you become, the greater threat you will become to the enemy. Satan will not take this lying down, and his desire will be to convince you that your testimony is worthless and to render you useless for the Kingdom of God. Do not receive this lie. If the Lord has delivered you from the slimy pit, you have a testimony and God desires to use it and you for His glory. Christ will be victorious in your life, over all things, if you let Him.

Know this with all your heart: the victory is yours in Him who loves you. Through Christ, God has already won the victory over the forces of evil that try to plague you; therefore, stand tall, Warrior Bride, in confidence and grace, because the Rider on the white horse is right by your side. And one day you will stand before Him; perhaps tattered and torn from the years of battle; your face streaked with tears, and blood staining your clothing. Your hair may be disheveled and the dirt from the battlefield may be embedded in your skin. But on that day, when you stand before your King, He will look into your eyes and proclaim, "Oh, how beautiful you are, my darling. How beautiful you are." He will take you in His arms and kiss you gently, and in that moment your war-torn appearance will become radiantly white.

God Desires You

Come into the presence of the Lord and listen to His ravished heart: "How beautiful you are, My love. How beautiful you are. You are more beautiful than anything I have created. You are more lovely than anything I possess. You are more radiant then the sunrise, and more elegant then the rose. You may not see your beauty, but I do; and I tell you that you are the most beautiful of all creatures. Come to Me in repentance and offer Me your worship. Come into the light of My glory and I will give you My splendor and My affectionate love. Come to Me, gaze upon My beauty, and I will reveal to you the radiant beauty that I know you to be."

Reflection and Response

How does the heart of Christ speak to you about your infinite beauty?

_____

_____

Are you convinced that you are very beautiful to the Bridegroom? Why or why not?

_____

_____

_____

Share with Christ your willing response to offer Him true repentance, the worship He longs for, and your willing desire to embrace His cross.

_____

_____

_____

If you could go back in time and be a person of the Bible, who would you choose and why?

_____

_____

_____

Which piece of armor do you find the most challenging to keep on or use? Why?

_____

_____

_____

Share about a time when you stood firm in the battle. How did you experience the deliverance of the Lord?

_____

_____

_____

Week Eight

Lesson Eight

Perfect in Beauty

Song of Songs 5:9-16 and 6:4-5

1. Christ _____ for you to be so taken with Him, so _____ on His Person and splendor that you cannot, and will not, live without Him.

2. The banners represent _____ and great _____ (Song of Songs 6:4)

3. You are made beautiful as you suffer for Christ. You are radiant when you endure for Jesus in the _____ _____ _____ His purified bride

4. This great warrior can be taken captive by one thing—the beloved who _____ Him against all odds.

5. The _____ is to become the _____ bride of the Lord Jesus Christ (2 Corin. 11:2).

6. Daily we are being _____ as His partner; a partner who will run with Him in intimacy and servanthood.

7. We are the inheritance of Christ. His eternal _____; His _____; His possession; His co-partner; and we are being _____ for Him.

He, a gallant champion among champions; a true noble, and the rightful king of all the land. Everyone in the kingdom knew that the king deserved to marry a princess; one suitable and equal to him; one who had the refinement and poise to be his queen; yet, in all the land, none could be found. However, there was one who had claimed his heart; a simple maiden, a servant among those who knew her. She was not worthy of him, but his heart was dominant over his decisions, and no one dared to tell him that he could not have her as his own. Nothing would stop Him; so, risking his life for her, he came against all the forces keeping them apart. His heart would find no rest until he had reclaimed his one true love. Rising victorious from the battle, the only thing left was to win her heart.

Desiring for his chosen one to enter his presence, a place of beauty and grace, he calls out to her, beckoning her to come. And in this place of elegance, the king romances her heart, enthralling her, and soon he captures her love and devotion. Then with humility and gentleness, he asks for her hand in marriage. Accepting his offer of love, she comes to the altar, the meeting place he ordained for them to join, and as she stands by the side of her king, he takes her hand in promise as they exchange vows, entering into a covenant union of love and commitment.

After the ceremony, the king escorts his bride behind the veil, desiring to consummate their marriage. And in this secret place, hidden from the world, he communes with her; sharing with her his tender affection, showering her with his love and filling her with his seed.

Week Nine

The Highest Level of Love

- Day One: *God Desires to Exchange Vows*

- Day Two: *God Desires to Exchange Wedding Rings*

- Day Three: *God Desires a Covenant*

- Day Four: *God Desires Your All*

- Day Five: *God Desires Fruitfulness*

- Reflection and Response: *God Desires You*

In this ninth week we are going to:

Hear the vows of our Groom
"I will betroth you to me forever" (Hosea 2:19a).

Symbolize the wedding
"For you have heard my vows O God; …then will I ever sing praise to your name and fulfill my vows day after day" (Psalm 61: 5, 8).

Understand the covenant the Lord seeks
"All I have is yours, and all you have is mine" (John 17:10).

Write a personal letter of covenant to the Lord
"This is what the LORD commands: When a man makes a vow to the LORD or takes an oath to obligate himself by a pledge, he must not break his word but must do everything he said" (Numbers 30:1-2).

Recognize that the covenant requires fruitfulness
"I will look on you with favor and make you fruitful and increase your numbers, and I will keep my covenant with you" (Leviticus 26:9).

Day One

God Desires to Exchange Vows

"Haven't you read," he replied, "that at the beginning the Creator made them male and female, and said, 'For this reason a man will leave his father and mother and be united to his wife, and the two will become one flesh'? So they are no longer two, but one. Therefore what God has joined together, let man not separate" (Matthew 19:4-6).

I witnessed a wedding recently. It was extravagant with its display of pink roses, and lavish in the love that was expressed between the couple. The music was enchanting, the guests overjoyed, and the ceremony itself—priceless. As I watched, I was enthralled by the glorious panorama, excited and completely amazed. Not by the beauty of the decorations, but by the love and commitment that was shared by the bride and her groom. Anticipation mounted as the groom stood in position at the altar. Silently, he watched and waited for his bride. And at that moment, I had a glimpse of Christ standing at the altar waiting for His bride.

The look on the groom's face was precious. His eyes melted at the thought of seeing her. His love for her was evident and it shone from the love in his heart that beamed from his face. When the bride finally appeared, she was radiant. Her dress was elegant and adorned with diamonds. She was beautiful; but, I couldn't help but think of how beautiful, how stunning and breathtaking we will be—the bride of Christ. And even though she was an exquisite picture of beauty, we will undoubtedly be even more beautiful.

Gracefully, she walked down the aisle to take the hand of her waiting groom. Standing before him, she looked lovingly into his eyes. Again, I could picture the bride of Christ who will one day stand before her Groom. His heart will swell with unbridled passion, and her heart will swoon with delight as they turn to face the altar to exchange vows of everlasting marriage.

What a joyous occasion it will be as we all gather at that celebrated time, when we finally stand at the Groom's right hand as the royal bride of Christ (see Psalm 45:9), united with Him as it was originally meant to be. I can get lost in just the thought of it. As little girls, we dream of being married, don't we? And as we grow into young women, we continually envision that perfect one who will make all of our dreams come true.

Unfortunately, our dreams seem to be shattered when we actually believe we have chosen and married the perfect man, only to find out as soon as the plane lands home that the honeymoon is over. Reality sets in and we begin to realize he is not perfect and we don't know how to cook. Life is messy and married life is hard. But the good news is that there is One who is perfect, and He understands us in ways that no human can.

Begin today by asking the Holy Spirit to give you a Spirit of wisdom, and then please read Revelation 19:5-9.

What is this great and glorious occasion? What two events are they celebrating?

_____

_____

Fill in the blanks according to Revelation 19:7b, NIV:

"For the _____ of the Lamb has come, and his _____ has _____ herself _____."

The word *wedding* or to wed means "to take for a husband or a wife; to marry; to join closely; a matrimonial contract."[30] It is a ceremony of exchanging vows, pledging oneself, promising to be wholly devoted. A *bride* is "a woman on her wedding day; who is about to be married; or has just married."[31] The word *made* means "to cause to be; to secure; to arrive at."[32] To be *ready* is "to be prepared; fitted for use; and willing."[33] Something that is *prepared* is "made ready for use; fit for a particular purpose; to qualify; to equip."[34] A little later in the week we will look at the definition for husband, but for now let's concentrate on the wedding and the bride who is making herself ready.

Compare Genesis 2:24 with Ephesians 5:31-32. What is the central theme?

_____

_____

God designed marriage to be a paradigm. In Genesis 2:24 we see the first example of this as Adam and Eve are joined into one, becoming one flesh. Then this extraordinary illustration is given to us again in Ephesians 5:31-32 as Paul tells us that the profound mystery behind marriage and the two becoming one is the joining of Christ and the church. Weddings, marriage, and the sacred union of two becoming one are meant to serve as images, living metaphors, of what we are to experience with Christ. Our wedding ceremonies are symbolic, and they are meant to give us revelation into the sacred union that we are to partake of with our eternal Bridegroom.

Our wedding ceremonies are symbolic, and they are meant to give us revelation into the sacred union that we are to partake of with our eternal Bridegroom.

Traditionally, when a bride and bridegroom wed they come to an altar. At the altar the bride surrenders her life, then takes the hand of her groom in marriage, becoming one with him in a sacred union. The covenant relationship Christ desires to share with us begins at the Altar of Sacrifice. This is the marriage altar; and it is at this altar that Christ waits for His beloved, where He calls out to her to come and *meet* Him (see Exodus 29:42-43, KJV).

The word *meet* in the Hebrew language is *Ya'adh*, which means "to appoint; to betroth; to give in marriage."[35] The Old Testament refers to this altar of meeting as the Altar of Burnt Offering (see Exodus 27:1-2). At the Altar of Burnt Offering the priests would sacrifice an innocent animal, shedding its blood for the atonement of sin. We no longer have to take the life of a blameless animal, because we have the sacrifice of our Bridegroom who laid His life upon the Altar of Sacrifice for us, giving us the opportunity to become one with Him.

At the Altar of Burnt Offering, your Creator and Redeemer intervened for you, becoming the substitutionary sacrifice for you, to save you from your undesirable condition, saving you from death and slavery to your sins. And now, He who made this atoning sacrifice of blood desires to share with you His unfailing, ever loyal and inexhaustible love, being completely joined to you in holy wedlock, a sanctified union of devotion and love expressed in an unending, faithful covenant.

Beloved, the very One who laid down His life for you at the Altar of Sacrifice, mounted on a hill at Calvary, is inviting you to come and take His hand in a faithful covenant. Listen to His vows of His heart: "Come now, let's make a covenant, you and I, and let it serve as a witness between us" (Genesis 31:44). "Yet my unfailing love for you will not be shaken, nor my covenant of peace be removed," (Isaiah 54:10). "I will remain loyal to you. My covenant of blessing will never be broken" (Isaiah 54:10, NLT).

Continue filling your heart with His vows of covenant found in Hosea 2:19-20, NIV:

"_____ _____ betroth you to me forever; _____ _____ betroth you in righteousness and justice; in love and compassion. _____ _____ betroth you in faithfulness" (Hosea 2:19-20).

"_____ _____ make an everlasting covenant with you, my faithful love…" (Isaiah 55:3).

Traditionally the words, "I will" are the response from a bride and groom as they exchange wedding vows; making each other promises from their hearts. These promises, at the time they are made, are most likely made with every good intention as they solemnly commit themselves to one another as long as they both shall live. Unfortunately, many marriages today end in divorce; couples fall out of love, cheat, leave the one they promised for another, have incompatible personalities, irreconcilable differences, and money problems. And every day people are getting divorced on the basis of these issues and many others, unable or unwilling to keep the promise, the vow, and the pledge they swore to uphold.

I have not personally experienced divorce, but I have experienced the heartbreak of losing someone very special. I know that my experience of lost love does not compare because I know people who have experienced divorce, and I have seen the pain and heartache that can be generated through this gut-wrenching trauma. I also understand that for those of you who have tasted the bitterness and pain of divorce, these promises of everlasting marriage from the Lord can be difficult for you to embrace. But take heart, Dear One, Christ promises He will never leave you nor forsake you (see Hebrews 13:5), and He promises to love you forever (see Judges 2:1, Psalm 105:8).

When we consider the covenant relationship offered to us in Christ Jesus, we must remember that we cannot look at this relationship between the Bride (the church) and Divine Bridegroom merely from an earthly perspective. Remember that weddings and marriage are living metaphors. Human relationships can disappoint us, but the love Christ offers us is pure. His love, the marriage covenant He offers, will never disappoint us. We need to allow Christ to be our soul's source of satisfaction. We must receive all we need from Him, and then what we receive from others will be a bonus.

Look again at the glorious promises of His love found in Hosea 2:19-20 and Isaiah 55:3b. Meditate on the vows of covenant that the Lord your God is making with you. How does this covenant speak to you? Share your heart with your betrothing Bridegroom.

_____

_____

_____

_____

_____

Our Bridegroom is saying, "*I will* promise to take you in marriage as my own forever. You are mine, and I am yours. *I will* promise to love you in righteousness; being upright, honest, moral and gracious, and *I will* promise to show you justice, fairness and integrity all the days of My life. *I will* be faithful, true, authentic, close and truthful with you. And *I will* promise to love you with that true and authentic love forever."

Bride of Christ, the Lord is faithful to all His promises (see Psalm 145:13). He has taken an oath; a pledge. He has made you a promise, an unfathomable promise of love and faithfulness that will last for all eternity. "God is not a man, that He should lie, nor a son of man that he should change his mind" (Number 23:19). So, do not hesitate to give Him your heart; pledging yourself to Him, because He will not break your heart the way others might. Christ will be loving and faithful to all who keep His covenant (Psalm 25:10).

Now, if you are ready, offer Jesus your vows of covenant marriage to Him. "Jesus, I will…"

_____

_____

_____

_____

_____

_____

_____

_____

_____

_____

_____

_____

_____

_____

_____

_____

_____

Day Two

God Desires to Exchange Wedding Rings

You will be a crown of splendor in the LORD'S hand,
a royal diadem in the hand of your God" (Isaiah 62:3).

Up to this point, we have analyzed the metaphor of the wedding ceremony by looking at the significance of coming to the altar and exchanging wedding vows. We reflected on the covenant promise Christ desires to share with us, and we observed this promise from His perspective and heard the vows of His heart. Today our lesson will be in two parts. First we will continue to look at the symbolism and significance of the wedding ceremony. Then we will attempt to understand this unfathomable contract of love offered to us in Christ Jesus by looking at the covenant that God established with Abraham.

Please pray that the Lord will give you eyes to see and ears to hear what He desires to share with you, then read Isaiah 62:1-5 and answer the following:

What important items do you see being paralleled to our earthy wedding ceremonies? (v. 2-3) What do you believe is their spiritual significance?

_____

_____

_____

According to verse 4, what will the bride be called? What does this name mean?

_____

What will her land be called? What does this name mean?

_____

I don't want to jump too far ahead here, but get used to the idea of being called "land." This will have significance later in the week. But for now grasp the fact that "as a young man marries a maiden, so will your sons (Builder) marry you: as a bridegroom rejoices over his bride, so will your God rejoice over you" (Isaiah 62:5).

In Isaiah 62:2-5 we find two more wedding symbols: the wedding ring and the changing of the bride's name. In every wedding ceremony that I have witnessed, the bride and groom have exchanged rings. And as they bestow on each other this precious gift, they may say something like: "With this ring I seal my promise to be your faithful and loving husband/wife."

Amazingly, our Groom desires to do the same. Isaiah 62:3 says, "You will be a crown of splendor in the LORD'S hand, a royal diadem in the hand of your God." A *diadem* is "a fillet or head band worn as the symbol of royal power; a headdress; or crown, significant of royalty."[36] A *crown* is "a diadem worn by sovereign royalty; bestowed upon as a mark of honor; to complete; a circlet."[37] Therefore, I think it is safe to say that Isaiah 62:3 is symbolic, our act of presenting a wedding ring to Christ. As the bride we offer upon our Sovereign Royal Husband a royal diadem, a circlet, a mark of honor, a crown, which He will wear as our gift every day upon His hand, and according to Revelation 19:12, upon His head.

So, where does the bride get these crowns to bestow on her Bridegroom? All throughout their journey together He first bestows them on her: "a crown of beauty" (Isaiah 61:3); "a crown of joy" (see Isaiah 35:10, 51:11); "the crown of righteousness" (2 Timothy 4:8); "the crown of life" (James 1:12, Revelation 2:10); and "the crown of glory" (1 Peter 5:4); and they shall be crowns that will last forever (see 1 Corinthians 9:25). And she will take these many crowns and have the extreme joy of presenting them to her Eternal Bridegroom. Glory to God!

Now the wedding ring Christ bestows upon the bride is so special, we must stop and pray and ask for an extra measure of God's grace. To help us understand the significance of the King's ring, let's open to the book of Esther.

In Esther 8:8, what stands out to you about the king's signet ring?

_____

What do you think is the spiritual significance of the signet ring in connection to the covenant?

_____

_____

A *signet* is "a seal used for authenticating documents."[38] A *signet ring* is "a finger ring which is engraved with a monogram or seal of the owner" and anything sealed with this signet ring is irrevocable. A *seal*, according to the *Vine's Concise Dictionary of Bible Words*, is "a mark of authenticity; a mark of the formal ratification of a transaction or covenant."[39] This *seal* is the mark of the King's signet ring. And with His signet ring He seals the covenant relationship, claiming ownership of His bride (see 2 Corinthians 1:22), and making the vow between them irrevocable.

An earthly wedding ring is a mark of ownership, saying to the world that we belong to someone else. The King's signet ring is His mark of ownership that He bestows upon His bride. Those who *belong* to Christ have been marked with a seal (see Ephesians 1:13). Those who meet Him at the Altar of Sacrifice, who take His hand in marriage, surrendering their life to join with Him, are the ones who will be baptized with the Holy Spirit and with fire (see Matthew 3:11).

In the Old Testament, the covenant relationship was sealed with Abraham when God sent fire down from heaven (see Genesis 15:17-18). In the New Testament, the covenant was sealed at Pentecost, when the Holy Spirit landed upon the disciples like tongues of fire (see Acts 2:3-4). The covenant is sealed with fire. The King's signet ring, which carries His monogrammed initials, is engraved upon our hearts, as the fire of love comes upon us placing its mark of ownership and sealing the covenant agreement.

Now let's consider the second wedding symbol found in Isaiah 61:2-5—the bride's new name. Look again at Isaiah 62:2, "You will be called by a new name that the mouth of the Lord will bestow."

According to Isaiah 56:4-5, what will the Lord give to those who choose what pleases Him and hold fast to His covenant?

_____

What is the significance of this name? How long will this name last?

_____

According to Revelation 3:12 whose name will the bride be given?

_____

What information does Revelation 19:12 give us about Christ's name?

_____

According to Revelation 22:4, where will His name be written?

_____

Upon His eternal bride, Christ will bestow the name that is above all names; a name that will last forever; a name that only He Himself knows. And she will forever more be known by His name; for the One who claims full ownership proudly displays His omnipotent name upon her forehead for all to see. Then, after the ceremony, together they will turn and face those who have come to witness their union. Beaming with delight He will smile and gallantly announce to all, "Behold, this is my bride."

It is wonderful to reflect on the significance of the wedding imagery, it helps us to understand more fully the covenant connection the Lord desires to share with us; and through this relationship of love and loyalty God reveals His covenant purpose: for man to be joined to Him; united; yoked together in union forever. With all that we have affirmed in mind, let's look at the covenant contract God made with Abram.

Please read Genesis 12:1-3

Based on the covenant vows of promise we saw in our lesson yesterday, what words do you see repeated over and over?

_____

_____

Who is making the vows? _____

What covenant promises do you see the Lord making with Abram?

_____

_____

In His "I will" statements, God is making a lot of promises in His covenant with Abram. Did He keep them? Was God faithful to His end of the deal? You bet. God said that "all peoples on earth will be blessed" through Abram (v.3). Think back to Week Seven when we determined that the word *bless* means "to make holy; to sanctify; to set apart; to consecrate."[40] God was promising Abram that through him he was going to make a way to sanctify, make holy, set apart and consecrate all peoples on earth.

How did God keep this promise?

_____

_____

Fill in the blanks according to Matthew 1:1 (NIV):

"A record of the genealogy of "Jesus Christ the son of David, the son of _____.""

Jesus is a descendant of Abram. And through Jesus, God desires to sanctify, make holy, set apart, and consecrate a people who belong to Him; a people who desire to take His hand in covenant marriage. God's covenant of love is offered to everyone, to all the peoples on earth. It does not matter who you are—your background, your nationality, how rich you are or what kind of neighborhood you grew up in. It does not matter. The covenant of love is offered to everyone. Unfortunately, not everyone will accept the covenant agreement.

End today by praying for someone you know who is struggling to accept God's covenant of love.

_____

_____

_____

_____

_____

_____

_____

_____

_____

_____

_____

_____

_____

_____

_____

_____

_____

_____

Day Three
God Desires a Covenant

"I will establish my covenant as an everlasting covenant between me and you. As for you, you must keep my covenant…" (Genesis 17:7, 9).

From God's own heart came the design for covenant relationship. It was His determined purpose, His idea, and it is His unwavering plan to make it work, no matter the cost. And from the beginning God has given us examples of what He longs for, and the design by which He would make it happen. In the relationship with Adam and Eve, for example, we see covenant marriage take place, and through this original marriage, we are given a direct connection to Christ and His bride in the New Covenant. In both the original covenant of the Old Testament and the New Covenant revealed in the New Testament broken flesh and blood were required, a sacrifice acceptable to God.

Today's lesson is a long one, and we will be digging deep into the Word of God, but hang in there; it will be well worth the effort. Pray that you may grasp the covenant to which you are called, and then read Genesis 2:19-25:

According to verse 20b, what was the dilemma?

_____

_____

How did God solve the problem? Explain how He did it—be specific.

_____

_____

What was Adam's response when the woman was presented to him? What did Adam call her? (v. 23)

_____

_____

What took place in verse 24? What was the woman now called in verses 24 and 25?

_____

_____

When God created Adam, God said that it was not good for him to be alone, and that He would create a suitable partner for him. God had already formed all the beasts of the field, yet as Adam named them, he could not find an appropriate companion in any of them. God then made Adam fall into a deep sleep; while Adam was asleep, God broke open his flesh and took one of his ribs in order to create woman.

God then brings the woman to him and Adam then declares, "This is now bone of my bones and flesh of my flesh; she shall be called 'woman' for she was taken out of man" (Genesis 2:23). Eve was made from Adam; she is a part of him. Then they joined together in marriage, one in flesh and the woman became his wife.

In order to draw our connection to Genesis 2:19-25, turn with me first to Genesis 1:26-27, then to John 19:34. What does Genesis 1:26-27 tell us?

_____

_____

What happened in John 19:34? What connection do you see between Jesus and Adam represented in this verse?

_____

_____

In the beginning, God made man in His own image. God then became man to make the ultimate sacrifice. John 19:34 tells us that Jesus' side was pierced, cutting into His flesh. The spear that tore into His side represents the tearing into Adam's side to create Eve, a suitable partner for him. And through Christ's pierced side, a suitable partner was made possible for Him.

This broken flesh, which made a way for the covenant to take place, was presented to the disciples at the last Supper. In 1 Corinthians 11:24, KJV, Jesus said, "This is my body which is broken for you; do this in remembrance of me." The *Vine's Concise Dictionary of Bible Words* refers to the word *remembrance*, as it is used in this verse, as "an awakening of mind."[41] And if you recall from Chapter Four, we concluded that the word *awakening* meant "to rouse from sleep; to develop; a beginning; a stirring of the heart and an arousing of the soul."

In His selfless act of love, Jesus offers up to God the acceptable sacrifice of His broken flesh; giving up His life in order to breathe life into hers; awakening the heart, mind and soul of His bride. Just as God breathed into man's lifeless body (see Genesis 2:7), Christ breathed life into the lifeless soul of His beloved, offering her the gift of life with Him.

And once the suitable partner had been formed and brought to life, they were *united* in a marriage covenant. "For this reason a man will leave his father and mother and be *united* to his wife, and the two will become one flesh (Genesis 2:24). We then see this same statement in Ephesians 5:31, with the added explanation of: "This is a profound mystery—but I am talking about Christ and the church" (Ephesians 5:32). If you recall, in Chapter Three we determined that the word *unite* means "to join; to make into one; to form a whole; to cause to adhere; to act as one."[42] Through Adam and Eve, God is giving us the planned model of marriage, that living metaphor of relationship that we are to share with Him, and the design by which He would make it happen.

Now, along with broken flesh, there is a second covenant requirement—blood. In John 19:34 it says when the soldier pierced Jesus, a sudden flow of blood burst from His side. Based on this covenant requirement, wouldn't it make sense that when God opened Adam's side there was a sudden flow of blood, which came pouring out?

The blood is very significant. If you remember, in Chapter Two we discussed the ceremonial meaning of the groom drinking from the cup of wine and handing the cup to his bride. If she drank from the cup, she was entering into a betrothal, a binding agreement of marriage with him. We then drew the connection of this Jewish custom to the cup that Christ offered to His disciples at the last supper, representing His blood being poured out for them.

In an attempt to put all of these covenant marriage requirements together, let's use one more portion of Scripture.

Read Genesis 15 and allow the Lord to pull it all together.

What was the sacrifice of flesh?

_____

What was the sacrifice of blood?

_____

How was the covenant sealed?

_____

Who was the covenant between? Who made the covenant?

_____

In this portion of Scripture, we see the pouring out of the blood as the innocent animals were pierced. The breaking of their flesh as they were split in half, and then the sealing of the covenant with God's signet ring as His Holy Fire from heaven came down and walked between the acceptable sacrifice. And on that day the Lord made a covenant with Abram… (see Genesis 15:18).

What does a covenant relationship mean to you? Why did God go to all of this trouble to set up this covenant? What does it mean to live in a covenant relationship with the Lord? The New Covenant is in place. The covenant requirements of broken flesh and poured blood have been satisfied. And for those who accept Christ's sacrifice, they are sealed, marked in Him with the promised Holy Spirit; however, just because someone has taken a vow at the time of salvation doesn't mean that he or she is automatically walking in the fullness of the covenant relationship. It takes time to grow and mature in relationship with Jesus.

The covenant relationship is utter commitment and loyalty; an unbreakable bond made in love that is so binding, so dedicated to the other, that nothing can break it. Bride, this kind of devotion takes sacrifice; a willingness to surrender everything you've got into this relationship. However this level of commitment cannot be accomplished in your own strength.

Read Exodus 24:3-8. When Moses mediated the covenant between God and the Israelites, how did the people respond? Check the correct response:

___ "Lord, help us to remain faithful to you."

___ "We will do everything the Lord has said; we will obey."

___ "The word of the Lord is faithful and true."

The Israelites were more than eager to take those vows of covenant with God. They desired with all their hearts to keep the vows they made to the Lord that day, but they couldn't do it in their own power..

After the people took the vows of covenant, what happened in Exodus 32:1-6?

_____

_____

_____

Now, let's be honest here. How many of us have done this same thing? With all our heart, we have taken the vows of covenant before God and then at a time of prolonged waiting, or when God didn't come through in a way we thought He would, we decide we want something else. God desires for each of us to take this step of covenant with Him, but it is impossible for us to maintain it and walk in the fullness of relationship that God has in mind. We cannot do this alone; and God knows that. This is why He has given us His Holy Spirit to help us keep the vows we make with Him.

When we begin our journey of relationship with Christ, each of us, I believe, takes those vows of committed promise seriously. We desire to please God. We desire to be the joy of His heart in total loyalty and devotion; to be surrendered in utter obedience, loving Him with our whole life. Unfortunately, we are human and weak. And when we begin to fail in our pure devotion, we often begin to withdraw from our promise with the Lord, convincing ourselves that we are not "good Christians" and we'll never get it right. But this relationship is not about being a "good Christian," because it's not based on our performance, it's based on God's love and grace.

Beloved, you need God; you can do nothing without Him. This is why surrender is so important. Only by the power of the Holy Spirit can you be faithful to the desire of your heart to keep the vows of covenant you pledge before God. Only by being completely yielded, under the full control and guidance of the Holy Spirit, are you able to enter into the fullness of the covenant relationship.

As I have studied and dwelled on the covenant, I have come to realize, just as there were four parts to the earthly Tabernacle that Moses and the Israelites built (see Exodus, chapters 25 through 30), there are four levels building up to the covenant relationship that God seeks, they are: *connection, cooperation, commitment,* and then, finally, *covenant.*

At the *connection* level the beloved is connected to the Lord through salvation. By accepting Christ's sacrifice, receiving His grace by faith, she has entered the Tabernacle and now stands at the Altar of Burnt Offering. Here she has taken the vow of covenant agreement, and has joined her life to His. At this level her faith is young, but she is learning to grow through prayer, Bible study, through fellowship with other believers, and by attending church regularly.

The second level is *cooperation*; here the level of relationship goes higher. Here she is, of course, connected to Christ, but now she is being cooperative with Him in willing obedience. She has embraced a greater level of trust and is learning to function with Him as a unit. At this level she begins to take risks, stepping away from the status quo. This level is represented by

Only by the power of the Holy Spirit can we be faithful to the desire of our heart to keep the vows of covenant that we pledge before God.

the Bronze basin which is located west of the Altar of Burnt Offering, just outside the Holy Place.

At the level of *commitment*, her loyalty to Christ takes a jump. Here, at this level, she is definitely committing her life, her heart and her love into His hands. She is committed to His desires and finds great joy in doing His will. Her level of hunger for Christ increases tremendously, as the awareness of His intimate fellowship intensifies. Through the elements found in the Holy Place He continues to draw her, allowing her to partake of Him at the table, experience the warmth of His Spirit from the Lampstand, and offer passionate prayers of intercession with Him at the Altar of Incense. Yet, even with all this, there is still more—the Holy of Holies.

Here, in the Holy of Holies, we find *covenant* relationship, a relationship that is as wide, as it is long, as it is high, as it is deep. At the covenant level we have extreme relationship. Higher than any bonds of earthly marriage, this level of closeness demands the highest level of commitment, unquestionable levels of *cooperation*, and a powerful *connection* of intimacy.

Here at this point in your relationship with Christ, you will lay down your life at all costs, because nothing, absolutely nothing, is more valuable to you than He is. Through covenant relationship you are one with God. His thoughts become your thoughts; everything you think, say, and do is with the mind, attitudes, and actions of Christ (see Galatians 2:20).

Now, look at these four "C"s through Christ's eyes. He has already taken this covenant oath, and absolutely nothing will remove or hinder His faithful promises. He is already at the highest level of commitment; desiring to share that powerful level of intimate connection with you, and He has already decided that you are more valuable than anything He possesses.

Beloved, reaching the covenant level takes time, at each level of relationship you are growing and learning to move as one with the Bridegroom. Through the power of the Holy Spirit, He is moving you through the Tabernacle, drawing you closer and closer to His heart.

But the question is, "Are you willing to submit?" If you are willing to say "yes" to the Bridegroom, He is more than ready to say "yes" to you. For the covenant response is when you joyfully, and without hesitation or reservation respond, "Yes, Lord," His direct response to you is "Yes, My love." When you give all you have, He gives all He has; when all you have is His then all He has is yours (see John 17:10).

Day Four

God Desires Your All

"Make vows to the LORD your God and fulfill them" (Psalm 76:11).
" In view of this, we are making a binding agreement,
putting it in writing and our leaders, our Levites and our priests
are affixing their seals to it" (Nehemiah 9:38).

This week we have been looking at the significance and symbolism of the wedding ceremony. We have heard the vows of our Divine Bridegroom and, hopefully, we have come to a deeper understanding of the covenant relationship that Christ desires to share with us. In light of all we've learned thus far this week, we're going to do something a little different in today's study. It is my hope, as you do today's lesson, you will be inspired to share with Jesus the desires of our heart in a personal covenant letter. Before you begin, in an attempt to give you richer insight, please indulge me and permit me to share with you one of my personal covenant letters.

Covenant Letter

Jesus, I give you my whole life. As my King, I will esteem you; I will respect (value and revere) You with sincere devotion (dedication, affection, care, loyalty) and love. As my Lord, I will honor you in absolute awe (fear, wonder), offering you my worship (adoration, love) and reverence (respect and admiration). As my Master, I will obey you, follow (go after, pursue and chase) You, abiding (basking, soaking, dwelling) every day in You.

Jesus, I give you my whole heart. As my Husband, I give You my total commitment (promise, pledge, vow) to love You first and in complete faithfulness (loyalty, closeness, dependability, devotion, and truth). I long to give You pleasure (enjoyment, joy, delight), loving You with full abandonment of self; offering myself to You as a living sacrifice and loving you the way you desire (wish, long for, yearn, crave). And as my Best Friend, I will laugh with you, cry with you, take your hand, and forever (eternally, forevermore) stand by your side in good times and in bad times; wholly devoted and forever (everlastingly, unceasingly) Yours.

Patty   *Dated: June 24, 2003*

This is the second of three covenant letters that I wrote to Jesus expressing my devotion, love and loyalty. However, when the Lord first asked me to write my third commitment letter, I remember taking several days to pen the words of my heart. I loved Him dearly and longed to enter into that higher covenant relationship, but I hesitated because at that time I was just beginning to realize the sacrifice involved; not to mention the fact that something special and very profound happens when we put things in writing.

Thinking back to that time, I remember His tenderness, patience and gentleness that simply overwhelmed me. I was in the midst of a difficult time of purification and I was still a little uncertain of what He was asking me to do, and I recall the struggle I went through writing this letter; yet, I also recall the loving way He continually encouraged me to complete the task.

Covenant Letter

A few days ago, I was asked by the Lord to write a covenant agreement. At that time I couldn't do it. I longed to write that letter with the confidence and heart that I had penned the others, but fear and an overwhelmed soul kept me from entering into that agreement with a steadfast heart and mind. Oh, Jesus, my desire is still the same; I long to love You and obey You with all my heart, but I realize now that this commitment you ask for is from your perspective and not mine. When I made the prior promises and vows with You, they were desires within my heart, things I eagerly longed to do with You, but now I realize that You desire a commitment based on the desires of Your heart and agenda and not mine. The level of commitment is deeper and higher and the cost is huge; it's one that I will pay for with my life. You are seeking a level of commitment that overwhelms me, and I know that You will not stop until You have obtained my entire heart, mind, soul and life.

I sit here pondering the first two letters of dedication and I am amazed at how easily those promises flowed from my heart, but this one is different. In the others, I promised to be faithful, to love You, honor, obey, respect You; surrendering completely, being wholly devoted to You all the days of my life. I am Yours and you are mine, and I meant it! So, why is this one so difficult? Then it hits me. At the time when these other commitments were written (by the grace of God none of them at this time have been broken), the situations and circumstances were pleasant. Now I am facing the cross, and this undoubtedly means a time of suffering. I realize that this is not a one-time thing but a daily surrender. However, a purification takes place during this time of "dying to self" that enables You to completely take over unhindered—a process where I become completely Yours.

Lord, I have prayed before: "Invade me; consume me; I am Yours; just take over." I meant those prayers then and I mean them now. I do not want to be afraid of the cross, the Refiner's Fire, or the opportunities to get better acquainted with You through suffering. Perhaps now I have a better understanding of the kind of commitment of which You speak, and it is not easy. So, with Your help, I desire to enter into this covenant relationship of intimacy and servanthood to which You call me. And I now know and understand in my heart that I must be prepared for the calling You have placed on my life here on earth and with You in the life to come.

Okay. This is big; but here we go. Whatever it takes. Mold me. Change me. Crucify me. Make me fully yours. Create in me the person You want as a partner and bride. I belong to You and I must be prepared, made ready to co-partner with You; taking Your hand to leap over the mountains, bound over the hills, and reach the nations with You. Prepare me as a bride beautifully dressed for her Husband; purify me to become that strong, pure, virgin for You— Your inheritance, Your treasure, and Your beloved.

Lord, I do not make these statements carelessly, but You are here, being merciful and gracious, holding my hand and giving me Your peace and strength. With Your help I will be faithful to the vows I have made today.

Patty   *Dated: October 28, 2004*

I understand this is not an easy step. I understand that this can be a very challenging task, but no matter where you are right now in your relationship with Jesus, I would like to encourage you to write your own commitment letter to Christ. What I have learned is that there is something much more vital and valuable at stake. More than anything else, I long to draw close to Him, to touch His heart and know Him better than I know myself.

Oh, how beautiful is this sacred romance, the true romance between two hearts and souls totally committed and held captive by one another. I can't find the words to express the truth of my heart, allowing the words to dance. I desperately yearn to come closer to Him, to go deeper in our connection and reach for higher levels of relationship. I long to be consumed and devoured by His presence, peace and love. I have already reached the point of no return. I am enslaved by the power He possesses over me. Yet, He helps me to take His hand and to follow Him into the depths of His being, to move in harmony with Him as He leads me in this magnificent dance, joined together in a pledge, a vow of covenant love.

Now it's your turn. Review Psalm 76:11 and Nehemiah 9:38 and pray for the Lord's help. Then open your heart, pick up your pen, and share with Jesus the desires of your heart. Write Him the covenant letter that you feel He is leading you to share with Him. Make it real. Make it personal—this is just between the two of you. Then sign and date it. God bless you, Beloved. May He give you His grace as you take this step of faith with Him.

Signature _____ Date_____

Day Five

God Desires Fruitfulness

"The fruit of your womb will be blessed, and the crops of your land. The LORD will grant you abundant prosperity—in the fruit of your womb…and the crops of your ground" (Deuteronomy 28:4, 11).

Today's lesson, at first, may not make much sense as to why it was included in this portion of our study, but I guarantee you, fruitfulness is the result of the relationship. And the higher we go in our relationship with Christ, surrendering daily in order to reach that higher level of covenant with Him, the more fruit we will bear for His glory.

Let's begin today by asking the God of our fruitfulness to reveal His truth as we read Deuteronomy 28:1-14. What is the theme for this portion of Scripture?

_____

In the margin, list some of the blessings mentioned in these verses? (Pay special attention to verses 4 and 11.)

What is essential in receiving the blessing and favor of God? (v. 2)

____ Living a good life   ____ Going to church   ____ Obedience to God

God's favor and fruitfulness are blessings for obedience. Obedience produces fruit. I love the word *accompany* in verse 2. Like a good dose of laughter shared with a cherished friend, or a warm blanket on a cold night, these blessings will accompany you if you obey the Lord your God; they will escort you, stay with you, and never leave you. Christ desires to accompany you today and every day, every minute of your life, walking with you and you with Him, so He can offer you His favor, and grant you abundant prosperity in the fruit of your womb.

The word *obedient* or *obedience* means "to subject to another's authority; willing to obey; submission to authority."[43] Do you want to be a man or woman after your God's own heart? Then pursue His heart with an aspiration for desperate obedience. It is through faithful obedience that your womb will be blessed with abundant prosperity.

With this in mind, it is time to shed some light on the blessings of favor and fruitfulness that Christ loves to bestow upon His bride.

What does John 15:16 tell us about bearing fruit? Check the correct response:

_____ Being fruitful is completely in our hands

_____ We must work hard to bear fruit

_____ We were chosen to bear fruit

I am moved by the words, "I chose you," here in this verse. According to *Vine's Concise Dictionary of Bible Words*, the word *choose* means "to pick out; to select; to choose for oneself, choosing with the subsidiaries of favor and love."[44] I don't know about you, but the concept of being chosen by God is huge for me. As a kid growing up, I was not readily chosen. I recall the days in gym class where captains would be selected in order to choose sides. I was the one who was selected last, or at best—next to last, and was received onto the team as someone they were merely stuck with. No one asked me to the prom—or on any date for that matter. And among the girls, I was the outcast. I was the one who usually played alone on the playground. That was if I wasn't being followed by taunting seekers who wanted the satisfaction of my company only to make fun of me.

So, when I came to the realization that I was chosen by God, hand selected, picked as a primary choice, and not because there was no one else left, it was tremendously touching for me. The Almighty, All-powerful God of the Universe, chose me for Himself because He loved me and wanted me as His very own, His treasured possession (see Deuteronomy 7:6), one whom He valued more than rubies (see Proverbs 31:10) and esteemed (see Isaiah 66:2), one who was of more worth than any country (see Isaiah 43:3-4), or anything else in the entire universe. God chose us. He chose you. He chose me. And it is the inexhaustible desire of His heart that none should perish, but for everyone to come to repentance (see 2 Peter 3:9), to turn toward Him and choose Him. Oh, Dear One, I cannot begin to tell you how cherished this makes me feel. Therefore, I am greatly humbled and honored to bear the fruit of His heart.

The word *fruit* according to the *Webster's Dictionary* is "an edible produce or seed of a plant; offspring."[45] *Vines' Concise Dictionary of Bible Words* refers to the *fruit* mentioned in John 15:16 as "the invisible power of the Holy Spirit in those who are brought into living union with Christ."[46] I would like to draw a connection here, so let's now look up the word *pregnant*. According to *Webster's* the word *pregnant* means "to be with child; to be fruitful."[47] Therefore, when we put all of our definitions together, we see that being fruitful means to be pregnant through our union with Christ, and to bear fruit means to give birth.

In Isaiah 66:9, what do you think the Lord is telling us about giving birth?

_____

_____

The word *deliver* means "to liberate from danger, captivity or restraint; to save; to give birth."[48] *Birth* is "an act of coming into life or being born."[49] Now, take the covenant relationship we have been discussing and equate it with what we just learned. It is like Christ is saying, "I have chosen you. Come be My life's partner. Let's devote ourselves to each other in love. You are Mine and I am yours. Share everything with Me: My heart, My passion, My joys, and My pain. Be a part of Me and I will be a part of you. And as we join in this committed intimate relationship, we will share a union of the heart and Spirit where you will conceive, and together we will bring forth an abundant harvest of life."

Bride, it is Christ's greatest desire that you be joined to Him in a sealed covenant relationship where the two of you will become one, and together you will conceive new life (see 1 Corinthians 6:16b-17); delivering the nations from their captivity and giving birth to the offspring who will bear His name.

Do you remember earlier this week when I told you to get used to the idea of being referred to as land? Well, it is because your heart (womb) is soil; and in this soil Christ desires to plant His seed. It is like a man who marries a woman, and as her husband, impregnates her womb with his seed, and together they conceive new life. This may be difficult for some of you, but keep an open heart as I draw the parallel.

The word *husband* means "a married man; …to till the soil; …a farmer."[50] Therefore, like a farmer plowing his field, the Lord plants His seeds and produces new life, bringing forth spiritual offspring. Remember in Isaiah 62:4 where it says "your land will be married"? When you become married, you become the property of your spouse. Christ is Lord. A lord is the owner of the property. Christ is the land owner, and in this land He desires to till the soil, and then plant His seeds that will produce a crop.

Prior to planting, however, the soil must be prepared. Read Matthew 13:3-9 and 18-23. List the four types of soil the seeds fell upon and what Jesus said they represented:

1. _____ - _____

2. _____ - _____

3. _____ - _____

4. _____ - _____

Why is it important for the seed to fall on the good soil?

_____

God's divine purpose is to cultivate, prepare, and till your soil, making your land ready so that He can plant in you His Holy passions. Beloved, is your ground tender and workable or are there clumps of hardened dirt and rock that simply resist being plowed into workable soil for the Farmer's hand? Is your ground hardened with bitterness, unforgiveness and self-centeredness? Is your ground free from obstruction or are Christ's seeds falling upon soil covered with thorns? Allow the Lover of your soul to come into your stony areas and till the land so that He may plant His seeds of righteousness within your fertile soil, that you may reap an abundant harvest.

Now, once the soil is ready, the planting begins. "I am giving you a promise now while the seed is still in the barn, before you have harvested your grain and before the grapevine, the fig tree, the pomegranate, and the olive tree have produced their crops. From this day onward I will bless you" (Haggai 2:19, NLT). The seed that was once bagged in the barn is now brought into the fields and lovingly planted by the hand of the Farmer.

In this planting process, you must remember that Christ has chosen you to bear His offspring, and it is His determined purpose to produce fruit in your life; fruit that will last and make a difference for the kingdom of God; but, you cannot become pregnant without intimate communion through His Holy Spirit and being in His Word. You must join with your Spiritual Partner if He is to plant His seeds within you because your fruitfulness comes from Him (see Hosea 14:8b).

What does Jesus tell us in John 15:4-5? Check all that apply:

_____ Remain joined to me and I will remain joined to you

_____ No one can bear fruit by himself

_____ Stay connected to me and you will bear much fruit

All too often, we think that we must "do" something in order to produce fruit, when all we really need is to "be" connected to Christ. Our capability to generate fruit has nothing to do with hard work, ability, or giftedness. We don't need to strive, struggle, or strain to produce fruit; our fruitfulness is a result of our intimate relationship with Jesus. Without that intimate connection through His life-giving vine, we can do nothing. Therefore, I say it again—the relationship is everything. Only through Christ, by the power of the Holy Spirit, can we ever truly hope to love God and others, be obedient in utter surrender, keep our vows of covenant to Him and fulfill our purpose in this life, bringing forth the glory of God in our lives. Without Him we can do nothing—absolutely nothing.

A few words of caution about planting seeds before we move on: We want Christ's seeds of righteousness, the seeds of truth from His Word, to be planted in our hearts. We need to be aware of the fact that seeds can come from other sources. Seeds can be planted by the flesh, which is our own self-ambition, through the influences of the world and the enemy. We only want the seeds that come from the Farmer's hand. This is the only good seed. So I ask you: What seeds are you receiving? What is it you are allowing to be planted in your heart? Remember, a man reaps what he sows (see Galatians 6:7); therefore, sow for yourselves righteousness and reap the fruit of unfailing love (see Hosea 10:12).

Also, understand that you cannot force fruit. John 15:9 says to abide in Christ. When we do this, the fruit will produce naturally. A good tree produces fruit naturally, like that tree planted by streams of water, which yields its fruit in season and whose leaf does not wither (see Psalm 1:3). You have been created for such a time as this, to bear good fruit, because the Fruitful One desires to plant His seed in you. The Bible calls it the Imperishable Seed, and it bears the likeness of the One who planted it (see 1 Peter 1:23). Therefore, yield to His great power of love and allow Him to plant the seeds which will, at its appointed time, bring forth a great harvest of grain, fig, pomegranate, grapevine and olive crops (see Haggai 2:19).

The words *at its appointed time* means that "there is a time God has chosen; a time selected on the Kingdom calendar," in which you will give birth. You cannot rush the birth or give delivery on your own. "Flesh gives birth to flesh, but the Spirit gives birth to spirit" (John 3:6). If you grow impatient and try to birth the fruits of His hand too early, you will have a miscarriage, or the baby will be stillborn. Ministries, tasks of service, divine appointments, church programs, and all other wonderful good works that the Lord has divinely chosen to bring into being through you will be cut off if they are not done in the timing and power of the Holy Spirit. Have faith and He will be faithful to complete the work He has begun (see Philippians 1:6).

Abide in the fact that Christ is wholly committed to you forever. It is a done deal. And if you remain connected, cooperative, and committed to the Bridegroom in a covenant relationship, He will look upon you with favor and impregnate you with His seed(s) that will bring forth a harvest (see Leviticus 26:9). Church, we are His bride, and Christ desires to have many, many offspring. Our job is to offer ourselves to Him; to be a willing partner, and to desperately desire to be obedient to His desires, so that He can produce fruit in our lives. Therefore, open your heart (womb) and yield to your Spiritual Husband; allow the Farmer to till, plant, and reap a great harvest in your life.

God Desires You

Listen, can you hear the heart of your Bridegroom: "Allow the sweetness of My love to cover you every morning with the rising of the sun in the eastern sky. I desire to love you so tenderly, revealing to you My intention and passion. Allow Me to overcome you with My affections and plant the seeds of My desires. This is the sacred romance, My Darling, where two hearts come together in an everlasting promise. And from this covenant union that we share, together we will produce the fruit of unfailing love. My treasured Bride, seek wholly after Me. I am your Spiritual Husband, and I yearn to lavish you with My love and from there I will bring forth a great harvest."

Reflection and Response

What speaks to you the most about this unfathomable relationship of loyalty and love that Christ desires to share with you?

_____

_____

_____

_____

_____

_____

How has your understanding of the covenant relationship deepened?

_____

_____

_____

_____

_____

How desperate are you for obedience? Obedience is the fruit of submission to Christ; in what areas of your life do you need to surrender to Jesus?

_____

_____

_____

_____

_____

_____

What areas need to be cultivated so that your land may produce a harvest of thirty, sixty, or a hundred times what was sown?

_____

_____

_____

_____

_____

_____

What evidence of fruit is being birthed in your life?

_____

_____

_____

_____

_____

_____

Share with Jesus the desire of your heart for Him to produce even more good fruit in your life.

_____

_____

_____

_____

Week Nine

Lesson Nine

Completely His

Song of Songs 7:6-10; 8:6-7

1. Christ desires to _____ our love with the _____ of His love (John 4:19).

2. When love, like the _____ of _____ , takes hold of you, it will never let you go.

3. The LORD God called Himself by the Hebrew name _____ (EL kan-NAH), which means _____

4. Christ is jealous _____ His bride (see Corinthians 11:2).

5. Christ's jealousy for His bride is not _____; rather Christ's jealous love is

   _____

6. Christ, who is the essence of love, wants to _____ His bride with His love, a love that will _____, a love that is _____, _____, stubborn and unstoppable; an eager and enthusiastic love that is full of _____ and passion.

7. This is _____ relationship, when your love for Christ is as strong and steadfast as His love for you.

The illness has taken over her failing body. Age has not been kind, and she struggles with every movement. Her once beautiful features are now wrinkled and worn from the years. Her skin that was once so soft is now thin and sagging, as time has played its theme in her life. The early morning sun shines in through her window and her soul rises with the dawn. Her body is weak and frail from the sickness that plagues her, but the spirit within her sings, full of life and love. As she looks out the window, her fading eyes lift toward heaven and she longs for the embrace of her First Love. She closes her eyes and thinks of His faithful love as a faint smile graces her delicate face. Her chest slowly rises and falls, finding it difficult to draw air as her tiny body struggles to breathe; but still she manages to speak the praises of her heart. Joyfully, she lifts her voice to love Him in her weakness as she did in strength. He had never let her down, and even now she finds renewed hope in the truth that she has carried in her heart for so long. A sense of peace washes over her, and she feels His presence in the room. He had come to her, not only to comfort her, but to lead her in her journey one last time; to take her hand in His and lead her home, to be with Him where He is, forever. Gently, He bends over her weakened frame. "Arise, my love." He whispers in her ear, "Arise, my Darling, my beautiful one. Come with me." (Song of Songs 2:10). With one final breath, she lets go and falls into the arms of the One she has loved for so many years.

Week Ten
The Story Goes On....

- Day One: *God Desires for You to Know Heaven*

- Day Two: *God Desires to Share His Kingdom*

- Day Three: *God Desires Celebration*

- Day Four: *God Desires for You to Take Your Place in Heaven*

- Day Five: *God Desires to Bring You Home*

- Reflection and Response: *God Desires You*

In this tenth week we are going to:

Reach for Heaven
"Now this is eternal life: that they may know you, the only true God, and Jesus Christ, whom you have sent" (John 17:3).

Draw the parallel to the parable
"The knowledge of the secrets of the kingdom of heaven has been given to you…" (Matthew 13:11).

Get ready for the celebration
"On that day I will purify the lips of all people, so that everyone will be able to worship the LORD together" (Zephaniah 3:9, NLT).

Grab hold of the prophesy
"Behold, I am coming soon! Blessed is he who keeps the words of the prophecy in this book" (Revelation 22:7).

Receive a foretaste of glory divine
"His kingdom will never end" (Luke 1:33).

Day One
God Desires for You to Know Heaven

*"Father, I want those you have given me to be with me where I am,
and to see my glory, the glory you have given me because
you loved me before the creation of the world"* (John 17:24).

I am not looking forward to being frail and weak with age, but I am counting the days until I am in the arms of my Savior. Death is not a threat to me. In fact, I long for the day when Jesus will come for me, and with great anticipation I dream of what that homecoming will be like.

Tears fill my eyes at the thought of being welcomed home—just welcomed—simply walking in the front door of heaven. There are many times when I think about meeting Jesus; standing before God; literally face-to-face for the first time. I often dream of a quiet tender moment filled with tears, laughter and unbridled emotion as I am finally embraced by Jesus. Sometimes I envision a small welcoming party made up of the 12 apostles, maybe a few angels, and the people I once knew and loved here on earth.

But lately I have been thinking about a different kind of welcoming home; a celebration beyond measure. Perhaps it will be simply an intimate gathering of loved ones, but then I began to think of the millions upon millions who will be rejoicing in heaven as the gates open and another precious one walks in. Jesus takes my hand and escorts me into the reception area where suddenly I envision a grand and glorious party welcoming me into my eternal home.

Oh, just think of the celebration as you, too, will one day walk into the full Presence of God for the first time. Perhaps, slowly at first, Jesus will walk you along the red carpet stretched out before you. You will look around, trying to get a visual of each face as you walk by. Confetti showers may fill the air as cheers and thunderous applause reverberates in the heavens as everyone shouts, "Welcome home! Welcome home!"

Ask the Spirit of revelation to give you an inspired view of heaven, and then read 1 Corinthians 2:9 and fill in the blanks according to the NIV:

"_____eye has seen; _____ ear has heard, _____ mind has conceived what God has _____ for those who love Him" (1 Corinthians 2:9).

No one knows—not one of us—what God has in store for us when we are with Him in eternity, but isn't it fun at times to stop and ponder the idea of being in heaven; standing toe-to-toe and gazing into the eyes of the Alpha and Omega; totally consumed in His presence?

When you think of eternity, what descriptions come to mind? How do you envision heaven? Are they images of white with angelic beings everywhere sitting on clouds playing harps and singing Hallelujah praises to the Lamb? Do you envision heaven as one big long church service? Or do you envision going for long walks with Jesus in a private garden? What is heaven to you? What do you think you will discover in eternity? When I think of heaven I can't help but wonder if each of our eternities will be personalized? Why not? Our experiences here on earth with Christ are personalized. So, as we ponder the things of heaven, let's think big!

What do you think? When you think of eternity, what do you envision? What do you long for?

_____

_____

_____

Jesus called heaven paradise. He said to the thief crucified along with Him in Luke 23:43, "Today you will be with me in paradise." What do you think God's idea of paradise is? Perhaps you've had the privilege of seeing exotic and tropical places firsthand; at least most of us have had the opportunity to see pictures of such places as Hawaii and Tahiti. But even with all the splendor, color and grandeur we have here on earth, I believe our infinity will be far greater than anything we can fathom; bursting with colors and creations we have never seen.

Jesus called heaven paradise. What do you think God's idea of paradise is?

Scripture tells us that God made the world in six days (see Genesis 1:1-31). He created everything from the mountain heights to the ocean depths; every living species of plant and animal formed. Every living creature and scenic landscape known to man was created in six days. It has been, however, more than 2,000 years since Jesus told His bride that He was going to prepare a place for her. Now, if God formed the earth and every-thing in it in six days and it is taking Him more than 2,000 years to prepare eternity, then what an incredible place our eternal home must be.

Isn't it wonderful to dream of the possibilities? But what if paradise, God's paradise, is not so much a place as a state of being; a utopia of soul and spirit where our sole source of existence is based on our connection with Him. From the beginning has that not been God's ultimate desire—to be joined with man forever in a covenant relationship? And when I am united with Him during our personal intimate time, I begin to experience paradise; an ideal state of being, as heaven seems to open up before me and I am lifted high above my earthly surroundings; given a taste of the ecstasy to come, overcome by His beauty and love.

We cannot even hope to understand fully now, yet Scripture affords us the privilege to glimpse into God's idea of paradise. No one completely knows what heaven will be like until we arrive; therefore, Scripture is the only safe place we can turn to find the answers to the questions that we seek to know. With this in mind, let's explore the promises together as we search God's Word this week in order to gain wisdom, insight, and understanding into our unfathomable eternity (see Proverbs 2:1-6).

Let's begin our search with Genesis 15:1, what did God tell Abram was his very great reward?

____ Gold and silver

____ Fine linen and a mansion in glory

____ God Himself

What is Christ telling His bride about her eternal reward according to Revelation 22:12? How will the reward be determined and distributed?

_____

_____

_____

We all know of, and wait for, His awesome return and the reward that will undoubtedly follow Him. And He will give to each one according to what he has done. Not what our neighbor has done or our pastor or even Jesus. Our salvation is based on Christ's sacrifice, but our eternal reward is based on what we have done with what God has given to us.

Our eternal reward is with Christ, and we begin to know Christ through His Word and through His Holy Spirit, which is given to us now, while on earth, as a promise of what is to come (see Ephesians 1:13-14). As we come to know Christ more and more through what has been deposited into us, we are to share it. Whether it is to bring encouragement and edification to the church, or hope to a lost and hurting world that doesn't know Him—the goal is to share what we receive from God as a result of our relationship with Him (see Matthew 10:8b). Most, if not all, believers know this, however, the way

Our eternal reward is with Christ, and we begin to know Christ through His Word and through His Holy Spirit, which is given to us now, while on earth, as a promise of what is to come.

in which we share, the motivation of our heart, will make all the difference in whether or not we receive the eternal reward that Christ has in store for us.

Read 1 Corinthians 3:10-15 and answer the following: What is our foundation?

_____

What are we to be building upon this foundation?

Check all that apply:

___ Hay	___ Costly stones
___ Straw	___ Silver
___ Wood	___ Gold

What do you think the gold, silver and costly stones represent?

_____

_____

What do you think the wood, hay, and straw represent?

_____

_____

Of these two groups of materials, circle the one you think will withstand the test of God's fire?

What will happen if what a man builds survives the flames?

_____

_____

What will happen if it burns up in the fire?

_____

_____

As one who has received salvation through the atoning blood of the Lord Jesus Christ, we will not be judged for our sins, but we will be judged based on what we did with God's precious gift; how we allowed Christ's love to radiate through our lives. One day each of us will appear before the judgment seat of Christ, so that we may receive what is due for the things done while in the body, whether good or bad (see 2 Corinthians 5:10). And we will either be given reward or have reward removed in accordance with what is left standing after our lives have passed through the flames.

So, what are you building with? Upon the foundation of your salvation, are you building with the gold, silver and costly stones, the riches of a love relationship with your Savior that will birth good fruit in your life? Are you allowing His love to penetrate your heart so that you can share His love with those who don't know Him? Or are you building with the wood, hay and straw—useless time wasters that will only burn up in the fire of Judgment? Are you forsaking your First Love and His Kingdom with the things of this earth that hold no eternal value?

Our relationship with Christ starts now. Christ is our foundation; and He is our eternal reward. From the start of our salvation, until its completion, we must fill the time in-between by building with the richness of a love affair with Jesus. Learn to sow the seeds of relationship with Jesus so that you can "reap the fruit of unfailing love" (Hosea 10:12), because only love will survive.

Love is the greatest thing (see 1 Corinthians 13:13). Love is the greatest commandment (see Mark 12:29-31). Only love will withstand the flames. Only what we did as a result of our love affair with Christ will endure the intensity of the fire. On that final day it won't matter what gifts of the Spirit you had, what kind of ministry you had, how much money you gave to the poor, how often you served the church, or how many people you witnessed to if you didn't exhibit love. Without love you have nothing, you gain nothing (see 1 Corinthians 3:1-3).

The fire will test the motives of the heart. It will validate whether the tasks of service were done out of duty and obligation or out of a love affair with Jesus. In the end, you will reap what you have sown. Beloved, without love you are forsaking all that God has given you. God is love; and when you allow God's love to be made complete in you, then you will have confidence on the Day of Judgment (see 1 John 4:16-17). Then you will receive the eternal reward that is founded on love, built up in love, sown in love, and reaped in love.

Life is short. Each man's life is but a breath (see Psalm 39:4-5). God has given you much in the gift of a precious personal relationship with His Son; you must not waste it. Spend every day of your life, every breath God has given you by building upon that eternal foundation in Christ with the treasures of what is most lovely and wonderful. Now *that* is a taste of paradise—that is a taste of heaven!

From the start of our salvation, until its completion, we must fill the time in-between by building with the richness of a love affair with Jesus.

Day Two

God Desires to Share His Kingdom

"What is the kingdom of God like? What shall I compare it to?"
(Luke 13:18).

God has given us many parallels in Scripture to help us to grasp the revelation of the Kingdom of God. We have the opportunity to experience much in this life if we accept the possibilities, but we will not experience everything, because if we did, what would we have to look forward to in eternity? Many people want heaven now. They cannot understand that we live in a fallen world, and they continually wonder why a loving God would allow bad things to happen. But, we were not meant to live in this world; our true home is not found in these days. Therefore, we must not have a death grip on this life, but wait with hope and great anticipation for the next.

Most assuredly, eternity means different things to different people, but to me heaven is Jesus. He is my supreme and heavenly Prize; the One on whom I have set my sights; the One who makes all this worthwhile. He is my very great Reward (see Genesis 15:1). It is not the mansion in glory; not the crowns of life and beauty; not the finest dress of linen or the jewels that will adorn my garments. No, Jesus, is the One and only reason for which I long to go home, and the One and only entity of whom I dream.

For me, heaven will be heaven simply because He will be there; and heaven will be heaven for Him because you and I will be there. Can you imagine? God does not need anything, but even with all He has, with all He created and possesses, something is still missing. Without His beloved bride, His kingdom will not be complete.

While Jesus was here on earth, He shared many stories that began, "The kingdom of heaven is like…." In most, if not in all of these parables, Jesus was trying to tell us something about Himself, something about His bride, and something about their relationship. Therefore, we conclude that the phrase, "The kingdom of heaven is like," translating into, "I am, you are, and this is us together." Basically, through these allegories, Jesus was saying, "Okay, now that I am here with you, let's get acquainted. Let me tell you something about me, our relationship and the destiny we will share in my Father's kingdom." We will not look at all of these parables; that would be a book in and of itself, but we will take a peek at a few in the hopes of gaining a little further insight.

Please begin by praying for God to give you a broader perspective of His Kingdom and a stronger sense of longing for eternity with Him. Then read the parable of the weeds found in Matthew 13:24-30; 37-43.

In this parable, what did Jesus compare the Kingdom of God to? (v. 24) Who does the man who sowed good seed represent?

_____

Based on the concept that Jesus is sharing about Himself, what do you think He is telling his bride in this story?

_____

_____

How does the bride come into the parable? What does Christ compare her to? At the end of the story, where does she end up?

_____

_____

What is the threat to their relationship? Who is the opposition?

_____

_____

We must not have a death grip on this life, but wait with hope and great anticipation for the next.

In this story Jesus called Himself the one who planted the good seed. "I am the Farmer," He is telling her, "who plants the good seed and sees it through until the harvest." Here we see Jesus drawing the connection between Himself and His bride, presenting Himself to her as a farmer—a husband. (Recall our definition for husband in Chapter Nine.)

I love this picture of Jesus. Can't you just visualize Him planting each seed in His field and watching over them all until the proper time, carefully tending each one, even as the obstacles and threats from the enemy spring up from the seeds of unrighteousness planted among them? But the relationship will prevail, and in the end, all who belong to Him will be gathered to live in His eternal barn of peace and love. Hallelujah!

Now read Matthew 13:44-46: In this parable, what is Jesus comparing the kingdom of heaven to? How does Jesus reveal Himself in the story?

_____

_____

_____

How do you see the bride in this parable? What is the connection to their relationship?

_____

I have heard it preached from the pulpit that Christ is the treasure hidden in the field and the pearl of great value; and we, like a man searching for buried treasure or a merchant in pursuit of a rare pearl, seek to find this one of a kind and priceless treasure so we may claim it for ourselves. If you are approaching this parable in this way, you are correct; this is the true biblical context of this story. However, allow me the grace to paint a word picture for you out of this same parable that simply blesses my heart to no end.

In our eyes, Christ is the most wonderful treasure one could ever find. He is the One of greatest worth; however, from His perspective, we, the bride, are His treasure and pearl of great value and worth. Think about it. Did He not give up everything He owned to come to earth to buy back His bride? Did He not lay down His life to redeem her, paying the bride price for our eternal future with Him? Can you see it? I hope so, because to Christ you are the most precious treasure; you are His most precious possession. In His eyes, nothing in heaven or on earth is of greater value to Him than His beloved bride, and for her He would give up everything.

Consider the following verses, how does each one communicate to you your great worth in God's eyes?

Deuteronomy 7:6:

_____

Isaiah 43:3-4:

_____

Luke 12:24:

_____

Are you ready for another one?

Read Matthew 13:47-50. What is the message to the bride? Follow the format we have been using as you attempt to gain understanding.

_____

_____

_____

Here we have a parable giving us a glimpse of the end time results. Jesus is the fisherman who let down His net, the gospel of His truth and love, into the waters of the world to catch the hearts of man. I find this ironic because I cannot tell you how many times I have felt like a fish caught in a net from Christ's glorious love. From the waters the Fisherman will draw out all mankind, all who heard the gospel, and bring them before Him (see Matthew 24:14). The good fish, those who accepted Christ's truth and love from every tribe and nation, will be collected into baskets, forming the bride. The others, those who rejected Christ, will be thrown away. Remember, as you consider this parable, it is God's extreme desire that none should perish (see 2 Peter 3:9). He does not want to throw any away, but desires for all to turn to Him.

Therefore: "Repent, for the *kingdom of heaven* is near" (Matthew 3:2, *emphasis mine*). Jesus is near you. "Therefore, seek first His kingdom and His righteousness" (Matthew 6:33). Allow this verse to remind you again to seek Him with all your heart because He is definitely seeking you. And keep in mind, Dear One, there will come a day when the book of life will be opened one last time and the King will settle all accounts (see Matthew 18:23).

What does Revelation 20:11-15 tell us about the accounts that will be settled? Who is being judged? What are they being held accountable for?

_____

_____

_____

Now we know that these verses are not referring to "good works" done on earth, because good works cannot get you into the kingdom of heaven. Ephesians 2:8-9 says, "For it is by grace we have been saved, through faith, and this not from yourselves, it is the gift of God—not by works, so that no one can boast." Beloved, the Lamb's book of life contains the names of those who have received Christ as their one and only Savior (see Revelation 21:27). They did not earn it; they simply received the gift based on faith. Revelation 20:11-15 is talking about the dead who are being judged for what they have done; the ones who refused the saving grace of God and tried to do "good works" based on their own effort.

Okay, one more. I know this lesson has already been a lengthy one; therefore, I will lay out this last one for you. Just sit back, read and take in the parable of the wedding banquet found in Matthew 22:1-14.

"The kingdom of heaven is like a king who prepared a wedding banquet for his son" (v. 22:2).

Who can imagine the feast prepared in advance, and, according to this parable, one that had been prepared for quite some time. "Tell those who have been invited that I have *prepared* my dinner: My oxen and fattened cattle *have been butchered*, and *everything is ready*. Come to the wedding banquet" (v. 22:4, *emphasis mine*). But those who were invited did not come. God the Father has prepared much for His Son and His beloved bride, yet the bride left the Bridegroom standing at the altar. Just the thought makes my heart sick with grief, as I am certain it does yours; but as we discussed in Week Two, the story did not end there. Hallelujah!

"'The wedding banquet is ready, but those I invited did not deserve to come. Go to the street corners and invite to the banquet anyone you find.' So the servants went out into the streets and gathered all the people they could find, both good and bad, and the wedding hall was filled with guests" (v. 22:8-10).

I am glad He did not give up the quest, aren't you; that He didn't abandon His unfaithful bride? Many have not received Him, but He is always ready to receive them as long as it is called "day." His arms are always open wide as they were on the cross that blessed day at Calvary, and He is ready, even now, to mark, with His seal, anyone who will receive Him. But remember the Day is swiftly approaching when the doors to the wedding hall will be permanently closed. Do not leave the Bridegroom standing at the altar, and do not think that you will crash this wedding party by getting in some other way.

"But when the king came in to see the guests, he noticed a man there who was not wearing wedding clothes. 'Friend,' he asked, 'how did you get in here without wedding clothes?' The man was speechless. "Then the king told the attendants, 'Tie him hand and foot, and throw him outside into the darkness, where there will be weeping and gnashing of teeth'" (v. 22:11-13).

Proper wedding attire is required to attend this Grand Affair. You must be prepared; clothed in that garment of salvation and arrayed in a robe of righteousness (see Isaiah 61:10), that glorious wedding gown we talked about in Chapter Seven. Therefore, if you still have not prayed to receive Christ as your personal Lord and Savior, please stop and do so now. A feast has been prepared in His honor, and He longs to share it with you. And I don't think we are only talking about food here. Yes, there will be wonderful treats displayed on that banquet table far beyond our own thinking, but let's remember what we will really be feasting on—Christ. Romans 14:17 reminds us that the kingdom of God is not just a matter of eating and drinking, but of righteousness, peace and joy in the Holy Spirit.

For me, heaven will be heaven simply because He will be there; and heaven will be heaven for Him because you and I will be there.

God the Father is preparing the wedding supper to beat all wedding suppers, but the one thing He spends the majority of His time preparing is the bride. And one day it will happen, the time will come for the grand celebration, and people will come from east and west and north and south, and they will take their places at the feast in the kingdom of God (Luke 13:29), and God will sit down at the table with man.

Oh, Beloved, the *kingdom of heaven* belongs to such as these (see Matthew 19:14, *emphasis mine*), the ones who have opened their hearts like little children and embraced Jesus with all their being. Please do not leave this life without your name being written in the Lamb's book of life, and on a name card reserving your place at the banquet table. Those who grace the banquet hall have been marked as His and He has become theirs. They are the true inheritance of each other, a treasure beyond any other treasure. Now, this is heaven!

Day Three
God Desires Celebration

David said, "I will celebrate before the Lord" (2 Samuel 6:21).

In my journey of coming to know Jesus I have made an interesting discovery. Jesus loves a good party. And with His festive heart He celebrates over us (see Zephaniah 3:17), because of us (see Luke 15:23-24), and with us (see Matthew 26:18). Hallelujah!

Therefore, with festive hearts let us declare His name in the congregation (see Psalm 22:22) and learn to celebrate!

Corporate praise and worship is wonderful and necessary, and I believe we will be doing a lot of it in heaven. Also, for the purposes of today's study, corporate worship will be our focus; but, to tell you the truth, what I am really looking forward to in heaven is individual worship; that one-on-one worship with Christ.

Our individual worship must be better than our corporate worship; if it isn't, something is wrong. Jesus said when you pray, do it in private, not while you're standing on the street corners for everyone to see (see Matthew 6:5). Our deepest, most intimate worship is expressed in our private prayer lives; then, what we share with Jesus in private will be expressed during our times of corporate worship. For that reason, let me challenge you to take time every day to come into the secret place and center all your attention on

Jesus to bring Him gifts of love from your heart. Come just as you are; no matter how you are dressed or feeling. Open your heart and pour everything you have upon the One who deserves all praise. Don't worry about it not being good enough. Give what you have and allow the Holy Spirit to take what you offer and multiply it to great abundance.

Begin today by praying for a heart of celebration and praise, then compare Isaiah 12:6, Psalm 98:4, Psalm 66:1-2 and Psalm 47:1. What instruction do all of these verses contain?

____ Stand somberly before the Lord

____ Mourn before the Lord in sack cloth and ashes

____ Shout with joy to the Lord

This life is practice for what is to come. And we will experience inconceivable and bottomless amounts of praise and worship in heaven, celebrating with exuberant amounts of rejoicing and rapture before His throne. Now, remember that worship is a lifestyle and not just singing and lifting your hands in church, but we are going to use this form or tool of worship and praise to illustrate the rapturous celebration before the throne that I think God has in mind.

The word *rapture* means "extreme joy; ecstasy; bliss and exultation."[51] Therefore, what I believe we will be experiencing in eternity is worship and praise so full of rejoicing that our hearts, spirits, and souls will be overflowing with resounding joy, ecstasy, bliss and exultation.

According to *Webster's*, the word *shout* means "loud, piercing cry; to utter a loud sudden cry."[52] Synonyms for the word *shout* are "yell; scream; to call out loudly." And for the word *joy*, synonyms are "delight, happiness, pleasure, enjoyment, bliss, ecstasy and elation." Now, I know in today's society it is not pleasingly correct to shout aloud, even with joy, unless you are at some sporting event, but Scripture clearly tells us to do this very thing—to "shout with joy" before the Lord; to go into raptures of praise with shouts of glorious exhilaration of spirit, full of extreme joy, ecstasy and bliss..

In your own words, describe the scene found in Revelation 19:6-7.

_____

_____

_____

_____

_____

What was it that John heard that sounded like the roar of rushing waters and like loud peals of thunder?

_____

Who was *shouting*? What were they *shouting*?

_____

_____

Based on this portion of Scripture, what would you determine to be the expression and behavior of the people?

_____

Since these verses are from Revelation, we can reasonably assume that these people are in heaven with the Holy Trinity (Father, Son, and Holy Spirit). With that in mind, let's examine their behavior. The people described here are making a sound like that of rushing waters; like loud peals of thunder. And because they are with God, wouldn't you agree that they are absolutely, and without reservation or hindrance, rejoicing before the throne with "shouts of joy," with hearts full and overflowing with pleasure, ecstasy, bliss and exultation? I'll even go as far to say that these people are on their feet, lifting their hands and waving their arms in the air, dancing and singing. Frankly, these people are downright celebrating.

This kind of outrageous praise begins with a willing heart; a heart full of love ready to express itself onto the One it adores by shouting, dancing, celebrating, rejoicing, and lifting up the voice in the name of the Lord. Now, I realize that not everyone is comfortable with praising God in this way because what I am explaining takes a physical action of the body. I want you to know that I understand. It took me a little while before I could even bring myself to raise my hands in the sanctuary—much less dance and shout loudly; but the truth of the matter is, God commands us to celebrate (see Leviticus 23).

We discussed this concept at the beginning of this study, but because it is so important, we must take a minute and look at it again. Please reread John 4:23-24. According to these verses, what kind of worshipers does the Father seek?

_____

How did Jesus say the worshipers *must* worship? Why do you think Jesus stressed that there is only one way to truly worship God?

_____

_____

To worship in spirit and in truth is to worship by the power of the Holy Spirit who is Spirit and Truth. The Holy Spirit gives you the love and ability to worship and praise God in the way He desires, in the way He deserves. And when you are truly focused on Him and bonded with Him through His Holy Spirit, you are going to worship and praise God beyond yourself—beyond what feels comfortable.

Focused worship ushers you into that intimate face-to-face encounter that the heart of God desires. And remember—the Lord inhabits the praises of His people, bringing them into that celebrated time of delight where the Lord utterly rejoices with His bride.

I am excited. Perhaps this very message will free some of you, giving you the release in your spirit that you long for in order to move out in this way (see John 8:36; Galatians 5:1). Yet, at the same time, my heart is heavy, because as I share these things, two possible criticisms may come to mind that some who are reading this may try to embrace. So, let's get them both out into the light and see if we can defuse them.

With all this talk about expressive and excessive worship and praise before God, it may come to mind that God is some kind of egomaniac. First, and let me make this very clear: God does not need us in any way. He does not need our love; He is the very essence of love (1 John 4:16). He does not need our approval, and He does not need our praise. He knows full well who He is and what He is capable of doing and He does not need our acceptance. The offerings of worship and praise are not only for God's delight but for your benefit. God greatly desires your fragrant offerings and takes great pleasure in the gifts you bring, but you receive, too. Do you recall when Jesus said, "It is more blessed to give than receive" (Acts 20:35)? Why do you think that is? Is it because when you give you experience joy and pleasure?

Try an experiment. The next time you are feeling down, worried, or tired, try giving of yourself to the Lord. Put on some Spirit-filled music and sing to Him, love on Him and lift a sweet offering of praise to Him. Nothing changes my mood, emotions, or level of fatigue faster than offering up to the Lord a good dose of focused praise and worship.

Also, keep in mind we are all unique in design, and God created each of us with different gifts and abilities. Therefore, the second possible condemnation may be to pigeonhole praise and worship. Not everyone is going to offer celebrations of praise to God in the same way. It is not fair to condemn or be critical of others because they do not share our attitudes and views on appropriate praise and worship etiquette. One of the greatest mistakes people make is that they put God in a box. For example, they stereotype

Him by believing that God only enjoys and honors respectable hymns and that the newer contemporary music of today is offensive to Him. On the contrary, God is diversified. He loves all kinds of music; in fact, He created it, and when it is offered up to Him in heartfelt worship and praise, He enjoys it immensely.

Consequently, we cannot make the mistake of putting people into a box, demanding that they worship and praise God in a way that is suitable to us. We must be open in heart and mind in order to receive the ministry of the Holy Spirit, which can come through the praises of others. When we see someone truly in unity with Christ through the Holy Spirit, moving as one with Him, worshiping in spirit and truth, it is beautiful and not of the natural. And through their praise and worship, we can and will see God glorified in their actions.

Beloved, if your focus is on God and God alone, you will burst with joy, bliss, ecstasy and delight as you lift your heart to Him in whatever way the Holy Spirit leads you to celebrate before the throne. So, go ahead and celebrate; rejoice for your audience of One.

Day Four

God Desires for You to Take Your Place in Heaven

"And I confer on you a kingdom, just as my Father conferred one on me, so that you may eat and drink at my table in my kingdom and sit on thrones, judging the twelve tribes of Israel" (Luke 22:29-30).

In this life, as the bride of Christ, at times we can go through great suffering and unspeakable sorrow, but take heart because it is not for nothing. Since the creation of the world, the Lord God knew us, personally and intimately, and since that time He had a plan for our lives (see Ephesians 1:11). God knew the place and generation to which we would be born, and He knew the specifics of our lives and the tasks He would ultimately ask of us. Beloved, your life is no accident, and neither is your place in eternity. God is preparing a position for you (see John 14:2).

Begin today by praying that the God of heaven will give you rich revelation of His eternal plan for you; then read Hebrews 12:2. According to this verse, what was the eternal destiny of Jesus Christ?

_____

_____

What took place prior to taking His place in eternity? Why do you think Jesus considered it joy?

_____

_____

_____

Why do you think we are told to fix our eyes on Jesus?

_____

Prior to sitting down and taking His place in heaven, Jesus suffered greatly. Before creation—before God created man—He chose the cross; the way of suffering by which Christ would be reunited with His bride, and God would be glorified. From the beginning of time, Jesus knew the joy set before Him, and He endured. And for the joy He sets before you, you too will endure. Salvation and the eternal hope of glory with the Lord is the ultimate joy that floods our hearts to follow Christ into difficult places of suffering and testing.

I do not know or understand all of what will happen in my life, but one thing I am confident of—during my lifetime I will find myself in places of suffering. I also understand that the honor and privilege set before me in heaven is unfathomable and that God desires to prepare me not only for the plans that He has for me in this life, but the life to come.

In His great mercy God is preparing each of us to take our place in eternity with Him. We may not fully grasp the situation now, or appreciate the process of being prepared; frankly, it will not be easy for any of us, but God desires for each of us to succeed, to pass the test, to overcome so that we may take the place that He has chosen. And one of the ways He gets us to embrace the process is by getting us to focus on eternal things.

Jesus will share eternal matters with you now so that you will continue to look up. At the time of His great suffering, Jesus knew and understood the end result, even though His soul was troubled and overcome with sorrow to the point of death as He struggled prior to the cross (see Matthew 26:38, Mark 14:34), His eyes were fixed on heaven and the joy that would ultimately prevail. Therefore, Christ will share with His bride the hope of her eternal

In this life, as the bride of Christ, at times we can go through great suffering and unspeakable sorrow, but take heart because it is not for nothing.

glory so that she, too, will choose to fix her eyes on heaven and on His glorious promises of the life to come.

Read Matthew 19:16-30. Focusing on verses 27-30, what comment and question did Peter present to the Lord?

_____

_____

_____

Look carefully at the statement Peter made in verse 27; how do you think he presented this question to the Lord?

_____

_____

What was the hope of eternal glory revealed to the disciples? Check all of the promises:

    ____ They will sit on twelve thrones, judging the twelve tribes of Israel.

    ____ They will receive a hundred times more than what they gave up in this life.

    ____ They will inherit eternal life.

In your opinion, why do you think Jesus added the "But" statement at the conclusion of his eternal promises to His disciples? Do you think that it might have something to do with how Peter asked his question? Why or why not?

_____

_____

_____

In this portion of Scripture we see that Jesus had a conversation with a rich young man who turned down His offer of eternal life for the riches he possessed here on earth. Upon hearing Jesus' remark on how difficult it is for a rich man to leave behind his earthly wealth so that he may receive heavenly wealth, the disciples became astonished and asked, "Who then can be saved?" (v. 25). Jesus simply replied, "With man this is impossible, but with God all things are possible" (v. 26). Peter then jumped into the conversation proclaiming, "Wait a minute!" You can almost hear the anger, yet panic in his voice. "What about us? We have given up everything for you. Our homes, wives, children, jobs—everything, so what do we get?"

Then in one glorious moment Jesus turns around and fixes their eyes on eternity by listing for them what awaits them in glory. Hallelujah!

Now, let's consider another promise by exploring Mark 10:35-45: According to verse 35, what statement did James and John make to the Teacher? What was their request in verse 37?

_____

_____

What did Jesus tell them would be the cross that they would bear? (v. 39)

_____

What was the confidence level of the two brothers to endure? In your opinion, do you think the brothers understood what they were asking? Why or why not?

_____

_____

Who did Jesus say would have the extreme privilege to sit at His side? Take a look at another version of this account in Matthew 20:20-28. According to Matthew 20:23, what added information is given?

_____

_____

According to Mark 10:43-45 and Matthew 20:26-28, what is the cost of being given a place of honor in heaven?

_____

_____

You have got to love James and John. Even though they were arrogant in their approach to eternal honors, they understood that they had an eternal destiny. Jesus told them, right along with Peter and the other disciples, that they would sit on twelve thrones judging the twelve tribes of Israel (see Luke 22:29-30). Perhaps they were jockeying for position, after all, someone would be sitting at the right or left, right? Frankly, I think they all believed this, why else would the rest of them get so upset when they heard about the brother's request (v. 41).

Not for one minute do I believe either of them knew or understood what they were agreeing to when they told Jesus they could drink from His cup, but they were willing. What about you, are you willing to drink from His cup? The honor of sitting by His side in His kingdom is costly. It comes with a high price, but Christ promises that it will be worth it. God's Word says that there are those who are being prepared to sit at Christ's side; precious ones who have been chosen by the Father to take this place next to His glorious Son.

For further evidence of the eternal hope set before us, please reflect on the letters to the seven churches in Revelation 2 and 3.

In these letters, Christ gave the church wonderful promises for overcoming their attitudes and legalism, sufferings, false teaching, sins, struggles, spiritual deadness, trials and rebellion, helping them to set their eyes on eternity and not on their present lives.

What were the promises of eternal glory given to each church for overcoming?

Ephesus:

_____

_____

Smyrna:

_____

_____

Pergamum:

_____

_____

Thyatira:

_____

_____

Sardis:

_____

_____

Philadelphia:

_____

_____

Laodicea:

_____

_____

To the church of Ephesus, Christ offered the right to eat from the tree of life, which is where? Oh, yes, in the "paradise of God" (v. 2:7). To Smyrna, He continued to fill them with encouragement to help them endure. He knew they had already suffered greatly, but He told them to remain faithful and He would give them the crown of life (v. 2:10). To Pergamum, He offered the hidden manna; He offered Himself (see Exodus 16:4; 31). Plus, He offered a white stone with a new name written on it, known only to the one who receives it (v. 2:17).

Great authority, the same as Christ's, was offered to Thyatira for overcoming and doing the will of God (vv. 2:26-27). The glorious wedding dress, becoming that vision in white as Christ presents His bride before His Father and angels, was offered to Sardis (vv. 3:4-5). The church of Philadelphia was told that it would be made a pillar in the temple of His God; and that God's name and the name of the great city, the New Jerusalem, would be written on him who overcame; and that Christ's new name would also be given to him. And to those in Laodicea who overcame, He would give the right to sit with Him on His throne, just as He, Himself, overcame and sat down with His Father on His throne (v. 3:21).

The ultimate joy is eternity with Christ. Never for one minute take your eyes off of it, for glorious promises await you, too. Make the decision to fix your eyes resolutely on Jesus, the author and perfecter of your faith; because the One who endured for you is more than ready and willing to help you endure so that you, too, may receive the fullness of His wonderful promises.

God greatly desires for you to take your place in heaven, the place He has kept for you since the creation of the world; but, in order to step into that place, you must be willing to pay the price; to overcome by setting your eyes on the prize in the life to come. For He who holds the seven stars; the First and the Last, who died and came to life again; Him who has the double-edged sword; the Son of God, whose eyes are like blazing fire and whose feet are like burnished bronze; the One who holds the seven Spirits of God; who is holy and true; the Amen, the faithful and true witness, the ruler of God's creation, He says to His bride, "He who has an ear, let him hear what the Spirit says to the churches" (Revelation 2:7, 11, 17, 29; 3:6, 13, 22). Focus on the eternal glory; set your eyes on what is most valuable and choose to overcome in this life.

The ultimate joy is eternity with Christ. Never for one minute take your eyes off of it, for glorious promises await you, too.

What do you believe Christ is revealing to you about your eternal destiny with Him? How is He fixing your eyes on Him, so that for the joy set before you, you also may endure and overcome so that you may take your place with Him?

_____

_____

_____

_____

_____

_____

_____

_____

_____

Day Five

God Desires to Bring You Home

"But you have come to Mount Zion, to the heavenly Jerusalem, to the city of the living God" (Hebrews 12:22).

Begin today by praying to the only living God, that He would grant you great insight, so you may see with your spiritual eyes the Great City—the New Jerusalem—and the life that is to come. Then read Revelation 21 through 22:6:

Can we breathe yet? I know I am anxiously holding my breath until that great and glorious day when the old order of things will have passed away and we will be home, in the city of the Great King, the New Jerusalem, reigning with Him forever. But for now we are in a time of waiting for the return of Christ. One day He will receive the word from His Father, the trumpet will blast (see 1 Thessalonians 4:16), the sky will roll back like a scroll (see Revelation 6:14), and He will then descend upon the earth in power and majesty (see Zechariah 14:4). Until then, we must, "Wait for the LORD; be strong and take heart and wait for the LORD" (Psalm 27:14).

It is good to wait upon the Lord; difficult at times, but good; because good things come to those who wait on God's perfect timing. Curiously, I think about the Lord waiting on us. How long has God waited upon His people? We complain about waiting on the Lord for some period of time—a week, a month or perhaps a year or two; but Christ in His long-suffering has waited thousands of years for His bride. We are here for a generation; our days are fleeting and few (see Psalm 39:4-5), but the Lord is here for all generations (see Ephesians 3:21). How long has He waited for the love and devotion of His bride? How much longer must He wait until He is united with her?

The good news is that the day is coming; a day perhaps marked in gold on the kingdom calendar, when Christ will return and we will be engulfed in God's incredible promises; and together, united as one, we, the whole bride, will come before the throne, loving our Eternal God.

Revelation 7:9-17 gives us a glimpse of this eternal promise. In your own words, describe the scene. Who made up the great multitude? What were they wearing? What were they doing? What did they witness?

_____

_____

_____

_____

Did you notice what they were holding in their hands? (v.9) Compare Revelation 7:9-10 with Matthew 21:1-11 and John 12:12-15. What similarities do you see?

_____

_____

What are the distinct differences?

_____

_____

Who did the elder say were those dressed in white robes standing before the throne of God and of the Lamb? (Rev. 7:14)

_____

_____

Suddenly, everything will make sense as the tapestry of our lives is stretched out before us in a colorful expression; then the Lord will display the work of His hand in each life for the display of His splendor.

What did the elder tell John was their eternal destiny? (v. 15) Check all of the promises:

_____ They will be continually in the presence of God.

_____ God will protect them with His covering.

_____ They will never be hungry or thirsty again.

_____ They will never again feel the burden of the hot sun upon them.

_____ The Lord will take care of them.

_____ God will wipe every tear from their eyes.

My heart swells and my eyes fill with tears at the wonderful word pictures that are painted in this portion of Scripture. It is truly beautiful. Close your eyes and try to take in the majesty and brilliance of that celebrated day when all of God's people from every tribe, tongue, and nation will behold the glory of God and see His face (see Revelation 22:4). Beloved, picture it! I am talking about seeing the very face of God, just as the Apostle John spoke of in 1 John 1:1-2 when he proclaimed: "That which was from the beginning, which we have heard, which we have seen with our eyes, which we have looked at and our hands have touched—this we proclaim concerning the Word of Life. The life appeared; we have seen it and testify to it, and we proclaim to you the eternal life, which was with the Father and has appeared to us."

John saw Jesus—the very face of God in the fleshly body of a man; and the people saw Him as they waved their palm branches as He made His way into the city of Jerusalem. And one day we will see Him, not as a man, but as the Eternal Word; the Lord God Almighty Himself, in the fullness of His glorious splendor. And as we come into His presence, I can imagine that we will be weeping tears of joy. We must be crying, because at that moment He will reach out and wipe away those tears one last time. And there we will be standing before the throne of God and of the Lamb.

Our once tattered war-torn garments will be radiantly white, and the crown of life will be placed upon our heads, and all at once we will forget what was behind us. Suddenly, everything will make sense as the tapestry of our lives is stretched out before us in a colorful expression; then the Lord will display the work of His hand in each life for the display of His splendor (see Isaiah 60:21). And then we will finally know every reason why we had to suffer the way we did; why the black threads were necessary to complete a picture of such grand design. Then, promptly, the pain and suffering once endured in this life will be no more, for our God and King will have made everything new, including us.

Celebrate, for it is His determined purpose that you be joined to Him. The bride and the Bridegroom shall be inseparable, living together as one forever.

Week Ten: The Story Goes On....

Our lives will pass through the fire revealing the depth of intimacy shared with Christ in the former life. Yet, because of the intensity of the covenant relationship that was chosen; because of the bonds of love and loyalty we allowed to adhere us to our First Love, only a few things will be lost in its intense heat, and most of what was built will stand firm. Without warning, the joy of the Lord will rise as our former lives generously reveal His glory. And in that moment, the bride will realize that, yes, she was faithful in love and obedience, committing her life to that which was most worthy and worthwhile. Then the bride, prepared by the Father, will be presented to the Groom; a pure virgin, strong and spotless. The angels will sing praises to God as the great multitude on his right comes forward, for at the Groom's right hand will be the royal bride (see Psalm 45:9). "Then the King will say to those on his right, 'Come, you who are blessed by my Father; take your inheritance, the kingdom prepared for you since the creation of the world'" (Matthew 25:34).

I am beside myself at this very moment, overcome with tears of joy. Oh, how I hope you are joining me in a joyful teary-eyed moment. These are only a few possibilities, images taken from my own heart, but can't you see it, too? The magnificence of it all; from the feast waiting in the banquet hall to the aroma of the re-birthed Garden of Eden; the resounding corporate worship before the throne, and Christ's splendor resting on the bride, revealing her radiant beauty, so elegant and fair; a breathtaking masterpiece formed from the moment she was conceived in His heart. I cannot contain myself. I am practically panting for the return of Christ; longing with everything that is in me just to be able to hold Him.

How His heart is waiting and longing in great expectation, too. Listen as He calls out to His bride in Zechariah 2:10-11. Paraphrase what you hear the Bridegroom saying:

_____

_____

_____

Oh, how the Lord touches my heart, but His Word pierces my soul. Shout and be glad for He is coming; He is returning with enormous anticipation for his beloved bride. Celebrate, for it is His determined purpose that you be joined to Him. The bride and the Bridegroom shall be inseparable, living together as one forever. Rejoice, bride, and be glad; allow the joy of the Lord to rise among you. Be ever mindful of His return; ever watchful in these coming days. Grab hold of His unconditional and extravagant love with everything that is in you and continue preparing. Keep the flame from your candle burning within your heart and those wedding garments white, because your Groom is calling out: "Be ready." He who testifies to these things says, "Yes, I am coming soon" (Revelation 22:20).

On that day the announcement will be, "Cheer up! Don't be afraid!" Your days of mourning will come to an end and the sound of weeping and of crying will be heard no more (see Isaiah 65:17-19). He will save the weak and helpless; He will bring together those who were chased away. "Violence will disappear from your land; the desolation and destruction of war will end. Salvation will surround you like city walls, and praise will be on the lips of all who enter there" (Isaiah 60:18, NLT). At last your troubles will be over, and you will fear disaster no more. With his love, He will calm all your fears. The former things will not be remembered, nor will they come to mind; for the Lord Himself, the King of Israel, will live among you!

"On that day I will gather you together and bring you home again. I will give you a good name, a name of distinction among all the nations of the earth. They will praise you as I restore your fortunes before their very eyes. I, the LORD, have spoken!" (Zephaniah 3:20, NLT).

Here's to Ever After....

Let it out; go ahead, everything you are feeling in this moment. Share with Jesus the desires of your heart.

_____

_____

_____

_____

_____

_____

_____

_____

_____

_____

_____

God Desires You

The journey of a lifetime begins with desire and it will continue for all eternity nestled in the intimate embrace of a covenant relationship with God. This relationship, that begins now, will last forever. Our happily-ever-after, fairytale endings are a foretaste of a much greater reality—the life we are meant to live with Christ as His bride. God's greatest desire is to join with you every day in a personal and intimate covenant relationship; one that is grounded in His word and prayer, one that is full of ardent, extravagant worship and puts Him first. He desires a relationship that lays aside every idol, making Him Lord and Savior. With all of His heart He longs to awaken your heart and soul with His power and love, and share with you the intimacy and wholeness found only in the King's chambers. He wants you to set aside everything; every attitude, every mind set, every obstacle that is hindering your relationship with Him and pursue Him with an intense, ravenous hunger, one that causes every ounce of your being to cry for Him and Him alone.

He wants to purify your love for Him, as He transforms you into the radiant beauty He knows you to be. His goal is to become one with you in a covenant marriage, a relationship that He sacrificed everything for so that He could make you His suitable partner for all eternity. Now is the time to be transformed, to be made ready for the Bridegroom. One day He will return and, we, as the Bride, cannot be found unprepared.

Beloved, the journey of a lifetime begins with desire—yours and God's. If you desire to be transformed by the desires of your heart, the ones that are buried deep within you, then you must open your heart so that the Lord may birth these desires in you; and, at the same time, you must allow God to unveil the many desires of His heart, because, Dear One, the truth of the matter is, His desires and your true desires are actually one in the same. And when you are joined with God through these desires, you come to life like never before, living the life you are meant to live; because, through this unity you are alive with His power, life and love, you are one with Him, purified by His love, transformed into His likeness, and prepared as a bride beautifully dressed for her Husband. Dare to dream, dare to be all that you can be, dare to answer the question: *What are the desires of my heart?*

Reflection and Response

As you journeyed with Christ through this Bible study, in what way(s) has He filled the desires of your heart?

_____

_____

_____

_____

_____

_____

_____

_____

_____

_____

_____

_____

How has this journey of embracing desire changed your life?

_____

_____

_____

_____

_____

_____

_____

_____

_____

_____

_____

_____

Week Ten

Lesson Ten

Come and I Will Show You the Bride

Revelation 21:9-22:5

1. The bride will reflect God's brilliant _____. Like Him, she will be _____

    a.) She will have the appearance of _____ (Rev. 21:11).

2. The bride will be ready, _____ and _____. She will be
    _____, and able to stand strong and firm (Rev. 21:12).

3. The bride has _____ to God on all sides (Rev 21:12-13).

    a.) And it will be _____ access.

    b. The number 12 symbolizes _____ _____

4. The bride was established from the foundation, the groundwork of the _____ _____
    implemented by the 12 Apostles through Jesus Christ (Rev 21:14).

5. Like a perfect square, Christ's love is _____ (Eph. 3:18)

    a.) And in perfect _____, God's desire is to _____ with His bride. (Rev. 21:16).

(continued on next page)

6. The bride's _____ and _____ (Rev 21:18).

    a.) The bride will be _____ of _____ (Matthew 5:8).

    b.) Purity also means _____

7. The bride will be adorned with _____ and _____ jewelry (Rev 21:19-20).

8. The bride will be filled with the _____ and _____ of God's glory.

9. God's _____ flowing through His bride, producing abundant _____ full of healing.

10. She will glaze upon Him _____. She is _____ and He is _____

11. His mark of _____ and His _____ will be upon her (Rev. 22:4).

12. She will _____ with Him forever and ever (Rev.22:5).

"I saw the Holy City, the new Jerusalem, coming down out of heaven from God, prepared as a bride beautifully dressed for her husband"
(Revelation 21:2).

Endnotes

Week Two

1 *Webster's Encyclopedia of Dictionaries: New American Edition* (Otterheimer Publishers, Inc: 1978) edited by John Gage Allee, Phd., 184.

2 W. E. Vine 1873-1949, *Vine's Concise Dictionary of Bible Words* (Thomas Nelson, Inc., 1999) Nashville, Tennessee, 73.

3 *Webster's Encyclopedia of Dictionaries: New American Edition* (Otterheimer Publishers, Inc: 1978) edited by John Gage Allee, Phd., 204.

4 Ibid, 41

5 Internet-website: encyclopedia.org: http://2.1911encyclopedia.org/B/BE/Betrothal.htm

Week Three

6 *Webster's Encyclopedia of Dictionaries: New American Edition* (Otterheimer Publishers, Inc: 1978) edited by John Gage Allee, Phd., 431.

7 Ibid, 408

8 Ibid, 408

9 Ibid, 198

10 Ibid, 79

11 Ibid, 429

12 Ibid, 137

Week Four

13 *Webster's Encyclopedia of Dictionaries: New American Edition* (Otterheimer Publishers, Inc: 1978) edited by John Gage Allee, Phd., 31.

14 W. E. Vine 1873-1949, *Vine's Concise Dictionary of Bible Words* (Thomas Nelson, Inc., 1999) Nashville, Tennessee, 155.

15 *Webster's Encyclopedia of Dictionaries: New American Edition* (Otterheimer Publishers, Inc: 1978) edited by John Gage Allee, Phd., 82

16 Ibid, 199

Week Six

17 *Webster's Encyclopedia of Dictionaries: New American Edition* (Otterheimer Publishers, Inc: 1978) edited by John Gage Allee, Phd., 182.

18 Ibid, 120

19 Ibid, 117

20 Ibid, 375

21 Ibid, 167

Week Seven

22 *Webster's Encyclopedia of Dictionaries: New American Edition* (Otterheimer Publishers, Inc: 1978) edited by John Gage Allee, Phd., 45.

23 Ibid, 141

24 Ibid, 38

25 Ibid, 372

26 Ibid, 73

27 Ibid, 83

28 Ibid, 156

29 Douglas, J. D. and Tenney, Merrill C., *NIV Compact Dictionary of the Bible*, 1989, Zondervan, Grand Rapids, Michigan, 466-468.

Week Nine

30 *Webster's Encyclopedia of Dictionaries: New American Edition* (Otterheimer Publishers, Inc: 1978) edited by John Gage Allee, Phd., 426.

31 Ibid, 51

32 Ibid, 227

33 Ibid, 306

34 Ibid, 290

35 Hebrew word Ya'adh

36 *Webster's Encyclopedia of Dictionaries: New American Edition* (Otterheimer Publishers, Inc: 1978) edited by John Gage Allee, Phd., 105.

37 Ibid, 93

38 Ibid, 347

39 W. E. Vine 1873-1949, *Vine's Concise Dictionary of Bible Words* (Thomas Nelson, Inc., 1999) Nashville, Tennessee, 331.

40 *Webster's Encyclopedia of Dictionaries: New American Edition* (Otterheimer Publishers, Inc: 1978) edited by John Gage Allee, Phd., 45.

41 W. E. Vine 1873-1949, *Vine's Concise Dictionary of Bible Words* (Thomas Nelson, Inc., 1999) Nashville, Tennessee, 309.

42 *Webster's Encyclopedia of Dictionaries: New American Edition* (Otterheimer Publishers, Inc: 1978) edited by John Gage Allee, Phd., 409.

43 Ibid, 257

44 W. E. Vine 1873-1949, *Vine's Concise Dictionary of Bible Words* (Thomas Nelson, Inc., 1999) Nashville, Tennessee, 54.

45 *Webster's Encyclopedia of Dictionaries: New American Edition* (Otterheimer Publishers, Inc: 1978) edited by John Gage Allee, Phd., 155.

46 W. E. Vine 1873-1949, *Vine's Concise Dictionary of Bible Words* (Thomas Nelson, Inc., 1999) Nashville, Tennessee, 149.

47 *Webster's Encyclopedia of Dictionaries: New American Edition* (Otterheimer Publishers, Inc: 1978) edited by John Gage Allee, Phd., 290.

48 Ibid, 101

49 Ibid, 43

50 Ibid 182

Week Ten

51 *Webster's Encyclopedia of Dictionaries: New American Edition* (Otterheimer Publishers, Inc: 1978) edited by John Gage Allee, Phd., 305.

52 Ibid, 345

Made in the USA
Charleston, SC
14 April 2014